Reputations of the Tongue

Reputations

University Press of Florida GAINESVILLE

TALLAHASSEE

TAMPA

BOCA RATON

PENSACOLA

ORLANDO

MIAMI

JACKSONVILLE

On
Poets
and
Poetry

of the Tongue

WILLIAM LOGAN

Copyright 1999 by William Logan
Printed in the United States of America on acid-free paper
All rights reserved

04 03 02 01 00 99   6 5 4 3 2 1

Library of Congress Cataloging-in-Publication Data
Logan, William, 1950–
Reputations of the tongue: on poets and poetry / William Logan.
p. cm.
Includes bibliographical references.
ISBN 0-8130-1697-5 (acid-free paper)
1. American poetry—20th century—History and criticism. 2. English poetry—
20th century—History and criticism. I. Title.
PS323.5.L645   1999
811'5409—dc21   99-23588

The University Press of Florida is the scholarly publishing agency for the State
University System of Florida, comprising Florida A & M University, Florida
Atlantic University, Florida International University, Florida State University,
University of Central Florida, University of Florida, University of North Flor-
ida, University of South Florida, and University of West Florida.

University Press of Florida
15 Northwest 15th Street
Gainesville, FL 32611–2079
http://www.upf.com

for Debora Greger
criticus critici

My selfe was once a student; and, indeed,
   Fed with the self-same humour, he is now,
   Dreaming on nought but idle poetrie,
   That fruitless and unprofitable art,
   Good unto none, but least to the professors. . . .

BEN JONSON, *Every Man in His Humour* (1616)

CONTENTS

I began to write criticism because I needed the money, but I kept writing because I needed the discipline. Many editors gave me a free choice of current books and—except when I was writing for newspapers—enough space in which to compose "Lalla Rookh." Still, there are poets I admire whom I've never written about and poets I should have written much more about. I have written criticism only by flashes of lightning, and later I hope to remedy a few of my omissions.

The pieces here have occasionally been expanded or rewritten, and some reviews have been gathered into small groups perhaps having greater unity than the haphazard or rough-and-ready form of their first appearance. A few revisions restore remarks blue-penciled by my editors.

Poets die by their hands but live by their words. What was an oral art is now almost always an artifact for the eye. People talk about poetry more than they talk poetry, and to a large extent reputations are still made and lost in table talk. If criticism is just a higher form of gossip, a critic must remember that only the conversation of decades and centuries, and not these will-o'-the-wisp sentences, will secure such reputations of the tongue.

When I think poetry, or the reviewing of poetry, might no longer be a high calling, I try to remember A. N. Wilson's report of his dinner conversation with the Queen Mother, the widowed consort of George VI. Speaking of a stranger's visit to the royal family, she said, "Then we had this rather lugubrious man in a suit, and he read a poem . . . I think it was called 'The Desert.' And first the girls got the giggles, and then I did and then even the King." The poem was *The Waste Land.* "Such a gloomy man, looked as though he worked in a bank, and we didn't understand a word." These reviews are for those giggling young princesses.

Many editors invited me to write these essays and reviews: Herbert Leibowitz of *Parnassus*; D. J. R. Bruckner of the *New York Times Book Review*; Joseph Parisi of *Poetry*; Alan Jenkins of *TLS*; Christopher Ricks of *Essays in Criticism*; Henry Hart and Robert Crawford of *Verse*; Reginald Gibbons of *TriQuarterly*; John Blades, Dianne Donovan, and Larry Kart of the *Chicago Tribune*; Jonathan Yardley of the *Washington Star*; and Michael Dirda of the *Washington Post*. I am equally grateful to editors who provided homes for wandering essays: Christopher Ricks once more; Willard Spiegelman of *Southwest Review*; George Core of *Sewanee Review*; and James McCorkle. I owe further thanks to David Gehler and Molly Tamarkin.

The
Condition
of the
Individual
Talent

That's one of the tragedies of this life, that the men who
are most in need of a beating up are always enormous.
The Palm Beach Story

Living so long after Mr. Eliot and his pronouncements, we ought to
be immune to the virus that pricked him into prose statement. The
reaction against Eliot has been a concurrent series of independent
and at times unconscious rebellions against tradition, or what might
even now be called "the tradition," though it is useless to complain
that there is never one understanding of tradition or that Eliot was
simplifying to get on with an argument. Tradition is still a word
anathema in some quarters, but I'm not going to abuse poets who
reject the poetry of the past in order to compose the poetry of the
present. The avant-garde is often a corrective to the complacent
blindness of our contemporaries, and even Eliot was avant-garde
once.

Many of the useful advances of the avant-garde have exploited a diction or syntax or subject poets of tradition have rejected out of hand. Perhaps earlier poets had thought in passing of skeletal lines approaching Eliot's parsonical manner or Pound's Chinese syntax, but could not bring themselves to commit them as poetry—such lines did not seem to *be* poetry as they understood it. The tenor of resisted advance could as well include Whitman's barbaric yawp or what might cruelly be called Ginsberg's mighty whine.

Breaches of tradition may be measured when one age follows another or is transposed into it. As Eliot suggested, such breaches are effective in reordering what we understand to be tradition, since tradition is not a set of monoliths or stone tablets, but a continually shifting set of understandings. The burden of the new is not that it is difficult—all new poetry is difficult because it evades a previous limitation, and so absorbs a limitation. The burden of the new is that it makes the past inaccessible in a new way. I might go further: no poetry can aspire to permanence without making our previous understandings of tradition inadequate.

I.

A poet must have an idiom and he must have a method. It is no use pleading that under certain circumstances idiom is as good as method. Without a method a poet is susceptible to the repetitive faculties of his imagination, to the unexamined correlations useful only in steering a safe course from morning's plate of eggs to evening's warm milk. Like Clare or Hardy, such a poet is condemned to write versions of the same poem, with intensifying virtues but also constricting responsibilities. Without an idiom a poet is doomed either to borrow an idiom from the past (and so exist as echo or afterthought) or to assume unconsciously the idiom of his period, which is rarely subtle or flexible enough for an attack on the ordered comprehensions of the past. To this degree a conscious decision must be made, which may not be material but must not be moral.

A poet may invent himself without a mastering design, but not without the attentions to which design progresses and in which design culminates. It is no adequate supplement, though it may be a defended position, for a reader to found an admiration on the political attitude a poem strikes, or the sociology its presence defends, or the history its content restores. There is no adequate supplement to poetry less ruinous than content or more dangerous. A poet can legislate a position, or make a museum of attitudes, or linger over history until it stops reeking of the dissecting room; but the only test of his poetry is its ability to exist independent of these measures, as well as to be a countermeasure to them. Content will not provide the idiom or the method.

Poetry does not, therefore, require a posture. Half the poetry of any moment strikes its pose within the ordinary comprehensions of poetry, as if on a billboard. The other half (there are exceptions, but too few exemptions) strikes the same pose, innocent that a pose has been struck. It is hard to decide which is the more culpable, the innocence or the calculation; but a reader may retain a fondness for ignorance (Blake's ignorances were massive, and responsible for his sweetness and penetration) while finding calculation pathetic, even if it is the calculus of fashion. Working in period style, taking dictation in current mannerism, poets create the innocence of their readers. Only by the reinforcement of mutual inauthenticities can one young poet, hardly the worst of his generation, call another's poems "brave" because she compares her father to Hitler and herself to the murdered Jews, a quarter of a century after Sylvia Plath proposed the marriage of household pastoral to Le Grand Guignol.

If poets suffer what Eliot called a dissociation of sensibility, it isn't for lack of sensibility, but from an overabundance of sensibility. That's why so much poetry offends not just by its manner, but by its voice. We may accept a dissociation that doesn't appear in the surface of the poem; and we may accept it as no more, and no less, than the burden of tradition.

We may also accept that Eliot was guilty of romance in believing there was a moment as late as four centuries ago when poets lived in the bliss before the dissociation of sensibility set in. There probably hasn't been a poet in four millennia who didn't believe his ancestors had a more immediate apprehension of thought, that thought was once as true as experience and as minutely modifying. I can think of various politic reasons why the phrase *dissociation of sensibility* should cause disquiet, when dissociation suggests quietism, failures to commit or inhere. But not all withdrawals are cold—many are kind. Such a dissociation in the poem (which implies and imposes no accompanying dissociation in the life) permits the texture and tension of the poem to erupt without the line-by-line intervention of grudging concern. Poems that flee the dissociation of sensibility seem to fare no better by the imposition of one. We too often witness instead the richly decadent deterioration of sensibility. But then few people are worth knowing at the close distances a poem requires.

II.

But, of course, only those who have personality and emotions
know what it means to want to escape from these things.

The joke is a dark one, especially when we think of Eliot in later life, closeted in his bedroom laying out tableau after tableau of Patience while John Hayward hovered patiently outside. I want to revise Eliot by drawing him out. It is a curse to realize a personality. A young poet may feel a fugitive anxiety over the estrangement of his common, habitual self from the self that composes, that emerges only in the bloom or canker of the poem. That other, uncommon self, whose regulations are often mysterious or deformed, was named by Proust *le moi profond*. A young poet may feel anxiety at this division, but the danger for the artist as he ages is that, rewarded for the invocation of that mystery, he may attempt to make the mystery manifest, to become what the poems behold. If he does so, a strange transaction occurs—as the secrets of that interior arrangement come open for display, become daily and vernacular themselves, the poems lose the force of those internal gestures and may even, by a startling inversion, become the common, sentimental self the poet began with. In the simple case the poet merely becomes *le moi profond*, with the attendant drainage to his work. As Frost became the cracker-barrel philosopher people imagined him, his poems grew brittle. Pound, Whitman, Stevens: in their late poems all show the debilitating effect of this transforming loss.

In practice the composing self may not seem all that profound. I refer not only to the difference between expectation and execution, between the immaculate conception and the muddy nativity, but to the persistent and even ennobling suspicion that the composing self is more deeply compromised, more fully crippled, more soiled and more disturbed by the close necessities and tragedies of life from which everyday life insulates us—that we are less profound in the act of art than crucially demeaned or comically sacrificed.

Biography can tell us little about interior arrangements: only when an artist has aged into literature, into the public aggrandized self, can we see clearly—on his face rather than in it—the lineaments of those private understandings. You must adjust your focus, take account of the mere accretions of age; but age hardens in plaster what was once private and elastic. An artist often becomes his own death mask.

We are drawn to biography because it is comprehensible rather than comprehending. The embarrassing circumstances of birth, the criminal neglect by parents, the lover's betraying touch: all these we understand. They are as satisfying as soap opera, their pleasures guiltily superior and shamingly voyeuristic. We can't feel superior to artistic achievement—not in this fashion—but we can reduce it to inconsequence, like the fisherman who rushes his trout to the taxidermist. What is returned to him is the skin and scales, padded to assume the form of the living and painted in colors that approximate faded glories. No one who ever knew a poet found him again in biographies, and no one who had forgotten his poems could rewrite them after the trail through literary dinners, small and sadistic love affairs, public sorrows and private angers, and anguish at the loss of dear Rover.

That doesn't mean biographies are without interest. Their very interest is venomous. I am fond of Byron's account books, which record the catchpenny details of keeping a courier or renting extra tableware for indulgent guests. Those who love the poems go least wrong in the small facts—the shade of a pair of shoes or the Tuscan crowns tendered to a spendthrift friend. These can't be confused with the inner self, and they invent a milieu. But the weights of larger sorrows and psychological speculations (all too much like stock-market speculations) give us only the superficial extravagance and nothing of *le moi profond*. Between the moral universe and the privacy of art falls the shadow—that is why public art is so shallow.

Most artists realize this, and those who don't are usually those who succumb to the dangers of division. You can protect that inner self only by descending into the deepest insulating privacy or by engaging in long-term fraud. In Henry James's story "The Private Life," the dull social appearance of the poet Clare Vawdrey and his inability to quote his own work drive the narrator to retrieve one of Vawdrey's manuscripts from an upper floor of the inn where they are staying. But there is *another* Clare Vawdrey upstairs, writing impassioned poems in the dark. "One goes out, the other stays at home. One's the genius, the other's the bourgeois, and it's only the bourgeois whom we personally know." Few poets can read this without an uncomfortable tremor of recognition.

And no one who reads the descriptions of young Eliot will doubt he worked very hard at his fraud. Though it had great costs, it guaranteed a private self able to withstand the early triumphs (nothing can be more crippling than an early triumph) and produce the great mature work about fraud, *Four Quartets*. Such defensive gestures often produce a second maturity. Yeats, Auden, and Coleridge were other poets who deliberated their early rise in a mature mask, though Coleridge lost his second maturity to opium (drugs may be a lasting investment, but the dividends are early and the penalties long).

The approach of biography invites us to define a literature in terms of a life; and to the degree we defer to the life to explain the literature, we misplace its true affect. It may be helpful to secure particulars, the particulars of a shilling life: when Auden wrote, in *The Orators*, "The couples are coming now out of The Tower," he was first referring to a local cinema (the point is made in Edward Mendelson's *Early Auden*). Critics have sometimes taken The Tower only as mythological or Jungian symbol, or as literary allusion. It is interesting to know the fact, interesting but limiting, since a private reference may be the most cunningly calculated. There the poem divides from the trifling fiction of outer life to the metaphors of the interior. Artists reveal the private in their private jokes, because in the fraud of a joke the interior life is permitted to emerge. If a reader limits his reading to the shell of that cinema, he has gained the joke at the expense of experience. Such duplicity has a sardonic aspect.

The real life surfaces in the ambiguity. I don't advocate utter license, whatever my liking of license, because I believe in the limitations language imposes, and fatally disposes. The artist flees into the limitations of language. The reader who finds each poem an index of the life loses the art, which means to force the reader into a private articulation, the register of his own experience.

Many poets have been tempted to confuse the substance of their poetry with the detail of their lives (critics aren't alone in supposing art a translation of the life, a translation that can be corrected by reference to the original). Poetry's access to prose has increased this temptation, because prose seems a more transparent medium. At the first simple rhyme a life is compromised for art. But no investigation of Donne's steps to the pulpit or Lowell's depressive mania can return us to the poems, which exist in a separate realm. We don't need to know much about psychology, about the fears absorbed in any representation, about the unconscious suppression or substitution of resonant detail, to realize how little of the real survives in the art. Every poem has its blanks, its terra incognita—no critic can provide the poem with language it doesn't have, with words it doesn't speak. It is easier to resort in confusion to the life because we cannot face the blanks of the art. What is left out is always absent for a reason—not to conceal the petty life from the art, but to divorce the life from the art.

This should not be taken as a license to invade the artist's necessary privacy, his sheltering silences, for the purposes of criticism.

(For the purpose of entertainment or moral lesson such invasion does no active harm to the dead, if no active good to the living. The burden of art may be precisely the reverse.) If we learned tomorrow Auden was a murderer, it would be no more trouble for critics to find the tremor of his sins in his art than if we were to learn he had been a closet heterosexual. The poems would not change. Only what we told ourselves about them would change. Wordsworth's affair with Annette Villon only *seems* to tell us more about his poems' governing anxieties. The facts only explicate; they never explain. And art will always accommodate.

No poet succeeds without holding his own personality in something like contempt. This doesn't mean the writer's highest state of development would be without personality at all.

III.

I therefore invite you to consider, as a suggestive analogy, the action which takes place when a bit of finely filiated platinum is introduced into a chamber containing oxygen and sulphur dioxide.

Eliot was not a chemist. If, as R. P. Blackmur has observed, criticism is the formal discourse of an amateur, it would be wise to remember that many of the intensities and anfractuosities of Eliot's prose were obtained by his status as an amateur. Criticism is the bias of a tendency, and in the tendency the critic is liable to errors of arrangement and errors of intimacy. If in Eliot the errors are less ingratiated, it is in part because he fended off adventitious concentration, so that finally he was able to write a poetry, as well as a prose, that personality might infuse but not corrupt. The corruption by personality is the corruption of personality: in such errors as remain we may find the residue, the exempla, of the primitive, private manifestation. Otherwise there would be no difference between *The Waste Land* and *Four Quartets*.

When the two gases previously mentioned are mixed in the presence of a filament of platinum, they form sulphurous acid. They form, in fact, nothing of the sort. Eliot confused his acid and mistook his process. Sulphurous acid is a weak dibasic acid useful as a bleach or preservative: it is created when sulphur dioxide is dissolved in water (SO_2 + $H_2O = H_2SO_3$). The process Eliot is attempting to describe in "Tradition and the Individual Talent" is the catalytic stage of the creation of sulphuric acid, the far more valuable and corrosive acid known to the Victorians, as well as the Elizabethans, as oil of vitriol. Unfortunately, mixing sulphur dioxide and oxygen in the presence of platinum or any other metal cannot produce sulphuric acid, because sulphuric acid contains hydrogen. There is no hydrogen in Eliot's chamber.

The chemical protocol is of some interest. In the contact process of preparing sulphuric acid, sulphur dioxide and oxygen are mixed in a series of converters or chambers at a heat of around 500°C. Once they were mixed in the presence of platinum, though now vanadium pentoxide is used because, though slightly less efficient, it is cheaper and less susceptible to poisoning or neutralization by the arsenic sometimes produced in small quantities when impure sulphur is burned to create sulphur dioxide. Platinum accelerates the reaction between the two gases by adsorption of the gases on its surface. What the gases form in the presence of a shred of platinum (trays of platinum, in the commercial process) is not sulphuric acid, but sulphur trioxide (SO_3).

$$2SO_2 + O_2 = 2SO_3$$

Sulphuric acid is formed only in a subsequent reaction. After cooling, the sulphur trioxide passes into a tower where it is absorbed in a circulating stream of 98–99% sulphuric acid, combining with the small excess of water in the acid to form pure sulphuric acid. The reaction is complex: sulphur trioxide and sulphuric acid form a viscous substance called oleum ($H_2S_2O_7$) that in turn unites with the water to form more sulphuric acid.

$$SO_3 + H_2SO_4 = H_2S_2O_7$$

$$H_2S_2O_7 + H_2O = 2H_2SO_4$$

I have indulged these complications not to fault the metaphor but to expose the honeycomb of significations and detours. When the particle of fact is infected, the language goes awry, and even a poet as austere as Eliot is not immune to the responsibilities of the word. It is the parcel of art to trim, but in science you cannot wrong an equation without amputating the delicate chain of chemical transaction. Science doesn't have luxury or latitude. The poet may have latitude, but when he believes he has luxury he is not just unscientific, he is no longer poetic.

If we take consolation from Eliot's errors,* it must be that the reaction would take place far less efficiently without the interference of the platinum shred; that the vitriol of art can be formed only in a later stage, an absorption in a concentration; and that the acid formed is not mild but murderous. Catalysts do not cause a reaction; they merely accelerate it by lowering the energy of activation. Equilibrium is reached much sooner, but the yield obtained under given conditions is no greater. The shred of platinum, changing but unchanged, is a tempting figure for the poet's mind—pure, rare, of marked value. Eliot's chamber might have been served more accurately, if without equal resonance, by analogy to the internal combustion engine and the spark plug. That reaction, which creates

---

*I'm not the first to notice them. "It is a pity that Mr. Eliot, in revising some of the earlier of these essays, did not consult a professional chemist—or even some friend with an elementary knowledge of chemistry," wrote a droll anonymous reviewer of *Selected Essays, 1917–1932* in the October 1932 issue of *The Criterion*. Eliot of course edited *The Criterion*. Almost entirely about the chemistry of sulphuric acid, the five-sentence review ends, "Whether the theory of poetic creation which Mr. Eliot supports by this celebrated metaphor remains valid, is a more difficult question to decide." Christopher Ricks kindly provided this citation. Mrs. Valerie Eliot has suggested to me that Frank Morley might have written the review, "for the fun of it," while Eliot was in America. It is odd but not uncharacteristic that Eliot never did correct the essay, though he made slight verbal changes—he was perhaps a man who preferred the mortification of certain errors. His mortifications were not wholly private (though they could be only obscurely public)—the catalysis of "sulphurous" acid is undoubtedly the "more than doubtful analogy" to which he refers at the beginning of *After Strange Gods*.

hydrocarbon waste and carbon monoxide (themselves capable of catalytic conversion, by platinum, to harmless carbon dioxide and water), cannot protect the artist's saintliness, though it might thereby dignify his salvations.

IV.

We never escape tradition, we merely debase it. Much recent American poetry has armed itself against a tradition that required the formal properties of technique. In every other way our age resembles the high Victorian period, when technique—a surfeit of technique— was used to embody the period's sentimental order. The Victorians roused to formal demand to distinguish themselves from the waywardness of the Romantics; we have lowered ourselves, into the pit, to evade a tradition that possesses and inhabits. The memorable poets of reaction (Whitman, Dickinson, Browning, Hopkins, the awful Melville and the sometimes less awful Clough) voided the Romantic values while not avoiding them. All these poets are difficult cases when considered as the imposed values of technique; and all, to a degree, are the victims and masters of prose. They didn't succumb to the personality of technique. The musics of Tennyson sound tinny in the presence of one of these poets, who conceived of tradition as a demonic angel, Jacob's angel, the spirit that outdistances the letter.

An avant-garde is sometimes a corrective, just as tradition is a corrective. Most of the poets of any period look neither forward nor back. They are content in their banked understandings; that is, in the idioms and methods that secure the local sentiment.

One might reverse Eliot here: only those who do not have a personality know what it is like to desire one. The way beyond artistic impasse is through the swamp of tradition, not around it. Even the most superficial analysis of artistic advance and decline suggests that, while decline is an act of repetition and rigidity, advance requires simultaneous revolt and surrender. Spectacular acts of decline, and of decadence, may be conscious and willed; but leaps of insight are often unconscious or innocent. No poet should take more than a necessary solace from the willfulness of his character or the grace of accident. If we take solace in error, it might be as a form of gratitude that the pedant in Eliot did not begin "Prufrock," "Let us go then, you and me."

Chemical reaction can transform only the elements present. Nothing is lost in reaction, and nothing gained ("In my beginning ..."). This elemental economy is chemistry's formal beauty, and why the sciences have always appealed to a poet like Donne. But why was *this* chemical metaphor so attractive, and why did Eliot not merely get it wrong, but persist in his error when it would have cost so little to correct it? (The versions of the essay in *The Sacred Wood* [1920] and *Selected Essays* [1932] are subtly different.) If poetry is the transubstantiation of the given substance, personality can be lost but not surrendered. Eliot's chemistry made something out of nothing. You might say he knew better, even though he was no chemist—he knew poetry required the confident belief that something extra, after all, must be created from the partial and inadequate elements of personality. On some subconscious level he knew the error was the poetry.

The poet may accept as his potential burden not to compose criticism as if it were poetry, but to compose poetry as if it were criticism. Every poem of value must have a residue. A residue is not a mystery or a withholding. It is the result of a continual ignition in the language, a combustion in the nearness of words—it is what lies beneath the surface value of words. We can wear out a poem as we wear out a favorite jacket or a joke. In a minor poem the residue is small and easily exhausted, but in the greatest it suffers a constant renewal. It cannot be exhausted because our lives are not long enough to do so. Indeed, in the greatest poetry the residue may seem to increase as our experience increases—that is, as we become more ruefully sensitive to the fire in its familiar words. We return to a poem not because of its symbolic value or its sociological carriage, but because of the waste, or subversion, or difficulty, or consolation of its provision.

Auden's
Dirty
Laundry

Auden's laundry list would be worth reading—I speak
as one who's read it many times, all rhymed and metered.
Randall Jarrell

Auden began as a major poet and ended as a minor one, the first
since Wordsworth to achieve such negative inversion. For Wordsworth the decline was the result of disregard and pigheadedness, but
for Auden it was a cool act of will. They were perhaps both poisoned
by Tory politics and the chill comforts of the Church of England,
though the search for philosophical comfort attends poetic decline
and is not necessarily the cause of it. Auden did not embrace failure
so much as the conditions of imagination that permitted it; and those
conditions operated so intermittently even the last works—those
peculiar, fussy poems slipping uncomfortably from the rough trade
of demotic (demotic no one ever spoke) to the mausoleum sweep-
ings of the *Oxford English Dictionary*, poems that seem to have been
commissioned by *Scientific American* or the *Reader's Digest*—even
those poems show on occasion the brilliant disabled mind and the

uncommon ear. Those who like the later poems often do so guiltily, out of a fondness for their disreputable virtues. I like them, but I also feel depressed and soiled by them; and half the time, like Fielding's Partridge at the performance of *Hamlet*, I want to break silence by saying, "No, no, Sir, Ghosts don't appear in such Dresses as that, neither."

Those who came early to Auden's poetry often did not forgive the formal change in sensibility, even if they forgave his betrayal of left-ist dogma or his decision not to return to England at the outbreak of war. For readers who came later to his work, there could never be the same sense of rupture; and felt appreciations of the first poems must now be even more shallow. The early poems will never speak as comprehendingly as they did to readers formed by the actions of the period, just as they will never again speak as obscurely.

Auden was old at a very early age, even if we discount the solem-nities he imported into his work to give it a political regard. To peel back the onion of attitudes he became to the early stinging interior is an act less of homage than of obligation, if his work is to have an organic comprehension and not become what it is so often treated as, a communion of anthology favorites and a ragbag of first lines. This removal of his concealing membrane has been made easier by the publication of a facsimile of Auden's early notebook containing drafts and fair copies of poems he wrote between 1927 and 1929, at the cusp of his early style, and, from a period twenty years later, when he was already too famous for his own good—or the good of his conversation—a volume of table talk.

Both these books belong to genres, with all of genre's difficulties of bias. Table talk has been with us for centuries—what are the Gos-pels, after all, but divine table talk? If table talk promises access to the private voice, the notebook—where the author is caught in the grip of literature rather then the pose of personality—anticipates secrets of the workshop, the undergrowth of mind. Literature may require personality, but the personality where its lessons inhere is an act of the page, as a conversation is a drama in air. The invasion of the workshop may seem less personal than the invasion of private conversation, though both books are invasions of privacy, and both species of biography.

Auden felt ambivalent about biography, which he deplored in principle but devoured in practice, like a priest with a private collection of French postcards. In his introduction to Shakespeare's sonnets he wrote, "A great deal of what today passes for scholarly research is an activity no different from that of reading somebody's private correspondence when he is out of the room, and it doesn't really make it morally any better if he is out of the room because he is in his grave." At Oxford, however, after he and Christopher Isherwood decided to publish a book of "confessions," he secretly entered the rooms of undergraduate friends and ransacked their desks for incriminating letters. The notebook therefore indulges a certain prurience not entirely scholarly. Just to riffle its pages is to succumb to an intimacy we rarely demand of our friends.

The "battered blue ledger," now in the Berg Collection at the New York Public Library, is a common lined account-book manufactured in Birmingham, where the Auden family lived, and purchased for one shilling thruppence, then worth about thirty cents. Auden has written his name inside and, as a title, *Poems. May 1927-March 1929.* The contents include almost all the poems in *Poems*, the pamphlet Stephen Spender began printing in the summer of 1928 on a press intended for making up pharmacy labels. Most of these poems were incorporated in Auden's first book, also called *Poems*, published by Faber and Faber in 1930. A little more than half of the thirty poems in *Poems* (1930) are present, with significant portions of the charade "Paid on Both Sides." Half a dozen or so poems are previously uncollected.

The library has lavished on this edition the same expensive attention given almost twenty years ago to the facsimile of its manuscript of *The Waste Land*. The notebook has been reproduced photographically and the transcriptions printed in red and black, to distinguish Auden's pencil from his ink. The editor, Patrick T. Lawlor, has for the most part meticulously transcribed Auden's crabbed scratchings. The editorial notes, a model of concision and enterprise, trace the poems to later publication, catch his allusions and faint echoes (always quoted), explain his references, and condense the relevant circumstances of biography. (The facsimile would have been improved by removing the melodramatic foreword, which says among other things that Auden's "cadences survive and flourish beyond his own, only too brief, lifespan." Auden died at sixty-six— he was no Chatterton. And he would have grimaced at *lifespan*.)

One could not wish for a more sympathetic or thorough job of embalming scholarship. If I have reservations and believe in this case the care has been misapplied, it is not because I object to the scholarship or think the editor and publisher have not produced an elegant edition. Rather, they have misunderstood the value of a facsimile or confused values better left discrete.

The poems must be considered in their early context. In June 1927, at the end of his second year at Oxford, Auden had submitted a collection of poems to T. S. Eliot at Faber and Gwyer, as it was then. Eliot, a little stiffly, wrote in rejecting them, "I do not feel that any of the enclosed is quite right, but I should be interested to follow your work." It was natural for Auden to have sent his poems to Eliot, who presides awkwardly over this early scrap:

The Megalopsych, says Aristotle
Never runs swinging his arms.
So when I saw the Reverend Bythesea Bubb
The customary fine for paucity was inflicted
But when I was drunk. "Goo goo' I said
'Lovely men."

The punctuation is all Auden's, but there is Sweeney, and there Professor Channing-Cheetah, and there the pub scene and "Goonight. Goonight." It is virtually the last time in these poems Eliot is heard so vacantly and so incompletely digested. The next leaf, against which Auden had written a note referring to Eliot's "Intimations of Mortality" (meaning "Whispers of Immortality," though sublimely whispering to Wordsworth), has been removed with the same ruthless authority that marked the sea changes of Auden's style or the suppression of poems he later thought dishonest. Auden was already appropriating the influences that would take him beyond the dry comedies of Eliot, and the notebook contains the first stirrings of early style as well as its first confident exploration.

Of the 192 pages (ninety-six leaves) in the original notebook, more than half were torn out, and only 60 of those remaining were written on. Nicholas Jenkins, who introduces the volume, believes nothing of value has been lost. But Auden was careful to destroy *something*. Since little can be deduced about the missing pages, I cannot share the editor's satisfaction that "it seems unlikely that Auden would have felt that a poem had reached a sufficiently advanced stage to be inscribed here, and not, as was his almost invariable habit, also have sent copies of it to his friends." I am disturbed by the "almost." Even if no poem has been lost, the drafts of poems now present only in fair copies would have been of value to the facsimile.

Consider the earliest poem that survived into *Poems* (1930). Auden replaced it in the second edition; but the clotted phrasing, lack of transition, and Anglo-Saxon rhythm and alliteration are (despite their anxious clumsiness) intrusively original, as if he were trying to out-Hopkins Hopkins. (Unless otherwise noted, the inset texts are from *The English Auden*, edited by Edward Mendelson.)

> *Bones wrenched, weak whimper, lids wrinkled, first dazzle known,*
> *World-wonder hardened as bigness, years, brought knowledge, you:*
> *Presence a rich mould augured for roots urged—but gone,*
> *The soul is tetanous; gun-barrel burnishing*
> *In summer grass, mind lies to tarnish, untouched, undoing,*
> *Though body stir to sweat, or, squat as idol, brood,*
> *Infuriate the fire with bellows, blank till sleep*
> *And two-faced dream.*

This passage reads like a schoolboy's raw translation, before the accommodation with English is made. Here, fossilized in Anglo-Saxon density, lack of definite and indefinite articles, compression of relation and suppression of subject, phrase attached to phrase like flat cars, is the first sign of the early method, if not the early conviction.

Until reading these drafts and seeing the poems page by page acquire and absorb each new influence, I hadn't recognized the comprehensions Auden reached through Anglo-Saxon verse. I'd thought the manner adventitious—the sort of literary notion that might occur to any undergraduate learning Anglo-Saxon. Perhaps his interest began as a slight attachment or novel idea; but in these drafts it is clear how deeply Auden saw into the medium of that earlier state of the language, how much it impinged and formed, and how his verse was altered. It was the addition of the right metal to the alloy, increasing its tensile strength as well as its ductility and conductivity. Thereafter his abstractions had, as in Anglo-Saxon, a more primitive substance, or what might crudely be called mass.

A poet knows in an early draft the concordance a poem has struck, its particular exactions of language and mood, and the boundaries limiting that concord. Most revision is simple in structure, if complex in effect. In the mathematics of revision (whose operations are insertion, deletion, transposition, and replacement), deletion and transposition ask the least access of imagination. Replacement is the most susceptible to brilliance. Auden already understood the demands of tone, deleting three lines that included the phrases "mucous tenderness" and "flesh dough suffits to spilling." He was not yet a master: in the printed version, the last line has been altered from "Seen yes or no. Before which argument my buts are impudent" (which does penance before Donne's "Here is no penance much less innocence") to "Seen yes or no, too just for weeping argument." This is slightly less labored, for dime-novel romance. Auden's shattering beginnings often shrivel to their endings—it is easy to quote a dozen of his first lines for every one of his last (with Larkin, for example, it is the other way around; but then Auden was a poet of life and shock, and Larkin a poet of death).

During the summer of 1927, Auden traveled with his father to Yugoslavia, where, he later told Spender, the boys were the most beautiful he had ever seen. Universities afford the young not just a private education but a private life. At Oxford, Auden devoted his idle hours to promiscuous homosexuality, carried off with considerable flair and bravado. (According to Humphrey Carpenter's biography, from which I have taken other shilling facts, Auden's method of seduction was to enter the room of his quarry, lock the door behind him, and say, "You know what I've come for.") Auden's private compensations were not always clear to his friends, who tended to take his nerve at face value: the assurance showed against his friends before it showed in his poems.

At this distance the moldy orange left on his mantle like a rotting globe, the loaded revolver (perhaps only a starting pistol) hidden in his desk, and the taste for outrageous clothing—the cane and monocle, the Panama hat, the medical jacket—seem the usual unfashionable gestures of an undergraduate who longs to be the fashion. It is not surprising that C. Day Lewis thought Auden was "perhaps best taken in smallish doses."

Yugoslavia provided the ripening metaphor of displacement for a poet who was physically and emotionally out of joint. In Dubrovnik he wrote the beautiful poem beginning

> No trenchant parting this
> Of future from the past,
> No idol fractured is
> Nor bogey scared at last.
> Yet still the mind would tease
> In local irritation,
> And difficult images,
> Demand an explanation.

It ends, "And that which we create / We also may destroy."

As so often, Auden proceeds by negatives, denying the "trenchant parting" denial calls to being. This is poetry as young as Keats's, reveling in the fresh exercise of power and the theft from elders (Yeats and Eliot here), deliberate in its aggressive mystification. Many of these poems of division ("Of future from the past") were written, I suspect, not in homosexual panic but homosexual bewilderment, as Auden realized he would never accede to the normal temptations. Except, perhaps, the temptation of loneliness.

The trip with his father was unhappy. On their return to the suburb of Birmingham, Auden wrote of a landscape whose tensions became characteristic, and then perhaps character itself.

Who stands, the crux left of the watershed,
On the wet road between the chafing grass
Below him sees dismantled washing-floors,
Snatches of tramline running to the wood,
An industry already comatose,
Yet sparsely living.

The familiar rarely feels more alien than after a trip abroad, the comforts less comforting than after failed escape.

Go home, now, stranger, proud of your young stock,
Stranger, turn back again, frustrate and vexed:
This land, cut off, will not communicate.

Only three small revisions have been made to the fair copy, but each shows the application of an artistry. The passive, thwarting description of "Snatches of tramline banked up from the stream" turns into the active, menacing "Snatches of tramline running to the wood," with its dark promise of exit. A responsive ear has adjusted "until this, / Its second office, grudgingly performed" to "Its latter office," echoing the "lay" of the previous line. Finally, "Stranger, turn back again, frustrate and vexed" began less memorably as the kittenish "nonplussed and vexed" passing through "frozen" to "frustrate," an adjective unusual enough to disconcert, with a noise that lies against "vexed" like skin against sandpaper.

The notebook does not contain the sonnet beginning "On the frontier at dawn getting down," written in Yugoslavia and redolent with the relief of crossing a border. As the poems were knotted into concealment and reticence, the various circumferences of Auden's reference began to overlap. By fall he had written the first poems that later resolved into "Paid on Both Sides." Much that is suggestive in the images of death, of anxiety before defeat, of men in bare rooms awaiting an unnamed enemy, Auden must have been unaware of—unaware, because history had not yet caught up with his imagination. His dawning comprehension that these poems "seemed to be part of something" only hints at the strangeness of their silent, repetitive relations. There is no convincing account of the gloomy intensity and eerie resonance of these images (so specific to Auden, and Auden's nature, their imitation was a disaster for Spender and others). Though I cannot offer a taxonomy of Auden's growth along lines of pressure and regard, these poems seem to proceed by negative influence. Invading the interior fiction of the thriller and the saga (the acrid melancholy of Graham Greene seems not far from Iceland), they force a cynical tone into political form, evading the philosophical and religious asperities of Eliot and the maudlin personal condition of Yeats. The atmosphere of the period was susceptible to such arraignment, but required a very private arrangement. Auden's early poems were written for himself and his friends, in the seclusion of their pleasure; but they changed when he discovered what he wrote would be listened to. The earliest poems achieve their statements; all too soon they are making statements. The secret world met a social condition.

Cultures in decadence and cultures in crisis are equally attracted to the private world and the private language. In the language of spies, whose declensions occupied Auden during his final year at Oxford (three years are the normal term at an English university), the tensions of homosexuality—of disguise, of secret knowledge, of distaste in others and discovery by others, of possible prosecution—found prior substance, a substance approximate to any affair of heart. As an idiom the poems exceeded their intimate virtues.

That note of private relation subjoined or corrupted intrudes even in poems most overtly politic, like "Control of the passes was, he saw, the key," of which three drafts exist in the notebook. The drafts are not diversely or divergently very interesting, though Auden shuttles the first lines about and momentarily wavers over the opening phrases, which briefly become "Control of the passes was the key, he guessed, / To this new district," and then "Control of the passes was he saw the key / To this fresh district," before returning to the form we recognize:

Control of the passes was, he saw, the key
To this new district, but who would get it?
He, the trained spy, had walked into the trap
For a bogus guide, seduced with the old tricks.

At Greenhearth was a fine site for a dam
And easy power, had they pushed the rail
Some stations nearer. They ignored his wires.
The bridges were unbuilt and trouble coming.

The street music seemed gracious now to one
For weeks up in the desert. Woken by water
Running away in the dark, he often had
Reproached the night for a companion
Dreamed of already. They would shoot, of course,
Parting easily who were never joined.

Isherwood remarked that Auden's saga world derived from the schoolroom. His spies were much like schoolboys (it turned out many schoolboys of the thirties were spies). A reader might be forgiven for thinking the first pair of lines a gloss on Yeats's "Among School Children," or the whole poem a parody of literary interpretation. The suggestion is serious, if in jocular form—Auden's darkest early poems often resonate in odd directions, as if a rich unconscious source had been tapped; some of their art lies in controlling the resonance. The final line's slight ambiguity as "Parting easily who had never joined," as if there were a party or a side to join, was clarified by changing "had" to "were." The notebook's evidence of imagination is mostly of this order. Even a poet's minute adjustments may be perversely fascinating, but they are rarely as unnerving as a complete set of drafts of one poem. These poems have almost reached final form.

To move from the flux of personal condition to the fascination itself is not to ignore the informing strictures of biography but to attempt momentarily to transcend their precise ingratiations and incised limits. Biography never explains the genius of the thing; it only wraps the genius in its conditioning hour. To take an example the notebook provides: after leaving Oxford with a disappointing third-class honors degree, Auden spent the summer of 1928 visiting family and friends as well as a psychologist in Belgium, possibly in an unsuccessful attempt to reverse his sexual disposition. His father promised him a small allowance until his twenty-third birthday (which would come in February 1930), and in the fall Auden moved to Berlin, where for the next year he indulged in working-class boys.

Each of these occasions might find effect in the poems, but the poems borrow almost nothing from their contingent circumstance. (We now know Auden wrote some intimate poems in German—this is an interesting self-division.) The securing anxieties were already in place, and the manner of speaking to them fully developed. Auden did not need to be in Berlin to write

If I lived in the country and you lived in the town
You would send books and the news
I, a brace of game or a hamper of fruit in season,

lines that never escaped the notebook, or

Under boughs between our tentative endearments, how should we
  hear
But with flushing pleasure drums distant over difficult country,
  Events not actual
  In time's unlenient will?

The attending imagery derives from English landscape and English concern. A bird or a habitat might have been discovered elsewhere, but there is little in the poems drawn tellingly from Germany in the twenties and much that continues the burdens of home. It is, in a sense, a biographical negative that in the middle-class suburbs of Berlin Auden composed

From scars where kestrels hover,
The leader looking over
Into the happy valley,

Orchard and curving river,
May turn away to see
The slow fastidious line
That disciplines the fell,
Hear curlew's creaking call
From angles unforeseen,
The drumming of a snipe.

An alien landscape may encourage a mood of self-absorption, and Auden freely absorbed fragments of his earlier English poems for this. The beauty of the opening has an almost moral stringency, the two nouns existing at first in strange relation; but as the meaning clears the birds take their patient predatory calm over the rocky cliffs, over a landscape where wounds have healed.

Auden was able to draw those anxieties into a language of beautiful pregnancy, often with the impression rather than the force of implication. The deliberate failure of routine or rendered meaning, the preference for the transient shudder over the hard effect, is perfectly adjusted to a poetry whose psychological singularity infects a reader not by insinuation, but by something akin to seduction. The delight to be taken from lines where language is brought into suggestive relation depends on balancing the pacing against the architecture:

Nor was that final, for about that time
Gannets blown over northward, going home,
Surprised the secrecy beneath the skin. . . .

Returned from that dishonest country, we
Awake, yet tasting the delicious lie. . . .

No, these bones shall live, while daffodil
And saxophone have something to recall
Of Adam's brow and of the wounded heel.

The poem from which these fragments come is not much longer, is perhaps not a poem at all in the sense of an argument. It is more a collection of small arousals, pleasures of disturbance, each relying on reference to matters unstated ("Nor was that final, for about that time . . .") or mysteries of provocation or juxtaposition. We must imagine what sins of the sax summon up Adam or Achilles, the high ideal brought low by small transgression. The argument is in the seductive nicety of the words; no other early passage shows so plainly the exotic (and neatly erotic) influence of Hart Crane.

People are more likely to be stirred by the private utterance, not because they bear secret loyalty to secrets overheard, but because they do not mistrust the sincerity of the private. Auden could write in a manner that permitted the wholesale lifting of lines from poem to poem, without any rupture of sense (Robert Lowell was also adept at such auto-theft). The manner allowed such larceny because it possessed the integrity of not argument but attitude. To parse such an attitude, to give it moral relevance rather than mere contingency, required the stroke of feeling more than the weight of tradition.

Many poets have sold the personal into exquisite artifice—some literary periods have been spent doing little else—but few have made flagrant artifice so private and personal. The impress of Auden's mystique on the homely, housebound fact left it the idiom of no one's life in particular but the condition of life in general. In Auden's detachment appears the necessity of moral engagement, as if the actions of analysis (as, in a very different way, in Henry James) required the integration of an observing intelligence. The private dramas never quite shredded to reveal their paltry circumstances, the seductions summoned in Oxford rooms, the German marks that bought the affection of Gerhart or Bubi or Pieps or Kurt. Grand gestures often come from sordid relations—that is what makes them grand.

The evidence of experience afflicted toward these gestures must be drawn from the small rages of revision, where the common is disrupted to uncommon form. The first cast of imagination often prevents further invention, it is so obvious. The imagination must descend to the second order of logic, to the oblique. First thoughts are followed by second thoughts:

Gauze pressed over the mouth, a sweet surrender
Gauze pressed over the mouth, a breathed surrender

Spring's green / Preliminary giggle
Spring's green / Preliminary shiver

The salmon feeds in the stream near Haykell
The salmon feeds in the tributaries of the Kell

And, understanding sorrow, know no more
An understanding sorrow knows no more.

Other revisions can be adduced by comparing the versions available here to the published versions:

One sold all his manors to fight, but winning trembled
One sold all his manors to fight, broke through and trembled
One sold all his manors to fight, broke through, and faltered

The song, the varied motions of the blood
The song, the varied action of the blood.

The small genius of such revision does not need attentive statement. There are changes to be quarreled with ("And streams are acid yet / To unaccustomed lip" is diluted to "And streams are acrid yet"), but in almost every case the critical eye has found darkening improvement. My selections have given weight to the striking verbal instance rather than to the rare replacement or deletion of stanzas. The examples show the mark of Auden's attention, though not the full score of his revising instinct, evident in the scrabble of lines that eventually become the passage in "Paid on Both Sides" beginning "To-night the many come to mind" or the half-dozen stanzas (including the memorably awful "Haemophilia is found in men. / He has tasted good, and what is it? / The White Wyandot is a fine hen") filleted for the charade's final chorus.

The examples are of a class, and in each Auden has introduced an ambivalence into the conduct of a word, once or twice by a mere shift of punctuation. The "motions" are mere physical routines, but the "action" of the blood is at once more occult and more implicating.

It may take in the oxygenation of the circulatory system, or the merest movements of that system; the effect of biochemical release, the fire of adrenaline, the rising of hot blood; or, more broadly, the entangling alliances of blood and family. Though some of these ambivalences might have been inferred from "motions," there they were passive and inert. Auden had a fine ear for the release of a word into ramifying structure—for example, in the way the salmon spreads from the simplicity of the stream to the reach of the tributaries, from the single case to the infecting generality, from the plain observation to the incriminating description, whose tributaries keep silent their tributes.

Without exhausting the interest of the notebook, these examples exhaust most of its evidence. Many of the other revisions are trivial, and few drafts compare to the single worked-over sheet of "O Love, the interest itself in thoughtless Heaven" published in Carpenter's biography. Of the forty-four notebook poems, more than half are unrevised or show labor over a word or two, a line at most. There are not enough crises of alteration, where the imagination seizes sudden advantage or opportunity in the language. Occasionally lines are shuffled or deleted, but it would take more imagination to root up weeds. The loss of more than half the notebook's pages, its purpose as a repository of fair copies rather than a book of drafts, and the very late state of the poems mean as a literary document it has negligible value.

As an emotional document, as the votive object for those responsive to the immanence of the poetry, it is of distinguished reliquary value—like a saint's withered finger—and has been so priced. A reader susceptible to such magics will find the hand of the author worth a premonitory shiver, however childish or illegible. Auden's hand is cramped, angular, almost geometric, the hand of an engineer's assistant or an intelligent crustacean, deciphered with admirable facility.*

*He does misread "Smith is therefore" for "And is therefore" (p. 158), and I would argue against reading "New land" instead of "New law," (pp. 58 and 59), though the reading is plausible. Auden probably wrote "on bark of elm," not "or bark of elm" (p. 37). Finally, Lawlor transcribes "Sever the yawing cloud" as "Sever the yaw[n]ing cloud" (p. 41), without explaining the word was printed as "yawing" in *Poems* (1928) and "yawning" in *Poems* (1930), after which the poem disappeared from the canon. Either reading may have been in error—Auden was a notoriously poor proofreader. If Lawlor has reason to choose, the reason belongs in the notes.

A facsimile edition has values mutually exclusive: the virtual and the circumstantial, the secular and the sacred, the essential and the contingent. The virtual or practical value for the scholar, and for the particularly attentive and devouring reader, lies in the subsidy of information. Our sense of *The Waste Land* must forever be enriched—and estranged—by knowledge of what Pound cut out and what Eliot did not. Even minor changes in a great work give us glimpses into the poet's cave of making, insight into habits of mind that conditioned the imaginative labor. Since this manuscript notebook is rarely of crucial literary importance, the practical value of the facsimile is somewhat vitiated. There is better argument for the emotional or contingent value, which approaches the magical and explains the lavish production and ransoming price; but an emotional object does not require quite such stringent scholarship or such meticulous definition. Literary manuscripts can have ravaging effect even without a footnote. Lamb almost wept when he saw the draft of "Lycidas": "How it staggered me to see the fine things in their ore! interlined, corrected! as if their words were mortal, alterable, displaceable at pleasure! as if they might have been otherwise, and just as good! as if inspirations were made up of parts, and those fluctuating, successive, indifferent! I will never go into the workshop of any great artist again."

Though few readers feel indulgent emotionally toward Auden's later work, many are obliged intellectually to the high architecture of "The Sea and the Mirror," "For the Time Being," "The Quest," and other poems of the war; the moral sequences ("Bucolics," "Horae Canonicae") and the dry insinuations of many of the lyrics; the magisterial horror of "The Shield of Achilles," which takes art more seriously than we are now permitted to; the homely and personal poems, all carried off fastidiously, with deep technical polish even when frivolous. If Auden had written nothing before 1940, he would still be one of the great poets of the century. There was a decline, however, and there was a cost. Auden's later poems—the poems after 1940—are one of the great achievements of this century, but they are not quite *of* this century. Despite their versions of the vernacular, they are cool and even cold, self-satisfied, repellent, and plummy—the poems speak *at* rather than *from*. Some of the poems before and most of the poems after *About the House* (1965) are poor imitations of a grand manner, and the very last poems are endearingly dotty. If the late poems make the early seem the work of a brilliant spotty schoolboy, the early can make the late seem halfhearted. Something goes missing from them—Auden had nothing to do with the unconscious anymore.

The reasons for the change in temperament include an aversion to his early readers. Always uncomfortable in the crowd, Auden found various strategies of insuring his recognition while preserving his detachments (he preferred to meet his Oxford friends one by one). The loss of political faith and the subsequent distancing of emotion was an artistic if not a moral disaster. A reader can be indifferent to moral disaster. In an old British movie called *Strange People*, set in the half-lit world of secret agents, a man refers to a line "the poet wrote": "We must love one another or die." The man believes in its militant, sacrificial necessity; and such is his belief, though the movie is unremarkable (apart from the debut of Audrey Hepburn), I am tempted to believe in it, too. When Auden altered the line to the cynical and resigned "We must love one another and die," he had chosen a different life and a different reader.

If Auden were subjected to Auden's habits of mind, his poems might be charted against two divergent axes representing the presiding genius and the imposed attitude. The first is usually uncontrollable, an affliction of spirit rather than an accepted burden (Auden was unusual in choosing his afflictions); the second is a tempering of impulse. In the matter of genius his poems were dominated by Tiresias or the Sphinx: the first blind, the second sharp-eyed; the first a changeling, the second a monster. Tiresias at the heart of mystery, able to predict the future, inhabiting the knowledge of both sexes; the Sphinx crabby and doomed, devouring, an outsider to mystery but a poser of riddles. If we imagine that each genius has contrary aspects—pure and impure, untempered and tempered, the sage and the fool—we can chart the course of his poetry in the following way:

	aspect as sage	*aspect as fool*
TIRESIAS	*Poems* plays *The Orators*	ballads, songs Yeats elegy "Letter to Lord Byron" "The Sea and the Mirror"
SPHINX	"New Year Letter" Freud, James elegies "For the Time Being" *The Age of Anxiety* "In Praise of Limestone" "Horae Canonicae"	"Thanksgiving for a Habitat" *Epistle to a Godson* *Thank You, Fog* clerihews and such

The individual poems may be variously displaced within these quadrants: the plays are almost early evocations of the Sphinx, while "The Sea and the Mirror" hovers on the borderline of Tiresias as sage and as fool. I have used the titles as exemplary and leave finer distinctions to the temperament of the reader. I don't want to wreck Auden's poetry on the shore of these divisions, since there are re-markable poems in three of the four aspects. Auden seemed more affected by internal division than many of the poets from whom he drew inspiration, who either lived under one dispensation or moved from one way of knowing to another. The divisions in Auden were less fatal than the lack of integration, just as a restlessness of style is less fatal than a disrespect for the integrities of style.

A poet under the dispensation of Tiresias understands more than he knows; under the dispensation of the Sphinx he knows more than he understands. Clare, Blake, Rimbaud, and Coleridge were poets of Tiresias, though as a critic Coleridge was a Sphinx. Hardy, Frost, Wordsworth, Dryden, and Lear were poets of the Sphinx. Though we think of the Sphinx as an inscrutable desert figure with a syphilitic nose, to Oedipus she was a gabby monster ready to gobble him up, and also ready to throw herself from a rock when he spoiled her tiresome riddle. Tiresias knew what it was like to be a man and a woman, with all the insight that comes after blinding. The Sphinx had 20/20 vision, but her knowledge of human behavior was a monster's. Their rivalries, the different sorts of knowledge and ignorance they could abide, inform much of our poetry still and are present in the various condescensions to which our poetry is subject. The Sphinx sounds like the voice of wisdom; Tiresias like the voice of truth.

It is usually a tragedy for a writer to discover that people will listen to him. The least likable aspects of Auden's personality intruded very early into his poetry; he quickly discovered ways of compromising his talent, though the minor poetry of the thirties, for example, aspires to more than the condition of privileged delight. When he turned public man, secure in his import, his poetry bloated with public statement. The grand Augustan poetry of the Sphinx in the forties and fifties was a poetry of bloat, but it reads like Dryden in a Brooks Brothers suit. You have to admire the Augustan manner to admire the poetic tact.

During this period of public honor and private regard, two mothlike young men listened attentively to what Auden said in private and wrote down what they could remember. One of these accounts, published some years ago, showed Auden as a garrulous monster, Jacques of all opinion and *maître* of none. The second has now been issued by a private press.

In the fall of 1946, Alan Ansen attended Auden's lectures on Shakespeare at the New School. After the lecture on *Merry Wives*, which consisted mostly of Auden playing excerpts from Verdi's *Falstaff* (Auden thought the play boring), Ansen, like a rapt schoolboy, helped carry the 78s home to Auden's apartment. He had already been collecting Auden's critical opinions in a notebook; as he collected Auden's friendship as well, rising to become a member of the inner circle, then secretary, then amanuensis, he grew obsessive about recording Auden's private remarks. In a year and a half he filled four composition books and eighty typed pages. *The Table Talk of W. H. Auden*, edited by Nicholas Jenkins, is the condensed version of these possessive conversations.

As talk it has enticements, because it catches Auden unawares, even if he is not a talker who ever seems less than conscious of having an audience. We must trust Richard Howard, who has supplied an acerbic and cautionary review of the book disguised as an introduction, when he says it reproduces Auden's "rhythm and interval." Nevertheless, this is Auden and not Auden. Passages have been cut, transposed, rearranged, moved from one date to another, in part to render comprehensible the random rush of talk Ansen wrote down from memory. The editor does not pretend the collage we are left with, the double distillation, reproduces precisely what Auden said or the order in which he said it. The result may seem little worse than the "memorial reconstructions" scholars used to invoke to explain the Bad Quartos, but the editing gives Auden the air of a Mad Hatter—rambling, a little nonsensical, quick to change temper or topic. Indeed, much of the time, where Ansen's questions or comments have been suppressed, Auden seems to be responding to inner voices. It is not the best way to make the acquaintance of a mind so original and so superbly discriminating.

Nor are the remarks themselves likely to endear him to a reader. The pleasure of Auden's prose lies in its clarity and eccentric brilliance. In prose he was able to control the waywardness of his prejudices; in talking, apparently, he just talked. His misogyny, for instance, is in full bore:

> *Do you know Dorothy Sayers' book on art and the Trinity,* The Mind of the Maker? *It's awfully cunty, but very good.*

> *Women should be quiet. When people are talking, they ought to retire to the kitchen. . . . Over here, though, the men are so dull it's sometimes a relief when a woman talks. It's all right for a woman to talk when she's really witty. But even then one has the impression she's really very unhappy and is being witty, not out of good spirits, but to cheer herself up. . . . One feels so sorry that one can't enjoy the wit.*

His mind flits over subjects, rarely alighting long enough for more than an ex cathedra judgment; and unfortunately such judgments are just the ones likely to be memorable to an attentive young man:

> *One thinks of Shakespeare as sitting quietly in a corner and then, when he'd had quite a bit to drink, becoming screamingly funny.*

> *As a matter of fact, the Quarto play [of Hamlet] isn't very good, you know. If an actor wants to do it, all right, let him. Really you would need a Southern Italian, a Sicilian, to do it properly, with tremendously theatrical gesticulations.*

The literary asides seldom rise to such ingenuity or consideration—they are often as useless and strange as the obiter dicta of my mad Aunt Margaret, except mad Aunt Margaret never wrote any serious poetry:

> *I shouldn't let anyone under 25 read Whitman, and Hart Crane is dangerous for the young.*

> *[Swinburne's] rather like Shelley—absolutely ga-ga. Well, Shelley may be ga-ga on a little higher plane. If Swinburne did just want to go on talking, why at least didn't he talk sensibly? I don't like the views of either Shelley or Milton, but one never thinks of Milton as ga-ga.*

It is easy to be this high-handed in private (though the high-handedness is sometimes cruelly funny), but I can imagine Empson talking in this fashion to greater and more brilliant effect. Auden's pronouncements never lead anywhere, never form the basis of a critical architecture. He talks to impress his listener, believes the listener will settle for the smart remark, is perhaps even eager for the smart remark. This sort of talk withers conversation and can most easily be inflicted on the young. The reader who desires different facsimiles of the talk of this period should inspect Howard Griffin's *Conversations with Auden* (published posthumously in 1981). Like

Ansen's, they were taken down from memory; but Griffin meticulously reworked them as literary artifacts, imagining himself as Eckermann to Auden's minor Atlantic Goethe. The talk is much more disturbing in its density and penetration. Either Griffin was a minor genius at doctoring raw speech or his questions put Auden under more pressure to perform. Whether it is Auden or not is a serious question. Auden claimed to agree with the opinions expressed but not to remember a word he was supposed to have said.

Auden's opinions were refreshingly mordant before Benzedrine and alcohol abuse turned his conversation into a rehearsal of his store of aperçus; but the final measure of Auden's respect for his disciple Ansen is that he escapes from a discussion of alliteration in *The Age of Anxiety*, the one technical discussion in these long talks, by saying, "I've got to go out now to see if the new Michael Innes is in the lending library."

The whole performance, or series of performances, is repulsive, tiresome, and condescending, like that of an Oxford don on poisoned port. Because it is Auden, it is also genuinely odd, fascinating in a fretful way, full of the accidentally revealed insecurities that drove the poetry. Sometimes the revelation is no more than a reminder of the poet's circumstance:

> *You know, for three years, I had to eat lunch every day with a horrible jukebox blaring away. It was in a drug store at Swarthmore. There was no other place to eat. I thought I'd go out of my mind if I heard "I'm Dreaming of a White Christmas" one more time. . . . The jukebox is really an invention straight out of hell.*

Anyone's sympathies would be aroused by this, by the pettiness of the affliction (if it is affliction); but mine were a little chilled when I remembered that, by spending the war at Swarthmore, Auden avoided the war in London. Poetry, even great poetry, must overcome the meanness of its inception; and it is dismaying but humbling to face the private consolations, the limited conditions of life that satisfied Childe Auden:

> *You don't like Betjeman? That's really my world—bicycles and harmoniums.*

I like the same country as Wordsworth but not the same places. My landscapes aren't really the same as Wordsworth's. Mine, and that's a point I haven't written about yet, come from books first.

Auden was happiest as a domineering and pampered youngest son, but his earliest poetry surmounted the Blimpish myopia of Edwardian England the later poetry reveled in. His critics could not make out whether the complacencies of the late poems defended a private insufficiency or attacked a public disorder. It is not unreasonable to think they did both, that the long argument with the twentieth century concealed the distress of the nineteenth, that the diction loud and public was also insulating and private. When Auden ventures into slang, or tries to talk like one of the boys, he never seems quite convincing. He's like an entomologist who has discovered—now what is this? Ah!—a squirming little bug. The effect is no different when he rummages through the *OED*, turning up his *foudroyant* and *sheiling* and *oggle* and *eloignment* and *malapert* and *disemboguing*—as a boy he paged through his father's medical books to impress friends with his deep vocabulary. A poetic diction requires more than impression; it requires nervous sensitivity to the history of nuance, to music, to the humidity of context, to the temperature of the line. That old fuddy-duddy don the late Auden might have said, with his Devil, "I've tried / To clothe my fiction in up-to-date diction, / The contemporary jargon of Pride."

Genius coexists with madness only in the rare instance. More often it inhabits an ordinary unhappiness, the constant irritant of loneliness or misery in love, driving the imagination to ever more insufficient sacrifice and propitiation. Who would have suspected that, still in love with the promiscuous Chester Kallman, Auden considered hiring Dahoman witch doctors to spell the faithless one home? Or that purity of religious instinct could find so secular (so dental!) an incarnation:

While I was under the anaesthetic [to have eight front teeth pulled out] I had a dream—it's the second time I've had it. It's all about Chester and salvation. Now I know I can't be damned. The margin of salvation is ever so slight—it was slighter this time than last—but it's there. It was a revelation that God cheats. He gives that extra little push. No, it wasn't a warning—it was an actual revelation.

Auden's poems about love would have a detached, almost clinical air, if not for the distaste they show toward intimacy. If we believe him, he would rather have paid for the physical spasm and been home in bed by nine. The distaste and the private sorrow rescue the detachment; yet Auden could be very moving about love, especially before he fell deeply in love himself.

These are perhaps poor consolations for a portrait so unattractive. And yet the evidence of his friends hints at some animating spark these lifeless sentences—or life sentences—do not provide. They are often merely peculiar, when the poetry was merely brilliant, or, after he chose to dissipate his talent, something almost more difficult, brilliantly good. I'm grateful—anyone would be grateful—Ansen thought such talk worth saving, but literature would be better for more notebooks of Tiresias than further table talk of the Sphinx.

Modernism's
Last
Aesthete

"At one of the later performances you asked why they called it a 'miracle,' // Since nothing ever happened. That, of course, was the miracle." To come to terms with John Ashbery's poetry is to come to terms with a sensibility deeply divided, nervously giddy, utterly fraudulent. How will those gimlet-eyed readers of the future judge our age's critical fascination with him? As a typical example of our culture's infatuation with fashion rather than meaning? As the inflation of a small, delicate talent for absurdity into a helium balloon six stories high, fit only for Macy's Thanksgiving Day parade? Or as the rare recognition of an innovative genius by a time with little else to recommend it?

If Ashbery's poetry is the acid test for contemporary criticism (one could compose a handbook of evasion from the critical responses to him), it is due less to its quality than to the questions it provokes. It would be a mistake to believe his fractured vision, his reflexive concern with the mind, and his radical technique have deep affinity with abstract expressionist painting or the structures of French philosophy and criticism, though it would be easy to align his work with either, given his long affiliations with the art world and matters French. That would be to mistake the movements for the mind itself. The "miracle" of his work is not what is present, but what is denied and effaced, and what does not happen at all.

As We Know, Ashbery's ninth collection, ranges from a quartet of one-line poems (whose titles in three cases exceed the length of the poems themselves) to "Litany," two sixty-six-page "simultaneous but independent monologues" printed in adjacent columns. It is hard to repress a weary sigh when turning to another long poem by Ashbery: the form—perhaps it should be called the length—has been responsible for his weakest, most indulgent experiments, as well as his finest poem, "Self-Portrait in a Convex Mirror," the title poem of a book that won the National Book Award, the National Book Critics Circle Award, and the Pulitzer Prize.

Unlike the focused intensities of "Self-Portrait," which possessed something very much like an argument, "Litany" has no center. Ashbery is at his most irritatingly ephemeral here, no moment sustained into stability, each sentence erupting at an angle to the last (and yet those angles sometimes charming and irresistible). The sensibility is there long after the sense; but what *is* erases what *has been*, the poem a linear palimpsest. The luxations of thinking, the random insertion of detail, and the reliance on deflations of mood limit the reader's attention to twenty or thirty lines that immediately vanish from memory, as if they had never been read, as if they had never been written. We are often told that modernism's disjunctions of form imitate the fracture of modern life, which is the imitative fallacy at its most brutal. Most of the protocols of our thinking are little different from those of Tacitus or Chaucer, and if there has been a fragmentation of consciousness it does not necessarily demand a technique so self-devouring.

Ashbery is modernism's last aesthete, a case of aestheticism so arrested he is often mistaken for a monument. However coldly au courant the strategy of his poems, they require a passivity toward (even a fatal ignorance of) feeling. I don't want to raise an intuition to the rigidity of a rule, but I doubt any poetry can exist beyond the manners of its moment—beyond the diction and syntax and even mannerisms the poet unknowingly reflects, which together might be called a medium—without providing the reader some recourse to emotional life, if only because the emotions have a grammar older than local circumstance.

The immediate pleasures of Ashbery's poems are so separate from textual analysis it is difficult not to be entranced by the surface—the wily gestures, the knowing tones, the great range of diction—and to dismiss a poem without attempting to dismantle it. Many of his poems will yield to an analysis far less rigorous than that needed for Hart Crane or even Emily Dickinson. Unfortunately, most of them resolve into an aesthetics of perception that would little trouble and little interest a freshman philosophy class. Ashbery is so adept at creating the illusion of thought it is depressing to find his dressed-up ideas just sweet banalities.

A poet can live on the banality of ideas far longer than he can live on the banality of expression. Ashbery's gift is a vague suggestiveness that is also a brilliant suggestiveness. When he writes, "Where day and night exist only for themselves / And the future is our table and chairs," he has supplied the small consolations of language (personification and metaphor being the core of etymology) in selfish nights and days and fateful meals. The adversities of logic do not interest him (it would be unfair to say they elude him), and a poetry deprived of logic always devolves into suggestion. It should not be surprising the only poet in our past to whom Ashbery shows any affinity is Wallace Stevens, the other great modernist aesthete, and also a master of pacing, wit, and galumphing off-centeredness. Ashbery's work, like Stevens's, is a tabula rasa for modern criticism—any theory interested in perception and reference can draw its symbols there.

Ashbery is a brilliant example of a condition, a fin de siècle sensibility with the attention span of a stand-up comic. "Taglioni danced what Kant thought," a dance critic once wrote, and Ashbery writes what Wittgenstein thought as he watched his beloved cowboy movies. *As We Know* continues the melancholy concerns of Ashbery's recent books, *Self-Portrait in a Convex Mirror* (1975) and *Houseboat Days* (1977), without altering or advancing his style. "Litany" is the litany of reciprocative prayer and the litany of monotonous account. The construction of vast rhetorical machines, spewing out meaning and non-meaning indifferently, defines the mocking originality of a poet who may have a lasting status as an American eccentric. It accounts as well for the cruel tedium of so much of his work.

In and
Out of
the Avant

Allen Ginsberg

The hysterical voice of Allen Ginsberg's *Howl* (1956) seems, a quarter of a century later, a young man's literary pose, no more threatening than a cap pistol. It is not only time that has stripped the emperor, though time is cruel to poseurs (even if the greatest English poetry has been the art of imposture). Much of the rude art and hapless sweetness of Ginsberg's early poems has been drained away by his subsequent trumpery. The more he has based his poetry on something other than his original exuberance and anger, the more desperate the howl has become. However admirable his study of religion and his devotion to social causes, Ginsberg has ended as a priestly shouter, further and further from a visionary like Blake (a poet, as Randall Jarrell once said, "whose favorite word was *howl*").

The title poem of *Plutonian Ode*, the cover helpfully informs us, "combines scientific info on 24,000-year cycle of the Great Year compared with equal half-life of Plutonium waste, accounting Homeric formula for appeasing underground millionaire Pluto Lord of Death, jack in the gnostic box of Aeons," and so forth.

> *Judgement of judgements, Divine Wind over vengeful nations, Molester of Presidents, Death-Scandal of Capital politics! Ah civilizations stupidly industrious!*
> *Canker-Hex on multitudes learned or illiterate! Manufactured Spectre of human reason! O solidified imago of practitioners in Black Arts*
> *I dare your Reality, I challenge your very being! I publish your cause and effect!*

In his sermonizing and hand-me-down Whitman, Ginsberg has the courage of cracked individualism, though the best weapon against plutonium may not be bad poetry. Poems from the Hyde Park Corner soapbox are jumbled here with "hot pants Skeltonic doggerel" ("Come twice at last / he offers his ass / first time for him / to be entered at whim / of my bare used cock") and some hilariously horrible punk-rock songs.

Drained of hopped-up rhetoric, Ginsberg's poems can still suggest the empathy rare in his work after *Kaddish* (1961). "'Don't Grow Old,'" a poem for his dying father, quietly attends to emotion:

> *Twenty-eight years before on the living room couch he'd stared at me, I said*
> *"I want to see a psychiatrist—I have sexual difficulties—homosexuality"*
> *I'd come home from troubled years as a student. This was the weekend I would talk with him.*
> *A look startled his face, "You mean you like to take men's penises in your mouth?"*
> *Equally startled, "No, no," I lied, "that isn't what it means."*

Only rarely, however, do moments of self-revelation ("my dharma friends think I'm crazy, or worse, a lonely neurotic, maybe I am") counter the shapeless rants, greeting-card rhymes, unerotic sex poems, and political diatribes of a numbingly obvious kind. Despite his interest in Eastern religions, Ginsberg's private note is not acceptance but betrayal—political, anatomical. Without the wit of a Rochester, an aesthetic can proceed only nervously on vengeance and philippic. Ginsberg has carried a bald philosophizing long past the era when its awfulness could be forgiven because of its politics.

Charles Bukowski

Charles Bukowski comes from the hard-boiled school of poetry. The antihero of the California poetry scene, he's worked in factories, slept rough, been knifed by a street punk. His short stories about life in the post office are raw and minor classics, what Orwell might have written if he'd stayed down and out. The poems in *Dangling in the Tournefortia* are the boiled-off residue of a life lived at the margin.

> *it was the 4th of July and I was*
> *living with an Alvarado Street whore,*
> *I was on my last unemployment check*
> *and we had a room on the first floor*
> *of a Beacon Street hotel next to a*
> *housing development.*
> *it was 11 a.m. and I was puking,*
> *trying to get a can of ale down,*
> *the whore in bed next to me*
> *in her torn slip.*

His gritty, lumpen-prole antagonisms are sociology, not pathology. Bukowski doesn't like his fans—he hardly likes anybody ("I lost my enthusiasm for / the masses at the age / of 4"). If he's pleased by his late success and his late wealth, it has made his poetry no less bleak. The repetitive subjects around which these hacked-off bits of prose orbit are women (mostly unhappy, or unhappy with him), alcohol, and horse racing. Only occasionally do the bitter anecdotes lapse into something recognizably poetic: "never again will I see all of your beauty sleeping, wide- / legged, immune to me: we've all been cheated." Mostly it's one sorry story after another.

Like most tough guys, Bukowski's sentimental at heart, and dozens of these poems are soiled by their own bathos ("she is sad. her walls cover her. she is alone. / I want to know her name"). It is tempting to dismiss such anti-poetry, so badly structured, so vain and misanthropic; after a period of intellectual self-castigation, when such poetry was overrated, I'd like to fight against underrating it. In an unemotive time it is a severe reminder that poetry stays close to strong emotion, to lives as they are lived. If the perception had the severity of the life, Bukowski would be our minor modern Villon (and how proud he would be of it!), our spoiled-by-wealth Genet. Unfortunately, life here has entirely mastered art.

Thomas Kinsella

Plain styles are all alike, but every obscurity is obscure in its own way. Thomas Kinsella has entered his seventh decade in full possession of his ancient angers toward the continuing corruption and crisis of Ireland. Kinsella has always been a poet most powerful when his politics were personal, when the shattered recollections of family were refracted through the impersonal brutalities of a state given to sentiment and the easy hypocrisies of religion. The ruptured style toward which Kinsella's verse has been tending was chipped out of an early sub-Georgianism, with its lays and legends, and a thin Yeatsian anguish and splendor. The poet who in his twenties could write "two lips / Were seen to break the crests of speech in fair order" and "O Rome thou art, at coffee-break, O Rome" seemed not to know whether he was mocking a style or being murdered by it. It is a distance to

> *Corded into a thick dressing gown*
> *he glared from his rocker*
> *at people* whispering *on television.*
>
> *He knocked the last drops of Baby Power*
> *into his glass and carried the lifewater*
> *to his lips. He recollected himself*
>
> *and went on with a story out of Guinness's.*

The emphasis on *whispering* absorbs the strain of overhearing as well as the volume of the old man's complaint. The old man is Kinsella's father, and in such whispers of mortality the poet discovers the "appalling, appealing" voices that counteract the susceptibilities of a culture gone from teleology to television in a generation.

Blood and Family begins with this elegy for his father and ends with a fractured sequence on Mother Ireland, inscribing the history of the Irish revolt in the ink of family and old engravings. That spread of subject, though consumed by the family drama that makes every parent a sovereign power and every government try to act in loco parentis, suggests the force required to make poetry out of an imagination now drawn to fragmentary organization and to utterances increasingly doubtful of their own sufficiency. The book itself is a willed construction, each of its five sections separately published as a pamphlet by Kinsella's own Peppercanister Press. The sections, which also include a sequence about the poet's childhood, a homage to Mahler, and an elegy for an Irish composer and musician, find their orders in disorder or in the imposed musical structure that serves as armature for the poem about Mahler:

For there are great iron entities
  afloat like towns erect on the water
with new murderous skills,

and there are thunderclouds gathered
  on our perimeter, and the Empire
turns once more toward its farrow.

That excoriating note, at once murderous and elliptical, is from the first movement of a poem that arrives, after an intermezzo and a second movement, at a coda where the Fall has become a pratfall ("I lift my / baton and my / trousers fall"). You can detect that murderous design in other poets, particularly in Geoffrey Hill, who feels a similar trepidation where the fate of empire and false hints of religion intersect. I haven't met elsewhere, however, the profoundly disturbing and disturbed meditative consciousness that can rise to the giddy delights of the conductor's falling trousers or "that last lovely heartbeat / of the whole world // like a low terrible string plucked / Ah Whoom / on the great Harp of Life."

It has been tempting to forget Kinsella as younger Irish poets, like Seamus Heaney, have taken the battered and bartered history of Ireland as a condition that can be accommodated or ignored, but not denied. Kinsella can still entertain the tragic possibilities, and his recollective passions serve as an affront to a present that can serve only the past. His new poems are his darkest, and the least vulnerable to easy understanding; they survive in the jolt of juxtaposition and the shudder of meaning beneath the surface. The poet's own thorny rectitude guarantees the precision and tonalities of this splendid, uneasy, moving book.

Michael Palmer

Amid the calm fatuities and self-satisfactions of so much conventional verse there is little that challenges, and poets swollen with the experimental impulse should not be blamed for attempting to overthrow a poetry so frequently submissive to triviality and caution. We are now almost comfortable with Mallarmé, Stein, and Ashbery, though there remains a delightful whiff of the con artist around the last two. Why should we not rise in rage at and later retire in delight with the L=A=N=G=U=A=G=E poets, or with Michael Palmer?

Reading Michael Palmer's poetry is like listening to serial music or slamming your head against a streetlight stanchion—somewhere, you're sure, masochists are lining up to enjoy the very same thing; but for most people the only pleasure it can have is the pleasure of its being over. *Sun* consists of six poems, two of them titled "Sun" and two others "C," appropriate in a poet who finds repetition a significant form of meaning, even when it signifies (as in Eliot, let us remember) drought rather than fruitfulness. *Meaning* is a fraught term for such a poet, whose work takes its form in violent juxtaposition, slips of syntax, in randomness and cacophony and the complacencies of the indeterminate, and in frequent reference to the act of writing and the theory of language. In "Baudelaire Series," the poet says,

A hundred years ago I made a book
and in that book I left a spot
and on that spot I placed a seme

with the mechanism of the larynx
around an inky center
leading backward-forward

That perhaps raises to consciousness the art behind the act; but it also trivializes art in favor of semantic theory, and does so in a fashion quite foreign to Baudelaire, who knew very well how to crush the reader's expectation without being a dilettante of the emotions. Baudelaire would have eaten Michael Palmer for breakfast, with salt.

In Palmer's work, language is frequently reduced to its surface gestures, which is fine if you're a gesture and if not, not.

Paper universe of primes
Flooded land flooded hand

House: herself in the mirror photographing herself

lies over then under

reticular figures

both speaking/

not speaking

When the field of meaning is so weakly generated, such fragments supply a coherence never more than contingent, and the disconnected particulars can flaunt but never inhere. A poetry that has fled the ingratitudes of meaning, that has abandoned so much of technique, cannot survive on the contemplation of technique alone.

My complaint is not that this poetry raises a challenge, but that it is not challenging enough. Palmer's tone is frequently mild-mannered and obliging, more retrograde than revolutionary, and his lines slip all too easily into the pretentiousness ("The opening is read by the tongue / momently for the dead now"—*Momently*!) and schmaltz ("You, island in this page / image in this page // What if things really did / correspond, silk to breath // evening to eyelid / thread to thread") they pretend to deplore. At such times obscurity is the pursuit of sentimentality by other means.

Even in the general collapse of impulse there are suggestive lines: "from moment to memory a swollen debt" or "And you married to that clown, that ape, that gribbling assassin of light," where *gribbling* seems a trouvaille on the order of Sir Arthur Conan Doyle's "Grimpen Mire." In one long passage the disjunctions fall brokenly upon the mutilated corpses of political victims, and there the method is suddenly justified by descent into politics of an enormity to which linear narrative cannot hope to be reconciled. Large claims have been made for Language Poetry, especially by critics who think derangements of semantics or syntax are revolutionary and likely to overthrow the existing orders of power. That is a romantic thought, and one that probably would not have occurred to Robespierre or Thomas Paine, Lenin or Frantz Fanon, who had more use for the plain statement, or the plain lie. Compared even to the revolutionary modernists, who reveled in disjunction, Language Poetry is a parlor game.

Millions
of Strange
Shadows

The Changing Light at Sandover

James Merrill revises his past, as Auden and Yeats did, and as Eliot
and Pound by and large did not. That the elegant and coruscating
lyrics of his earlier books are different in inspiration, if not enforce-
ment, from his recent wrestling with the occult is recognized by the
issue of two volumes to collect his work. But even in the first poem
of *From the First Nine: Poems 1946–1976*, where "the black swan
draws / A private chaos warbling in its wake," there appears the
personal estrangement, the private disorder a public grandeur trails,
that has become as characteristic of Merrill's poetry as his command
of form.

Form is always a resistance, and there is a danger anyone skilled
in such resistance will come to believe that a poet who masters form
masters spirit. Charming and suave, Merrill's short poems have an
elegance of surface that cannot conceal the brooding shapes within.
Whether a childhood home accidentally bombed by Weatherman

or a bank vault deep under Manhattan, the Hall of Mirrors or the Hôtel de l'Univers et Portugal, the settings of his poems imply all drama is domestic, an etiquette of relations gone wrong. Each reflection is a brutality, whether from mirror or mind; and the recurrent glass props in his poems—mirror, window, plate glass—never offer protection from what lurks beyond, or within (as, in an aquarium, "There are many monsters that a glassen surface / Restrains").

In technical virtuosity (and occasional ostentation), wit, variety of form (from the ballad to the villanelle), and range of feeling, Merrill's short poems are unmastered. Among his formal contemporaries, only Richard Wilbur and Anthony Hecht can claim to be his equal. Since the mid-seventies, Merrill has been at work on a long poem, separately published as "The Book of Ephraim" (in *Divine Comedies* [1976]), *Mirabell: Books of Number* (1978), and *Scripts for the Pageant* (1980). The most ambitious long poem of his generation, these three books and a new, thirty-page coda have now been collected and titled *The Changing Light at Sandover.*

Merrill and his friend David Jackson began their sessions at the Ouija board thirty years ago, but no one who read Merrill's early poem "Voices from the Other World" could have expected to what ends this parlor game would lead. To the two auditors, as disclosed in "The Book of Ephraim," came the otherworldly Greek named Ephraim, a murdered favorite of Tiberius. In his witty, gossipy manner, he revealed to his ephebes a supernatural system of patrons, each overseeing a "representative" on Earth who must return through successive lives until himself promoted into their hierarchy. Ephraim's flawed chronology and schoolboy Latin mirrored the shadowy learning of JM and DJ, as they are called in the poems; and there was a strong suggestion the Ouija board sessions were a mere folie à deux, a harmless mutual deception that allowed them "To sound each other's depths of spirit."

Divine Comedies seemed to close the matter, but in *Mirabell* new and darker spirits appeared, voices "WITHIN THE ATOM" demanding from Merrill "POEMS OF SCIENCE." Frightened but intrigued, JM and DJ began a long dialogue with these dark spirits, who looked like red-eyed bats and called themselves the fallen angels of man's mythology, creatures who had lived on Earth before man: "WE TRIFLED & FELL . . . / IT IS OUR DUTY TO WARN MAN AGAINST THE CHAOS ONCE / WORSHIPT BY US." (The other world is always shouting in the capital letters of the Ouija board.) JM and DJ were lectured on the structure of the other world, ruled by two gods, God Biology and Chaos (the latter also known as Nature or Psyche). The spirits of W. H. Auden and other dead friends helped interpret teachings often frustratingly couched in metaphor. The lessons, having been continued in *Scripts for the Pageant* by four white angels (Michael, Gabriel, Raphael, and Emmanuel—each representing one of the four elements), culminated in JM's and DJ's encounter with God Biology.

How can the physics of heaven be abridged for two unmathematical students? The angels struggled toward a figurative language more useful to the mortal poet. The metaphorical surplus points at once to matters micro- and macrocosmic, to the neutrino and the nebula, the boson and the black hole. Raphael's cave, protector of man, is also the cranium. Man, his arms reaching for the stars, is also the hourglass of time. Even so, the poetic tropes confound the poet as much as calculus might—"What this fable means / In textbook terms, we've long despaired of learning!"

By the last lessons the poet and his friend, formerly skeptical, now completely credulous, are the pawns of the world they have invented or mediated—the innocent mutual distraction has become an obsession. The poet, however reluctantly, finds in the deaths of his friends only new material for his poem.

Merrill's revelation cannot have the immediacy of Dante's vision—the distance from here to the other world is greater than it was seven centuries ago. Merrill's five senses have been reduced to the words laboriously spelled out by a blue-and-white dimestore teacup. The emotional movement must therefore derive not from a man's encounter with spirits, but from the effect of enlightenment on two men at their table, from their trouble interpreting and believing the hazy metaphors of heaven. The drama is a function of what occurs between men, not beyond them. Appropriately for a revelation that proceeds entirely through writing, the levels ascended are levels of diction, from the wry gossip of Ephraim through the historical fables of Mirabell to the apocalyptic lessons of the four angels.

It doesn't matter whether you believe in the other world—does anyone seriously credit Dante's system? Revelation tells us more about this world than the next. The secrets of the other world have less substance, less intuitive substrate and less conversant standing, than the poet's symbolic and dramatic use of his surroundings and his intimacy with David Jackson. One example only: the fine opening scene of *Mirabell* involves the solution of a domestic problem by purchasing a rug and designing a wallpaper—both covered with bats. These bats, the spirits later claim, were chosen unconsciously in their image, serving equally the poet who believes in the power of the world beyond and the reader who sees that world as a reflection of two lives.

The assertive occasions of the poem are all life, not lessons. The canzone "Samos," one of the poems set gemlike into the text, uses the angelic properties (water, fire, land, and light) as endwords to counterpoint, within the homely turmoil of a visit to Samos, the wish to become the island the travelers merely behold, to become the mere property of light; yet the poem is a catalogue of postcard detail not transcendent at all. The assumption into spirit of household experience is Merrill's gift for the implicating pattern, the pattern that arranges language into meaning. Poetry is less imagination than the imagination of an appropriate language.

A reader in need of final answers, from a poem that breathes teleology and eschatology, will find here no commandments for the conduct of moral existence, only a troubled search by two men in midlife. The real lesson in the silly and longwinded rigamarole of the other world may be that the imagination conceals "all of life imbued / With the dead's refining consciousness." The world in which the dead exist may, after all, be the cathedral of the imagination. This might seem the gloss of a skeptic who happens to admire Merrill's poetry, and there have been critics enough who have seen this slightly dotty epic as yet another sign that too much attention to meter makes a poet go off his head. It would be all too easy to criticize the faults in such a long poem: the tedium of the angelic lessons, as clumsy as bad carpentry; the ludicrously fashionable occult details (the secrets of the pyramids! Akhnaton!); the gabble of goofy jargon (God B, the 12%, No Accident, the R/Lab, 741, V Work); the unpleasantly elite nature of the other world (not only is the mass of humanity doomed to have "rat souls," but Merrill's friends turn out to have uncommonly high places in heaven). The later sections of the poem are never as poetically articulated, or even as articulate, as the wrought surface of "The Book of Ephraim." Even if Merrill's short poems come to seem, as I think they will, the important medium of his imagination, *The Changing Light at Sandover* continues the revelatory tradition of Blake and Yeats, a tradition that speaks for faith and belief in an age of science and here attempts to corrupt science to its own purpose. No one has yet fashioned in poetry an adequate reflection of the social and emotional life of homosexual men, the dependence on friendship instead of family, the ruptures of death when there will be no sons or daughters: the presiding figure of the poem may be Proust, not Yeats. The tangled ambitions of *The Changing Light at Sandover* go beyond the Ouija board, and even beyond faith and belief. But that may also be beyond poetry.

Late Settings

James Merrill has been much honored and much understood, if we allow that the critical undertakings on his behalf have not been failures as much as private understandings of a poetry that has grown ever more public and difficult. After the publication of *The Changing Light at Sandover,* one critic privately suggested that Merrill would never write again, that the epic had exhausted the psychological desires, or devotions, that had driven his poetry. Much of the real criticism of our time is privately suggested, but rarely do critics so nakedly express the wish to murder the body of work they are mastered by. Poets have never been surprised that scholars prefer to consort with the dead.

It is not the duty of poets to lessen the burden of critics. *Late Settings,* however darkened by its finishing gestures, represents the third or fourth time Merrill has resurrected his poetry from the death of an earlier style or earlier subject. Merrill's new work, as always abounding in houses, takes leave of his epic in a poem about the purchase of a home in Key West, "Clearing the Title" in both the legal and authorial sense.

> *Such a mistake—past fifty and behaving*
> *As if hope sprang eternal. At the baggage claim*
> *Armed with* The Power and the Glory *(Greene),*
> *I notice, finger-drawn in a soaped pane,*
> *One black sun only, spokes in air*
> *Like legs of a big bug flipped on its back,*
> *Above a clumsy* WELLCOME TO THE KEYS.

An inauspicious welcome. *The Power and the Glory* is a title that underlines the dismay with which the narrator approaches change, or endings. Merrill controls the ironies of his social scenes (his longer poems are often about socializing of one sort or another) largely by rendering the actions of an unsympathetic narrator increasingly intelligible and human. The cranky and querulous man who steps off the plane only gradually accepts the splendor of his new surroundings and the necessity with which "what at first appall precisely are the changes." A poem that begins by admitting an absence—"My poem (what to call it though?) is finished"—allows itself in its final line to acknowledge a silent presence, the title of the epic toward which these stanzas have been tending, "Juggled slowly by the changing light."

That sort of cleverness, wicked and self-congratulatory, is just what so many readers resist in Merrill; and it is worse for such readers to have to concede that if cleverness is Merrill's great weakness, it is also the source of his strength. Where that ingenuity is most consistently absent, in the final two sections of *The Changing Light at Sandover,* his poetry must rely on the psychological magnitude of its obsession with the other world, the folie à deux that threatens to become the Folies Bergère. For readers who cannot take seriously the lessons of the other world (lessons in any case contradictory and unhelpful—no one could hope to base philosophy or behavior on them), Merrill's epic is largely a social and psychological document, often of great subtlety, about two men who spend much of their lives and many of their fantasies together. The longueurs of those two sections, despite their great theater and considerable local delights, demonstrate how much of Merrill's poetic intelligence depends on the drive toward compression wit exacts.

Merrill has never been by nature a narrative poet, despite countless indications and many attempts to the contrary. He is more attracted to the dramatic scene, the epiphany whose implications are not limited to the actors who frame it—indeed, who are sometimes ignorant an epiphany of any sort has occurred (that ignorance is the criticism at the heart of much of his social poetry). When the tourists are rowed into "The Blue Grotto," they find it impossible to react to a spectacle long anticipated and often described: "Diane fingered the water. / Don tested the acoustics / With a paragraph from Pater. / Jon shut his eyes—these mystics— // Thinking his mantra." One shuts his eyes! The list of reactions continues, quietly desperate; even the names of the tourists, so blandly American, speak of a culture that has lost its ability to respond to the foreign:

> *Then from our gnarled (his name?)*
> *Boatman (Gennaro!) burst*
> *Some local, vocal gem*
> *Ten times a day rehearsed.*
> *It put us all to shame:*

> *The astute sob, the kiss*
> *Blown in sheer routine*
> *Unselfconsciousness*
> *Before one left the scene . . .*
> *Years passed, and I wrote this.*

The boatman humiliates them with his banal song, taking its richness from the richness of the scene, showing how much emotion the most tedious rituals can contain, not because they are tedious, but because they are ritual. The lives anxious to display their originality are measured by the grotto and found unoriginal. Merrill never excuses himself from his own judgments, though that may be only a higher form of evasion. If he reveled at the time in the ironies of the situation, he is canny enough not to admit it. Implicating himself in the failures of all, he stands back only after a lapse of time ("Years passed . . .") that will not imply a superiority to his fellow tourists.

Yet Merrill is frequently an observer, and many of his poems concern or contain damning observations. He can hardly pretend his interest in behavior is merely casual, that others are not constantly subject to an inspection as careful as it is clinical. Even the reader may feel the scrutiny of a steady and perhaps professionally ironic gaze (his wordplay is so arch and arcane it seems to contemplate the reader, rather than the reverse). An island in the making ("From air seen fathom-deep"), manatees observed underwater, a fish tank, the fish beneath a pier, Palm Beach seen as if underwater: these are poems of a world submerged, where the skin diver is at times the only spectator, distant and detached. Add to them the poems about watching the world through the plate-glass window of a bar ("an airless tank"); being on stage in a school play; gazing out a window whose panes become a sheet of commemoratives, a building, calendar, street grid, and chessboard; a series of poems about lenses; add these and the poet becomes both watcher and watched, his own behavior no less subject to inspection.

A narrator so giddily self-aware is difficult to criticize. Bursting with exclamations ("The trees!") and interjections ("Starlings by now have joined—safety in numbers—/ Forces"), he is alive to his own hesitations ("If one could do as much—A last drag. Wrong / To be so—so—"). The examples are drawn from a dozen lines of one poem, but in almost every poem these simulations of speech contrive a voice capricious and ingratiating—and sometimes irritating. If this is speech, it is speech of a peculiarly artificial sort, and the constant questions into which it erupts ("a bus? a jeep? a peasant's cart?" "*Now* Florence?" "Unpack the picnic here?" occur within a few stanzas) remind us how different interior monologue, even at its most colloquial, is from actual conversation. That interior is carefully guarded:

The doctor probes and listens. Powers failing?
A shot of hormone? The syringe he fills,
At tip one shining droplet, pure foreplay,
Sinks into muscle. And on the third day
Desire floods the old red studio.
A figure reincarnate, wings outspread,
Full quiver, eager lips, from years ago—
My Eros to the life—awaits unveiling.
Friends, here is salvation! Are you blind?
Here, under *the dumb layers which unwind*
I somehow cannot. Tanglingly opaque,
They're nothing if not me. The hidden god,
Unknelt-to, feels himself to be a fake.

("Bronze")

No reader could hope to fathom the depths this poet insists on (indeed, his occasional obscurity seems part of this pleasure in concealment), but he insists on them as if he fears they may not exist—as if he were an Invisible Man, vanishing when the bandages are removed, the wrappings unwound. Much of Merrill's work has been an elaborate confirmation of identity, yet the character of his poems is more mercurial than that of any of his contemporaries. If he has confounded those early critics who found in his work only surfaces, it has not been by denying the fascination with surface. Part of this book is defined by the weaker poems devoted merely to objects: an arc light, say, or a radiometer. In his most brutally elegant work his subject is the *concern* with surface or social being, the unease even elaborate defenses cannot fend off. He has never been a superficial poet, only a poet whose surfaces are meant to defend against his depths.

The atmosphere of Merrill's poems has often been a disadvantage. Cultivated, leisured, privileged with "the mixed blessings of a first-rate / Education exquisitely offset / By an inbred contempt for learning," he can afford to be the tourist, ever at home in the elsewhere. Americans generally distrust the traveler, so insecure are they with the idea of home (it is, after all, a borrowed country). They are even more likely to distrust a poet whose contact with the world is not emotional but verbal. Samuel Johnson said, in one of his moods, "A quibble is to Shakespeare, what luminous vapours are to the traveller; he follows it at all adventures; it is sure to lead him out of his way, and sure to engulf him in the mire." Substitute Merrill for Shakespeare, and you have the modern audience's opinion of wordplay, though the language of opinion would not be so picturesque.

Merrill is not a serious poet whose wit defeats him; he moves toward seriousness only through his wit. The poets of our century have rarely been funny, and when funny have often been childish (the wit of Wallace Stevens is not far removed from that of Ogden Nash). Auden has been as so often our great exception. The young Frost and the Eliot of *The Waste Land* knew more about the seriousness of wit than most of our contemporaries. Merrill belongs to their tradition, though his wit is more lapidary and feverish. If he shares with the metaphysicals the idea that language is pregnant with its own jokes, he has not scrupled to drag the twentieth century into his work. In this he has learned from Auden. "Days of 1941 and '44," a series of sonnets about a schoolboy tormentor, turns on the bully's death—"Three more years and you would die, / . . . in France, at war":

Word reached me one hot twilight. It was raining,

Clay spattering the barracks. I
Fell back onto my bunk, parched for decor,
With Swann's Way. *Basic training.*

The pun on *basic training* gives moral dimension to the recruit's passive situation, but its wry ambiguity is prepared by the preceding lines. The young man falls back, onto a bunk rather than into a bunker; the novel, like the death, is French (and part of a culture destroyed by the war); it is the first book of *Remembrance of Things Past* (a title that might encapsulate the subject of the poem); and, given the English title, it is being read in translation, emphasizing the unworldliness of the narrator. Then a pun to ready the pun, the swan song hidden in *Swann's Way.* Only wit allows such an infusion of meaning into the last line, an infusion that must be as ambivalent as the reaction it records. Our childhood enemies often know us better than our friends.

Late Settings (a title with its own ambiguities) is a book of death and departure, distances from the future and the past. Even when the poet accepts the inevitability of death ("Turning the loose knob onto better-late-/ Than-never light, we breast its deepening stream / Along with others who've a date / With sunset"—the lines also refer to going to watch a sunset), his language is still the heady vehicle of the profusions of this world, not the other one:

> *Close-ups: hibiscus broad as garden hats.*
> *Large winged but nameless insect excavated*
> *By slaves; the abdomen's deep strata*
> *Primitive-intricate, like macramé.*

("Clearing the Title")

Not many poets sustain the invention of their early work. Something hardens or clenches in them as they age; they become their own imitators. Merrill is one of the few (Anthony Hecht is another) whose poetry thrives on the intelligence of its demands. The slight or frivolous pieces prevent this from being among Merrill's strongest books; but the finest poems extend the dashing performance of our man of manners, a Fred Astaire (at times, a Nureyev) with a touch of the lonely and the tragic. Those poems include "Island in the Works" (in the voice of the island, yet), "Developers at Crystal River," "The Help," "Palm Beach with Portuguese Man-of-War" (one of those now-you-see-it, now-you-don't magical tricks with syntax), "Days of 1941 and '44," "Ideas," "Month," "Santo" (a delightfully ebullient Elizabeth Bishop piece), "Last Mornings in California," "The Blue Grotto," and others scarcely less fine. Three long travel poems are more ambitious but artfully overcomposed. Of them "Bronze," full of missed connections, of life in transit, sketches the slow deteriorations of aging from which travel is a flight (*"Quit / Dreaming of change. It is happening / Whether you like it or not"*).

Merrill loves to make poetry of the most unlikely material (no one has found such treasure amid the trash of culture, though some of the trash remains trash nonetheless). His epic was compelled by a drive for order, a universal order, but its revelations could not forever satisfy a mind entranced by the secrets of the mundane. Merrill's gaze always reverts to the world in the wardrobe, or the word.

c h a p t e r 6

Beyond
Psychology

The disarray of a poetry like Elizabeth Bishop's might be called instinctual, a matter of artistic sensibility deeply formed but not always consciously developed, and so not methodical. An artist does not have to be aware of her sensibility—she merely has to know when to let it run its course. A poet could find special advantage in being ignorant, or at least unconscious, of the workings of sensibility. Such an artist might be less likely to fall afoul of a theory of art, a preening self-regard, or an overestimation of intelligence. At the level of artistry Bishop offers an integrated sensibility, while at the level of personality she remains just idiosyncratic. Critics of her poetry must remember they are confronting an artist whose coherence cannot be reduced to coarse psychology.

In Bishop's poetry the appearance of intimacy does not secure any intimate access to the poet's condition. This was the common understanding of the relation between poetry and biography, before critics lost a skeptical distrust of the evidentiary value of poetic statement. To understand a poetry as reserved—as shy and full of indirection—as Bishop's requires a criticism of formal tact, and a will-ingness to treat with unusual care the artist's stray critical judgments, which may be less bound by those reserves and so less cautious ("these worries about . . . whether I'm going to turn into solid cute-ness in my poetry if I don't watch out—or if I do watch out"). The two critics considered here betray that trust—and the responsibili-ties attached to it—without being immune to the texture and con-text of the poems, their wayward and permissive charm.

The available clues to Bishop's life are misleading to the degree they are seductive. As a child she was deprived of her parents by death and insanity, and she became a lesbian and an alcoholic: the authority of these circumstances is almost entirely absent from the poetry. Lorrie Goldensohn is a lover of gossip, and it is hard to adapt the solicitations of gossip to the drier torsions of criticism. *Elizabeth Bishop: The Biography of a Poetry* would be peculiar in its breathless piety if it were not simply another example of what among Bishop's critics is a reverence nearly religious. Though not yet subject to miracle literature, among postwar poets she has become the object of (perhaps the irritant for) a devotional following almost larger than Larkin's. An examination of the criticism of veneration might have provided an interrogative center to what is often a naive, rambling, unfocused personal essay and travel journal, though that would have required a critic more self-possessed. During her pil-grimage to Bishop's former home in Ouro Preto, Brazil, Golden-sohn nearly succumbs to the temptation to steal one of the saint's relics, an old magazine.

The critic seeks out the signs of Bishop's presence in Brazil with a sublime haplessness. She wants to see some statues Bishop de-scribes—but they're half a day's distance away. She goes instead to see the sculptor's work at a local church—but it's closed for restora-tion. An inn-owner tells her "a few grumpy facts," but apparently they're not worth reporting. She meets the woman who now owns Bishop's house, but the critic's French can't keep up with her infor-mant. "Why hadn't anyone else come to see this woman?" she asks, ingenuously. To which the reader might reply, "Why hadn't anyone thought to bring a translator?" The critic expands on the difficulty of eating Brazilian melon with knife and fork.

Among Bishop's papers Goldensohn discovers a vaguely erotic unpublished poem ("All my signal systems are awash. I can't quite take it all in"). Despite a longish chapter of nerve-by-nerve exposition, in which a rather openhearted poem comes to have Grail-like gravity, it doesn't occur to her that Bishop failed to publish it not because of its lack of privacy, but because of its lack of character. The poem's touching and slyly charged ending ("The world might change to something quite different, / As the air changes or the lightning comes without our blinking, / Change as our kisses are changing without our thinking") cannot repair the thinness of expression elsewhere. The critic has stumbled onto a suggestive negative case, which begins to explain Bishop's preference for the oblique ("I believe in the oblique, the indirect approach, and I keep my feelings to myself," says her "Strayed Crab"): in an art essentially reactive and passive, she was incapable of absorbing the disruptive impulse of direct emotion. Emotion did not make her shallow; it made her inattentive, and her art thrived on the attentions plain emotion could not provide. The critic takes the wrong lesson: that Bishop was afraid of intimacy. Intimate emotion did not overcome her critical self-possession.

Goldensohn is alert and responsive to the underbrush of Bishop's language, but she lacks sympathy for the neutrality of Bishop's tone, its quiet sense of improbability, of the genial awkwardness of encounter. The critic wants meanings, and meanings she gets. Bishop's "Going to the Bakery" might be called mocking and mordant, even mutely disheartened; but not, I think, a poem "where neither the foreign American resident nor the home government nor the helpless population is denied corrupt or unpleasant roles." It is too full of the vitality of observed and rendered detail (Bishop's *present! present!*) for such bleak or blatant politics (politics were usually beneath Bishop's eye).

Now flour is adulterated
with cornmeal, the loaves of bread
lie like yellow-fever victims
laid out in a crowded ward.

The baker, sickly too, suggests
the "milk rolls," since they still are warm
and made with milk, he says. They feel
like a baby on the arm.

These stanzas are not tortuous. Goldensohn believes that here Bishop "finds the freshness and whiteness of bread is fever pallor, fever brightness. Bread itself is the helpless flesh of infants, and the baker of it is sick." Not exactly. The loaves aren't white—they're a jaundiced yellow, like yellow-fever patients, because the flour has been cut with cornmeal. The "milk rolls" (*not* the bread) are warm and soft, *like* a baby on the arm—the critic would have us think they are baked babies, an image out of Auschwitz.

Criticism is the poetry of false emphasis, of the inability to register the difference between simile and metaphor. Let Bishop write to a friend, in a fever of convention, "I'm afraid I do like Boston," and the critic will mutter, "Bishop is 'afraid' . . . that she *does* like Boston." Goldensohn is ungainly where her subject is subtle (she has no ear for metaphor: "Her only partly credulous readers rose to the bait on that hook, but in the end forebore to swallow"), and therefore most useful when dogged by fact. As a factual critic Goldensohn has surprising perseverance: she has added significantly to the context of a dozen or more poems. She has gone to the trouble to investigate minor circumstances and has made particular use of Bishop's letters and notebooks. She is, however, attached to the version of psychological criticism by which the life becomes a lived myth: fraught with meaning, meanly suggestive, subject to allegorical reading and the displacement of literature, and always the unique subject of the literature.

In securing an argument about a supposed conflict between Bishop's identities as poet and woman, the critic notes—with acuity—that "particularly when troubling emotions are at issue," Bishop's protagonists are male. The problem isn't that such a tendency doesn't have psychological bearing, but that it may bear in many directions at once. Bishop might as easily be praised for not succumbing to a simple version of the feminine or not suggesting that to be female is to court trauma. It seems odd to criticize Bishop for choosing troubled male voices, and to criticize her again for writing a late poem ("In the Waiting Room") in which "femininity is seen as problematic." (The critic is alert to the poet's least deviation from current pieties, and a little too confident in saying what Bishop *must* have decided or *must* have felt.)

Goldensohn as a biographical critic still believes in something called an "authentic self." Poets are a mass of barely connected selves, working in concert and in opposition (barely speaking at times), and their most grossly inauthentic selves sometimes have custody of the poetry. A poet may exploit an inner violence without responding to it, may respond to it in hints and misses, may find irony in using what in life has been of little use. May use it coldbloodedly. In a serious and severe sense great poetry is beyond psychology in a way that mediocre poetry never is. Mediocre poets are at the mercy of their psychological concerns, but great poetry requires a transfiguration that removes it from simple analysis. This is not to claim that psychology is irrelevant to poetry, only that such analysis tells us almost nothing about what makes a poem work as more than a mechanism. A poem may lie for reasons of construction, or symbolic use, or language, economy, or whim. For a critic of Goldensohn's temper, who sees the right fractures but asks the wrong questions, every movement forward and backward from the petite facts of life has a psychological supplement. For the artist there are dreads more pressing and more pertinent than the psychological.

Bonnie Costello's *Elizabeth Bishop: Questions of Mastery* avoids the conditions of the life in order to mark the inner carriage of an art that has often seemed deceptively simple, even deceitfully simple. Her "aim," she says, "is not to discover what specific events and places from the past determined Bishop's vision, or how these events were transformed to poetry and narrative." This is just as well, since her comprehensions of that life are sometimes comically crude ("It is not surprising that Bishop would find in travel a metaphor for consciousness. Her father, who died in Bishop's infancy, was connected with the shipping industry"). She has a more acute and more detached intelligence than Goldensohn, and conducts her inquiry of Bishop's poetry—sometimes her inquisition of it—on a more abstract plane.

The virtues of the abstract critic must be formed in particulars. The "questions of mastery" to which the study returns, increasingly vaguely and warily, are never reduced to a set of practices, but exist murkily as "modes and critiques" in the thematic realm. They determine, or are said to determine, the habits of seeing in this most visual of poets, both in the structures of sight (distortions of scale or perspective, symbolic horizontals and verticals) and in its application to travel, to painting, to memory, in which the poems find containing force. (Since in *most* poetry mastery may be a question of craft or of psychological adequacy—of fineness of vision or perhaps infirmity of memory—these "questions" may not seem specific to Bishop, however susceptible her poetry may be to their judgments.)

Reading a poet is a matter of getting not just the identities right, but the proportions. Bishop is a poet of unusual visual freshness (not only in her rakish sleight-of-hand descriptions) and moral form, and critics have tended to ascribe these qualities to the local influence of Marianne Moore and Robert Lowell. Costello has read Bishop against a richer spirit, a more comprehending anthology, and measured the poet's alignments with and antagonisms to the Romantics, the surrealist artists, modernists like Eliot and Stevens, and religious poets like Hopkins and Herbert. These influences have been noted and articulated by other critics, but rarely with such subtle gestures or such sensitivity to the contradictions of influence, the pull of a particular voice and the poet's push against it, like Odysseus binding himself to the mast.

These transverse angles of influence—to which the book might have been more devoted—calculate the resistance of a poetry predominantly private in its means but impersonal in its reference. A poetry as calm and matter-of-fact or as guileless as Bishop's rarely has such a dark interior architecture, and it is difficult to remember that the charm is the poems' and the dark architecture—like some scribble out of Piranesi—the poet's. (Costello, like Goldensohn, rather artlessly takes the voice of the poem for the voice of the poet—I agree that poems start there, but they often end somewhere else.) Costello has extracted the unguarded statements of Bishop's early notebooks, and found there informing glimpses of a spirit later more hedged and obscure, even as the poems became more open and transparent.

Here the limitation of the abstract method is laid bare. In her letters and interviews, Bishop was a witty and unsparing reader of her own temperament, and her phrases are sharply poised and weighted: "My outlook is pessimistic. I think we are still barbarians . . . But I think we should be gay in spite of it, sometimes even giddy,—to make life endurable and to keep ourselves 'new, tender, quick.'" *Even giddy.* Much of Bishop's poetry opens from that "in spite of," that incautious "endurable." But the critic is protected from such insight by the dull armor of her abstractions.

> *Certainly there is a subversive element in her violations of decorum, but most often it is tied to a representational aim. She emphasizes the betweenness of seeing form against conflicting form, the perceptual challenge of the world as process.*

And so on, sentence after sentence, for paragraphs and pages. This does not compare favorably with Bishop's "I am very fond of molds and mildews."

The thematic and tactical categories into which the book is divided (a chapter on travel, a chapter on perspective) offer few advantages to an integrated reading of this poet. The individual readings of poems, however, are attractive and finely detailed, not organized so much as tumbled forth. Costello is a subtle and finicky reader, and I wish—ungratefully, perhaps—to suggest where those readings go wrong. Do the five hooks grown into the lower lip of "The Fish" have more than a fragrant factuality? "Five wounds on a fish make him a Christ figure," says the critic flatly, but they are not quite the same as stigmata (Bishop does not call them wounds), and if they were we would only have Christ of the Martyred Mouth. Such a far-fetched conceit is little help to the clumsy Freudian reading the critic offers, which misses the terrible moral weight of the poem, the approach of something near to sin.

Many of her readings are slightly off-center. The critic believes the speaker in "Love Lies Sleeping" has awoken from a nightmare, though bad dreams are never mentioned, and it seems more likely she has awoken with a hangover, and with the woozy, scattered anxiety common to the aftermath of drinking ("Hang-over moons, wane, wane!"). Such an opening would make sense of the ending, where a man lies on a bed, his head hung over the side, drunk or dead, seeing ("if he sees it at all") the city "inverted and distorted. No. I mean / distorted and revealed." Where Bishop has fragility, the critic sees fear and danger, and "the routine oppression of the industrial culture," itself a description hardly less than routine. A writer on vision shouldn't miss the vision here—the critic thinks the city is revealed as a place not clear but distorted, but the force of Bishop's construction (a construction precisely pitched) is that, up-side-down, the city is distorted and *thereby* revealed. Through the distortion you can glimpse its real nature. It *is* a revelation, perhaps only a rueful revelation (especially if granted to a man dead or drunk, or dead-drunk), and scarcely what the critic calls "inchoate dark-ness."

This might seem a matter of critical disagreement, but much of criticism is a mere shifting of weight, the bearing of slight inflections. The critic claims that Crusoe's fifty-two volcanoes in "Crusoe in England" represent "the weekly eruptions in a year of Bishop's life," though how a year of *Bishop's* life is at issue is not clear, nor why these should be characterized as "eruptions," when the volcanoes are described as "miserable, small," and "dead as ash heaps." Her reading of "Pink Dog" smoothly deemphasizes, almost to the point of nonexistence, the terrible politics in the background—the death squads rounding up and drowning the beggars. She wants to read the poem against fashionable critical notions about the body, but the violence is hardly "impersonal violence wielded against [the body] by society"—it isn't wielded by "society," and it isn't impersonal, at least not to the beggars. The poem is as much about ugliness in the body politic as in the body itself. The critic is often intimate with the staging of a poem, but distant from the sense.

Her readings are more effective when orphaned from critical practice. Describing "A Miracle for Breakfast," she refers to the "grumbling, matter-of-fact, commonsense voice." There, in a book where the world of sensibility and the world of intellect are so often mutually incomprehending, the critic actually hears the poet. Costello's criticism is otherwise victim of its dotty formulations ("He has erased the belatedness of the figure and achieved a rhetorical mastery in which the fiction shows no sign of its invention," "Indeed, war is a crisis of difference on a national scale"). Her impressions of form are ill-considered or cursory (she approves of a passage's "alliterative g's" when alliterative g's are few and far between); she is not always comfortable with the vocabulary of vision; and her complaints against hierarchies and privileged beholders would be informing if she weren't blithely setting up hierarchies and privileges for herself.

In remaking the poet in her own image—as a poet who "challenges norms" and "complacent or repressive thought"—the critic has lost Bishop's messiness and scumbling, her delicacy, her emotional frailty, even her whimsicality. (The critic refers in one of her notes to the "intentions behind style," in the confident belief that there *are* any intentions behind style.) She has no comprehension, and little suspicion, of why a poem invents, or fabricates, or alters, and why to the poet the differences between source and solution do not "merely compete." To the poet it is incomprehensible to say, "This view from the midst of things is forfeited in favor of ironic detachment." A poet does not live in the realm of such forfeits.

The
Habits of
Their
Habitats

Amy Clampitt

Amy Clampitt is not a poet of silence. The vast shoreline of *What the Light Was Like* is filled with such profusions, from boulders down to barnacles, they require less a field guide than a phone book. After the beaten-down intimacies of recent free verse, it would have been hard to predict, except for those schooled on reversal, the sudden reappearance of baroque sensibility:

> *Force, just here, rolls up*
> *pomaded into vast blue curls*
> *fit for the Sun King, then crumples*
> *to a stuff of ruffs and kerchiefs*
> *over ruined doorposts, the rubble*
> *of an overthrow no one remembers*
> *except through cooled*
> *extrapolation—tunnels*
> *underneath the granite,*
> *the simmering moat, the darkened sill*

we walk on now,
prowling the planar windowpanes of tidepools
for glimpses of kelp's ribboned whips,
the dead men's fingers.

("Low Tide at Schoodic")

Details! Details! you can hear her exclaim. *Details!* Like a young architect forgetting all she's learned about buttress and carrying beam in the delight of pure ornamentation, Clampitt makes virtue out of the violence of compulsion. Never content to add when she can multiply, she is drawn to images of fecundity, especially pointless fecundity:

> *Boulders*
> *smothered in a fur of barnacles*
> *become a slum, a barrio*
> *of hardened wigwams, each*
> *(notwithstanding a seeming armor*
> *that invites, when added to the fate*
> *of being many, the hobnails*
> *of a murderous indifference)*
> *holding an entity no less*
> *perishably tender than any*
> *neonate delivered, red*
> *and squalling, in the singular.*

("Low Tide at Schoodic")

If this profligacy is at the edge of starvation (slums and barrios are failures of *human* architecture), it is not the baby but the barnacle that draws the sympathy of the eye—the baby is held at arm's length by that clinical Latin. The subtle inversion that occurs when the newborn becomes mere neonate, becomes an object of scientific classification rather than congratulation, shows how distant this poet is from the merely human or, rather, how the merely human falls in her work into a more consequential scheme than is usual in our poetry.

Clampitt has a naturalist's passion, and like a true convert's her enthusiasm is irresistible:

Stealth of the flood tide, the moon dark
but still at work, the herring shoals
somewhere offshore, looked for
but not infallible, as the tide is,
as the August darks are—

stealth of the seep of daylight, the boats
bird-white above the inlet's altering
fish-silver, the murmur of the motor
as the first boat slips out
ahead of daylight

into the opening aorta, that heaving
reckoning whose flux informs the heart-
beat of the fisherman—poor,
dark, fallible-infallible
handful of a marvel

murmuring unasked inside the ribcage. . . .

("The August Darks")

The sentence goes on for almost another twenty lines: punctuation can scarcely impede her plunging into image after image with a finely weighed abandon. Which of her contemporaries would begin a book with five poems whose longest sentences measure fourteen, thirty-four, fourteen, thirty, and fifteen lines? Who would have so many poems that *are* single sentences? If this is an abandonment to the ideas of order, it is no less complete than her abandonment to language. Preferring a language argued through its association, Clampitt embraces Keats—who else?—as a forebear, his romanticism a source profuse with permissions. Her eye turns toward each new observation with an excitement verging on frenzy, with an exhaustiveness lapsing finally into exhaustion.

The most severe of her texts rely on their exchanges, not their emotions, and such poems are the terrain of their transitions. The

violence of these juxtapositions, the logic not entered but entertained, is itself a kind of moral particular, as if encyclopedias were
trapped in the DNA. Whatever is is also something else:

> *The geranium and the begonia*
> *bloom with such offhand redundance*
> *we scarcely notice. But the*
> *amaryllis is a study in*
>
> *disruption: everything routine*
> *gives way to the unsheathing*
> *of its climbing telescope—*
> *a supernova of twin crimson*
>
> *tunnels, porches of infinity*
> *where last week there was nothing.*

("High Culture")

This is a mind determined by its elsewheres, by the *concordia* of its
discors, a disruption that is never quite corruption. The poem ends
with "the slave marts of the East, / the modes of Paris, the gazing /
ramparts of the stratosphere," and Clampitt is often tempted to
make of nature a travelogue, its ancient splendors noted by an eager
but overworked guide, constantly pressed to be on to the next painting, the next pitcher plant. She has established herself as a poet of
place without establishing herself in any place in particular. Maine,
the Midwest, New York City: the American locales recur, but are
just as likely to be intruded upon by an overnight to Italy or a leisurely sojourn in Keats's England. Wherever she is, she takes possession, not by imposing onto landscape the template of her own
sensibility (as happens with poets of stronger temperaments, like
Auden, or more lurid ones, like Lowell), but by engaging the intimacies within each horizon as if they were her own.

   As if: even at home, Clampitt is a poet of exile, her sense of place
conditioned by her uprootings from it: "What the stripped root,
exhumed / above the mudhole's brittle skin, discerned / was exile."
Each memory contains its murders: "the memory / of the seedleaf in

the bean, the blind / hand along the bannister, the virgin sheath / of having lived nowhere but here." This is the exile from childhood; it is also exile from the haven of a home, growing up inextricably linked to growing out of, someone waking "to find the gray world of adulthood / everywhere, as though there never / had been any other, in that same house / I could not bear to leave." The child torn from its home must be rooted everywhere, and nowhere: the promise of travel is the permanence of arrival. What finally betrays Clampitt as a tourist, as an orderly but outside observer, is that she cannot take her surroundings for granted. Everything must be mentioned in order to be mulled over, and at worst her poems become a kind of nervous chatter, though chatter of a particularly vivid sort.

Like Marianne Moore's, Clampitt's is a life lived through literature, but literature turned back toward the world. Where Moore preferred the tidy intelligences of the zoo, nature comprehended in its compartments, Clampitt is more likely to be hip deep in a bog:

> *Rancor*
> *is rarely simple, least so in the dank*
> *sector of organic*
>
> *chemistry. Likewise*
> *its lack, as in these strangely sallow-*
> *tinged, blandly baked-apple-*
> *flavored thimble nubbins, singly borne, no*
> *more than inches from the bog's*
> *sour surface. Could so odd a crop*
> *be edible? Yes,*
>
> *it could. Called*
> *hayth- (but spell it* heath*) berries by*
> *the populace Down East, they're*
> *known and relished as cloudberries farther north.*
> ("Cloudberry Summer")

Clampitt has reintroduced the section of endnotes to books of poetry, and like Moore's hers are a ragbag of intriguing and sometimes pointless elaborations to her poems as well as scraps of prose she cannot bear to leave unquoted. She is not some backwoods natural- ist who has learned the nutritional content of every root and stalk by rash experimentation. Field guides have been her faculty, and her lines sometimes sound like barely rewritten field notes—her tone is more often the schoolteacher's than the scout's.

Even when the transcriber lavishes the language with the insults of excess, nature is only so interesting as language—many of Clampitt's poems have been deprived of their color plates. The grand Victorian travel narratives, sexual and social repressions loosed in the safe precincts of the foreign, disturbed the familiar in part by being familiar. Clampitt's celebrations of the natural often seem a similar flight—toward a world whose luxuriant perfections are year by year renewed. When, deep in her boggy observations, she offers the most brittle ecological sentiment ("And a rare thing / pleasure is too, even for the mammal who / in effect invented // and then lost no / time polluting it, in ways the wretchedest / den-foul- ing lemming would surely / find astonishing"), it is out of a despera- tion deeper than politics. A poet who embraces the pleasures of the transitory fears their extinction. The annual deaths are deaths of resurrection; recording them, you don't have to record the deaths that are not.

Do not have to, but Clampitt's resolve is to confront those deaths nature provides a harbor from. The sequence for John Keats, whose life was thwarted in almost every way his art was not (and who even in his art could take little pleasure from his critics), is written in almost wretched fascination, as if this life and this death could reveal what other deaths cannot. The figure of the poet, frustrated in his art, turning gradually and inevitably toward his own death, might too easily serve another poet as a scapegoat, warding off death by accepting it for himself. That Clampitt cannot indulge in such sat- isfactions is all too evident in the unpleasant observations she is forced, perhaps even forces herself, to make:

He saw it: saw the candle in the icy draft
gone out, the little smoke, the moonlight,

the diamond panes, the stained-glass colors
on her as she knelt to say her silly prayers.
Saw her, smelled her, felt the warmth of the
unfastened necklace, the brooch, the earrings,
heard the rustle as the dress slid down;
backed off, became the voyeur of a mermaid.
Discovered, while she slept, that the sheets
gave off a sachet of lavender. Admired but
did not taste the banquet his senses had
invented, and whose true name was Samarkand.
He was in fact too excited to eat. What is
a poet to do when he stumbles onto such
excitement? He was not sure. He was also
somewhat embarrassed. Later he'd declare,
hotly, that he wrote for men, not ladies
(who are the ones who dream such things),
that he'd despise any man who was such a
eunuch as not to avail himself . . . It was
the flaw, as he must have known. He'd
imagined it all. He'd imagined it all.

("Chichester")

This is the Keats of sexual frustration, the earthbound and sultry Keats. Christopher Ricks has written *Keats and Embarrassment,* but Clampitt might be the critic for *Keats and Sex,* so well does she understand the dark erotic nature of his art. Critics tend to apotheosize artists when they do not destroy them; but either verb is a polite euphemism for castration, and it is well to remember that even Shakespeare wrote his version of a pillow book. Too often the sequence is versified biography, Keats week by week, even day by day. The nature that elsewhere achieves only its own renewal lurks in corrosive contrast to the poet who will father no children. From elegy and ending Clampitt derives the most adequate definition of her talent.

That talent has not been fully measured in either of her books. *What the Light Was Like* has its share of failed designs, poems of second nature that are also second intensity. (Her ear is a prose ear, and her breathless syntax distracts the reader from the clunky, pot-banging music of her lines.) Clampitt has only begun to trust the intelligence of her whimsy. How many of her peers would attempt, for example, a pseudo-sestina with these unpromising endwords: *reeds, asphodel, Hackensack, ugly, fraudulent, civility*? Or would have the ironic self-regard to suggest in the notes that the poem is a "last-ditch effort to associate the landscape familiarly known as the Jersey Meadows with the tradition of elegiac poetry"? Clampitt's sensibility provides what formal constraint alone cannot: an intelligence adequate to the reader's attention. *Mature* is an edged word when used of this poet, whose first book, *The Kingfisher* (1983), was published later in her life than Frost's or Stevens's in his. Though Clampitt is now rumored to be in her sixties, she is a poet mature and immature at once. She has come fully formed to her voice if not her vision, so the unsophisticated perception may be couched, and even concealed, in a sophistication of style. Her lapses remind the reader that for an older poet Clampitt is distressingly ingenuous, and for a newer poet disconcertingly shrewd. That conflict has made her voice one of the few real additions to the poetry of this decade.

Gjertrud Schnackenberg

Amy Clampitt reads herself into nature; Gjertrud Schnackenberg reads herself out of it. The rich and even decadent particulars of her verse frequently answer some literary text, and when no text is available she is not above creating her own, by love letter or embroidery thread. Schnackenberg has such an easy command of poetic technique that even when her lines are ungainly or bad the reader wants, not to set them right, but to find out what set them wrong. She is comfortable in a formal tradition that for twenty years has not been a tradition at all—one looks toward aging masters like Merrill, Wilbur, and Hecht, forgetting that when *they* were young they seemed as elegant and precious as the Cavalier poets. The first thing to be said about Schnackenberg's poems is that they are memorable *as* poems, when from book after book of current poetry I can remember only the smell of a sensibility or the texture of an attitude. Formal poets are often accused of formal distance, but the world is at times more deeply entered through an isolation from it.

The long "fictional portrait" of Chopin that opens *The Lamplit Answer* draws from the scattered facts of journal and biography to invent a world removed from the world:

> *The swan's neck of the teacup, her black vizard*
> *Plunged underwing, conceals her face like a modest cocotte*
> *Who can't bring herself to look up at the honored guest,*
> *As the silver hammer of the tea service practices*
> Chings *in runs of triplets, and the tea steam hangs*
> *Phantom chrysanthemums on long, evaporating stems*
> *In the air of the winter apartment. The guests,*
> *Having gathered for games, for mimicries,*
> *For gossip's intricate, expensive inventions,*
> *Crowd toward the pianist who, leaning forward,*
> *Clasps his hands, like a child's prison for butterflies,*
> *To begin a tale, perfected in his room, of his*
> *Reception on a tour in the South, where they had hired*
> *A sedan chair with servants to bear him to the theater,*
> *"Like a captured king from a remote, Saxon metropolis,"*
> *And then killed him in the reviews—a smashing joke,*
> *And his hostess snaps her fan shut when she laughs,*
> *In the city of slaves to mirrors, of rivalries*
> *Championed for less than a day by charlatans,*
> *Of politics lending heat to the rented rooms*
> *Of exiled virtuosos, and of cholera warnings affixed*
> *To the posts of the streetlamps, whose heads*
> *Flare with fever from here to the outermost districts.*

("Kremlin of Smoke" 1)

The bedroom and salon scenes composing this sequence divide Chopin's triumph in Paris from his childhood in Warsaw, a Warsaw from which the Russian invasion of 1831 has forever cut him off. Severed from his childhood, he is severed from himself, and the lavish entertainments cannot repay the losses of serenity such excess ignores and affronts. The childhood sickbed and childhood piano lessons convict the sickly and overdeveloped Parisian culture these scenes have led to. The images of that childhood are plundered as the home itself is plundered, the Russian soldiers hurling his piano from a fourth-floor window.

The judgment is in the form, as so often with this poet; but the attitude is in the style, the verse responding to the memory of meter with a lushness, a feverish vision of the salon, that excludes any easy reflection:

> *And overarching the cream cakes, the pale-skinned meringues,*
> *And the candied violets arranged among the bibelots of the old*
> *Legitimist Bourbons, the pipes and cigars of bespectacled*
> *Millionaire guests fling a kremlin of smoke overhead,*
> *Dome upon dome, rising up to the mauve-tinted heaven*
> *Of trompe-l'oeil clouds, as Chopin, stolen from*
> *The* Comédie *by the piano gods, with a tablecloth over*
> *His shoulders, enacts "My Viennese Laundress."*

("Kremlin of Smoke" 3)

The troubled and confusing stimuli of these lines recall the opening of the game of chess that haunts *The Waste Land*, the swan's neck of the teacup earlier summoning up Eliot's golden Cupidon, the one who "hid his eyes behind his wing." Here, too, scenes of arousal mask scenes of denial: in the final poem of the sequence, an entry in Chopin's journal, the composer recognizes how thin a veneer coats the world around him. Half a century after the fall of the Bastille, "Mottles of corruption edge the petals": the flowers have been "decapitated" like aristocrats. For this impotence, there is no cure. Like so many of Schnackenberg's characters, the composer has outlived the scenes of his strength, and the triumph from without shadows no triumph within—"I too," he is forced to write, "am an outcome withering from my cause."

"Darwin in 1881," reprinted from her first book, *Portraits and Elegies* (1982) (one eager reviewer, confused by the duplication, wrote that "her fascination with him continues"), shows a similarly belated figure the year before his death. In the smoldering superfluity of his age, the old campaigner avoids the public ceremonies that mark a private emptiness. He putters about his garden, reduced to memoirs and the naps that leave him an insomniac:

> *Sleepless as Prospero back in his bedroom*
> *In Milan, with all his miracles*
> *Reduced to sailors' tales,*
> *He sits up in the dark. The islands loom.*
> *His seasickness upwells,*
> *Silence creeps by in memory as it crept*
> *By him on water, while the sailors slept,*
> *From broken eggs and vacant tortoise shells.*
> *His voyage around the cape of middle age*
> *Comes, with a feat of insight, to a close,*
> *The same way Prospero's*
> *Ended before he left the stage*
> *To be led home across the blue-white sea,*
> *When he had spoken of the clouds and globe,*
> *Breaking his wand, and taking off his robe:*
> *Knowledge increases unreality.*

("Darwin in 1881")

Schnackenberg is led to her symbols by her emotional states, and the "broken eggs and vacant tortoise shells" take from his investigations the adequate signs of desolation. To cast Darwin, who made the whole biblical fable transparent, as Prospero bereft of his island, Prospero after the renunciation of magic, suggests by gesture as much as by meaning the unreality to which she refers knowledge.

That unreality appears in a different guise in her retelling of "Sleeping Beauty." There the princess, that creature of sublime unconsciousness, is neglected for the lives destroyed around her— the kitchen maid, for example, whose beloved woodcutter is trapped in the briars outside the enchanted castle, long a skeleton while she remains suspended in youth. That is the selfishness of fairy tales, to ignore the lives at their edges (Auden's "Musée des Beaux Arts" is subtly inverted here):

The gardeners gazing through their open shears
Or staring sightless from their wooden ladders
Stand helpless by and dream they cannot lower

Their upraised sickles poised a hundred years
Above the labyrinth of stems, as briars,
Even while dreaming of their destinies

As smoke and ashes in the gardeners' fires,
Fasten themselves around the spellbound blades
And steal the dreamers' hats in mockery

To lift them out of reach of stick and ladder,
Then lose them on their way to taking over
The twilit walls and roofs and hundred chimneys

Against whose edifices chimney-swallows
Have woven for their families habitations
With rosebud twigs and dust of crumbled mortar

And threads they've tugged gently as milliners
From out the silken shirts and ruffled trousers
Of failed princes hidden in the brambles,

The swallows unaware these men have starved
Entangled in their struggles with the briars.

("Imaginary Prisons")

Each character's life is tested by the predicament, each finding his disaster in the form of his desire (these are the real prisons of imagination): the kitchen maid who would entangle her lover will wake to his corpse in the briars, the insomniac will dream a hundred years he cannot sleep, the king who would postpone the future will have the future postponed past bearing. Each gains his desire at the cost of that desire; and the poem, as overlong as the enchantment itself, collapses into the falseness of appearance, the fruitlessness of hope, and the comfort of a sleep that will be uncomfortably broken. Except for Sleeping Beauty, each will awake to an individual unhappiness, "When grander schemes that mock our calculations // Reveal that we're the emblems standing for / The consequence of what we cannot master."

Even Schnackenberg, after three hundred and sixty lines, seems entranced by her own designs, the sleepy iambic pentameter enjambed so lightly each line makes a dying fall, a fall often encouraged by a feminine ending (it is, after all, a poem about Sleeping Beauty). Schnackenberg has an odd relation to her technical gifts. At times they seem beautifully surrendered to, at others purposely thwarted. Her free verse seldom escapes the echo of meter, but her forms seem ingenious indulgences conducted with the attitude of "What would happen if we started every line with a stress?" What distinguishes her from poets who haphazardly impose form upon unruly subjects is that each form is exhausted by the demands of the poem—she finds her moods within her meter. She never tolerates the self-congratulation that accompanies much formal poetry ("Look, gentlemen, I've written a sonnet!").

The variety of forms obscures the mythic continuity of these poems. The portraits, when they do not reveal the secret wound of the Fisher King (the invasion for Chopin, his wife's death for Ivan Generalić), at least show the decline and impotence that attend it. When such portraits have been peeled away, something darker is exposed, and nowhere more openly than in the poems self-consciously funny. The two Clumsy and No-No poems may derive from Punch and Judy (at one point Clumsy's hands "Fly up as if on strings"—Punch was originally a marionette), but the adventures of the hapless Clumsy and his nemesis No-No owe as much to the dark conflict of self and superego, Faust and Mephistopheles:

> *When Clumsy harks the gladsome ting-a-lings*
> *Of dinner chimes that Mrs. Clumsy rings,*
> *His two hands winglike at his most bald head,*
> *Then Clumsy readies Clumsy to be fed.*

He pulls from satchel huge a tiny chair,
And waggling his pillowed derriere

He hitches up his pants to gently sit.
. . . .
                    But oh, alack,
Quite unbeknownst to Clumsy, at his back
The circle of a second spotlight shows
That No-No has delivered fatal blows

To Mrs. Clumsy since that happy time
She summoned Clumsy with her dinner chime.
And there is Clumsy's darling lying dead.
How like a rubber ball bounces her head
As No-No drags her feet-first from this life.
Then No-No dresses up as Clumsy's wife.

("Two Tales of Clumsy" 1)

The purposely clumsy manner, all awkward poeticism and inversion and nicety, distracts from the violence of the murder but not the violence of its significance. This is a land of cartoons without happy endings. The masquerade in the poem above is as unsettling as the travesty of the classroom scene in its companion piece, where the illiterate Clumsy signs away his soul.

Schnackenberg employs light verse again for two love poems, "Love Letter" and "Sonata." Their studied ungainliness, however, cannot conceal the pain of underlying emotion:

I went to bed when you went to Hawaii,
And shut my eyes so tightly I saw stars,
And clenched my sheets like wadded-up memoirs,
And made some noise like wah-wah-wah, i.e.,
I find your absence grimly problematic.
The days stack up like empty boxes stored
In ever-higher towers of cardboard
Swaying in senseless-lost-time's spooky attic.

I'll give the-atic rhyme another try.
To misconstrue the point-of-view Socratic,
Life is a painful stammered-out emphatic
Pronunciation of the word Goodbye.
("Love Letter")

Comedy, even of this depraved sort, allows insights seriousness can ignore, insights that can only be stated, if at all, with a ludicrous and lucid irony. In "Sonata," the poet toys with the impossibility of mixing two themes (1: "My life lacks what, in lacking you?"; 2: "Does the material world exist?"). The lesson for lovers should be clear. The other love poems are more traditionally serious, and more traditionally bereft and bewildered; but they contain much further meditation on absence and loss. For this poet the present scarcely exists; and when it does exist (in the presence of her lover, say), she has no need to write. Writing recovers, and almost all these poems turn back toward or acknowledge an Edenic past, like the paradise Ivan Generalić's paintings occupy, from which he has been cast out by the death of his wife:

Once distant villages hung in the trees
Like God the Father's stars, and pigs transformed
The grass with wedding feasts, and goslings swarmed

Running like kindergarteners from the geese,
Glad in the farmyards of the sacred heart,
The windows of the Lord where sunsets brimmed

Around the heads of sheep, as gold-leaf rimmed
The gospel pages where we played a part
Until God chased you crying from the world:

There we were saved.
("The Self-Portrait of Ivan Generalić")

As a writer, Schnackenberg is such a reader because prose devours; it creates a visionary world. She reads herself out of nature because hers is a nature that cannot be inhabited. In "Paper Cities" she writes of Saint Clare that she "could see / Events in places where she was not, / The way readers do," but readers have no control over events in other cities, Flaubert's cities or the city of the absent lover. Composed on paper, these dream cities are easily destroyed: "The moth's tiny wrecked skull, its rumpled face / Preside weightless, hushed / Over paper cities: / Little one, in whose papery jaws, / As it is written on paper, / The world is crushed."

For Schnackenberg, biography accounts for loss, and her poems are biographical when they cannot be autobiographical. The losses are suffered by artists (Chopin, Generalić, Flaubert) or figures doubling for artists (Darwin, Simone Weil, Sleeping Beauty); they fulfill their artistic economies at material cost to themselves or others. Given the mythic incursions of many of these poems, their self-conscious absorption of sacrifice and expiation, it is not surprising the three poems that end the book undertake Christian themes: passion, advent, incarnation. The innocent gravity with which these themes are explored contrasts nervously with the savaging of religion in "The Self-Portrait of Ivan Generalić," where Christianity can neither absolve nor console ("our windows darken into squares / Of night, from which you've vanished, window squares // Like Bibles closed forever, squares of black"), and in her blasphemous and horrifically funny "The Resurrection" (published in *Kenyon Review*, Summer 1979, and never collected).

In "The Heavenly Feast," the first of that trinity, the pathos of Simone Weil's self-starvation is carefully implicated by the grass growing at her grave, the common symbol of imperturbability and renewal revealing instead a natural order based on "the shocking might / Of hunger and of thirst." This sudden unmasking of an apparently benign nature finds its complement in the following poem, "Advent Calendar," where the bitter northern sky "Opens door by door by door." These are only the paper doors in the nativity scene, of course, but they assume a more disturbing significance as the doors of childhood ("This is childhood's shrunken door"). To such innocence there can be no return:

Give me entrance to the village
From my childhood where the doorways
Open pictures in the skies.
But when all the doors are open,
No one sees that I've returned.
When I cry to be admitted,
No one answers, no one comes.
Clinging to my fingers only
Pain, like glitter bits adhering,
When I touch the shining crumbs.

("Advent Calendar")

This duplicates the situation of Chopin, divided from *his* childhood; but the specific images by which it is enacted, particularly those of shrinking and dwarfing, recur throughout the book and partly explain its unnerving psychology. When Clumsy pulls from his satchel a tiny chair, he becomes not just an adult sitting in a child's chair, but a child holding an adult's giant silverware. His relation to No-No is, not least in their names, that of child to admonishing adult; and other images of contraction or reduction suggest similar confusions of scale: the moth presiding over paper cities ("Paper Cities"), giant galaxies "tiny, tiny on my windowpane" ("Snow Melting"), and "vanished insect faces / So tiny, so intolerably vast" ("Darwin in 1881").

This dark affinity between child and adult transfixes the book's final poem, "Supernatural Love," where the poet as a child watches her father "through the needle's eye." Bent over a dictionary, he searches for some etymological reason for the child's insistence that carnations are "Christ's flowers." He finds first, to his discomfort, that the carnation, a variety of clove, derives from the Latin for flesh. Then

He turns the page to "Clove" and reads aloud:
"The clove, a spice, dried from a flower-bud."
Then twice, as if he hasn't understood,

He reads, "From French, for clou, *meaning a nail."*
He gazes, motionless. "Meaning a nail."
The incarnation blossoms, flesh and nail,

I twist my threads like stems into a knot
And smooth "Beloved," but my needle caught
Within the threads, Thy blood so dearly bought,

The needle strikes my finger to the bone.
I lift my hand, it is myself I've sewn,
The flesh laid bare, the threads of blood my own,

I lift my hand in startled agony
And call upon his name, "Daddy daddy"—
My father's hand touches the injury

As lightly as he touched the page before,
Where incarnation bloomed from roots that bore
The flowers I called Christ's when I was four.

("Supernatural Love")

The father's astonishment is genuine but mistaken; and the attentive reader, alert to the poetic faculty of this child, will have heard the echo the child heard between carnation and *incarnation.* There are delicate ironies here, about the scholar's path from knowledge to ignorance, about criticism's failure when faced with the magics of poetic insight, about poetic insight itself. (When the father reads that the carnation is "A pink variety of Clove, // *Carnatio,* the Latin, meaning flesh," he is wrong even more thoroughly. The spice known as the clove is the dried bud of the clove tree. The carnation is a variety of flower known as a pink, and specifically a clove pink, for its heady clove-like fragrance. What the father probably read was "a variety of clove pink.")

With symbolic neatness (and in an appropriately Clumsy way), the child pricks herself with the embroidery needle and brings forth her own blood. Here is the Sleeping Beauty tale, spindle changed to needle, mingled with the blood brought forth by thorn and nail at the Crucifixion. The child's cry, "Daddy daddy," rehearses in a slightly forlorn fashion the final cry from the cross, "My God, my God, why hast thou forsaken me?" That is the unspoken question of all Schnackenberg's work. Readers of *Portraits and Elegies* (1982) will recall the sense of loss and even betrayal that infused the elegies for her father. Her poems look toward an idyllic past, from which she is divided, because the past is where he is.

These interactions suggest, not that Schnackenberg's work derives from one psychological myth, but that the myth and its attendant images sustain and complicate the variety of her poems. I cannot read that the child's "dangerous, bright needle's point connects / Myself illiterate to this perfect text // I cannot read" (the text is "Beloved") without remembering how illiterate Clumsy came to grief with a different text, or how often these poems issue from the relation between a text and a reader. When, on the Advent calendar, "Joseph lifts his lamp above / The infant like a candle-crown," the image resurrects all the images of fire and light that haunt this poet, from the streetlamps "whose heads / Flare with fever" to the "sunsets brimmed // Around the heads of sheep," from the lily pollen that "Scatters like crumbs of fire across the floor" to the "furnace-stoker / Around whose lifted shovel embers sparkle // And hang like bumblebees around a flower." The unstated question in the final poem explains why these poems incorporate so many questions that cannot be answered, or can be answered only ambiguously ("Where is the snow from?" asks the boy Chopin, and his mother answers, "The snow—it comes from Moscow").

Most poets waste their sensibility on their early poems and have nothing to waste on their maturity, but Schnackenberg's poems betray only the glimmerings of sensibility. While Amy Clampitt's work is a vast and stately mansion you may tour a room at a time, with hallways radiating in many directions, each of Schnackenberg's poems is shaped and complete, like sculpture, exposing everything and revealing nothing. She risks much in this volume (in current terms, at least—more broadly considered, perhaps she risks too little, since she rarely tests her strengths), and a reader cannot predict, despite her preoccupations, what her next subject will be or how the attack on it will be managed. She is not willful so much as surprising; unlike so many poems hers demand a response, not simply an assent. Her poems are difficult not in what they say, but in what they have said.

Schnackenberg is the most technically shrewd and most technically gifted poet of her generation, the generation now in its thirties, though she is fulfilling a tradition rather than furthering it. I could praise these poems more feverishly than they deserve because they appear in an unfeverish time. To poets who lived through earlier years of the tradition, her talent may seem all too familiar, but perhaps all the more gratifying for demonstrating how radically fresh formal conventions can seem. I have lingered too long over her thematic intricacies because it is easy in Schnackenberg's work to be dazzled by immediate delights and to forget that something beyond the dramatic precision of image and the welcoming quality of voice makes these poems attractive. If Amy Clampitt is, like Marianne Moore, an entrancing but special case, Gjertrud Schnackenberg, whose tasks are traditional, has increasingly written to a standard by which her contemporaries must be judged.

Younger
Poets

Tess Gallagher

Tess Gallagher writes in one of the period manners: her free verse is prosy without being prosaic, breezy in tone though capable of a dash of bitters, informal, never too weedy, never terribly interesting as language, and finally more like a letter than literature. In *Willingly* she repeats the thematic tangles of her earlier work—severed love, minor events with major implications, consolation in the family drama. Like so many poets of her generation, she speaks relentlessly in her own voice, or in what the reader is encouraged to construe as the voice of the poet in suburban tranquillity. Such a voice is annoying when it cannot take itself seriously:

> *Are they filming this? I mean you*
> *putting your mouth to the receiver*
> *personally. I'm doing it too, naturally,*
> *out here in my cabin on the bay. Lots*
> *of windows to let in water, weeds*
> *sitting around drying up in mason jars.*
> *All that woodsy romance.*

Gallagher's free verse, elegant by opportunity rather than design, borrows the rhythms of prose without becoming enslaved to them. "Naturally" leads naturally to nature, and even when the subjects are so scatty and vacant she attends unconsciously to what she is saying.

She attends as well to what others are saying—over half of her poems rely on direct quotation ("'Today, today!' / the light says"—something's always talking in these poems). The poet's rambling voice is checked by the words of others, though other characters are almost never allowed to commandeer a poem—no one muscles this diva offstage. The most afflicting and afflicted character is her father, and in a series of poems she reflects on his life and his death:

> *What not to do for him*
> *was hardest, for the life left in us*
> *argued against his going*
> *like a moon banished in fullness, yet*
> *lingering far into morning.*

The consuming scenario of her poetry is a brief moment of physical connection, with lovers or strangers. Something in the self is released when it touches the other (Gallagher's first book was *Instructions to the Double* [1976]), and the tension of these slight intimacies is most heightened when most in danger:

> *Your silence is leaning toward judgment.*
> *Yesterday I bragged, writing to calm*
> *my paranoid friend, that I never assume*
> *the worst when my pals don't write. Now*
> *assuming the worst, I think what I must have*
> *done, or not done.*

She understands the rhetoric of emotion—or, better, the pacing of emotion—without having the full resources to exploit it. She tends to sound fraught, to sharpen into phrases like "cold plenitude" whenever she tries to make public what is private about loss. Gallagher's poems too often *seem* public, and not merely private utterances we have the privilege of overhearing.

Increasingly her poems have become minor fictions, with beginnings, middles, and ends, often in that order. Her weaknesses are all too poetic—she adores ludicrous epic similes ("I am in a state of mourning / for your coat which traveled with us that while / like a close relative concealing a fatal illness / in a last visit") and displays of overeager emotion (in a rainstorm: "Until I'm looking up / to let my eyes take the bliss"—you'd guess it was raining manna). Who would have thought so many bland poems could be written about the thorniness of love?

Richard Kenney

The Evolution of the Flightless Bird, chosen for the Yale Series of Younger Poets by James Merrill, is the most striking addition to that series since Robert Hass's *Field Guide,* published almost a dozen years ago. Richard Kenney's very formal music might have found a place in an earlier period, were it not now part of a gradual return to form among younger American poets. His poems are composed of "sonnets," fourteen-line stanzas of roughly metered verse, rhymed by glance more than rigor. They have the feeling more than the fixture of form, and their intricacies are as much verbal as visual:

> *The chimney of the spine*
> *still burned its gray electric fire, where neural*
> *fibers rose in braids above the heart's narrow*
> *perch and frayed as if to part and yet held on.*

It may be counted as courageous, in a time that rewards its poets for plainness, to speak of a broken neck (as the poem eventually makes plain) in this intransigently opaque fashion, unless you believe imagery can create an empire of the senses wholly different from the straitened language of prose (even prose isn't as prosaic as the prose now common in poetry). In the long opening sequence, "The Hours of the Day," Kenney explores the house where accident has confined him, reading the histories (of glassmaking and navigation) and examining the objects (a collar box, an icon of St. George) that become outer riggings for an inner convalescence. The architecture of the house becomes the flawed architecture of the body, the dense and heady imagery the claustrophobic invention of a mind alone with itself. Elsewhere Kenney's systems of imagery can seem mere scholastic involution, and his sequence "Notes for Greece" is so headlong in its annotation it can serve as neither Baedeker nor bibliography.

For Kenney, as for many difficult poets, the natural world is an irresistible accumulation of visual fact:

> *I've jewelled*
> *old memories in mind with such care: eventually*
> *the shore-ice weakened, the lake changed, its drumhead*
> *having rotted unnoticed in the March winds,*
> *the red-sailed iceboats having disappeared all at once,*
> *like birds. Then the lake split open,* doomed
> *and* snapped, *hollow, implausible, awful as stage-thunder.*

The rotted drumhead prepares that thunderous ripping drum, that shaking of tin sheets—the real action is offstage. Before accident, the life had a calm surface.

The stage Kenney otherwise prefers is the stage of history, where he takes a radical approach to narratives, some private, some public record. The Scottish bard Aneirin, as he sings his heroic poem "Y Gododdin," reflects on the bargain an individual makes with his time. A man almost loses his hand at a sawmill. The British Navy engages American ships under the command of Benedict Arnold:

> *The* Carleton
> *was totally unresponsive by then, caught*
> *bows into the breeze like a shivering compass needle,*
> *helpless to come about, hulled, her flame-*
> *lit decking raked by every shot from the galley*
> Congress, *and at the same time powerless to lay*
> *her own traversing guns.*

Trapped in a sound, the Americans slip by at night "like teal through marsh-reeds," like these lines through their meter or these "sonnets" through their form. Form has become a refuge for poets who have found the late manner of free verse an exhausted office. The logic of fashion has been to announce that the complications of mind have moved elsewhere, though the most Byzantine form can absorb the simplest expression. A poet of Kenney's deep appointments is not susceptible to fashion, however it stirs, and will follow his own peculiar line of development. It is important to have available again techniques recently out-of-favor and to find them used in a style uncompromising and triumphant. Such poetry is not afraid of having intellect, or requiring it.

Melissa Green

Melissa Green's first book, *The Squanicook Eclogues*, is flagrant with fault, garrulous, given to whimsy, and deeply derivative. It is also flooded with grace. No other young poet is so contented, so thrilled, merely to catalogue nature's metamorphosis, or to craft it into a deliberately turned formal verse that takes an almost shocked delight in its own daring. The title sequence records, in a hexameter of great flexibility and formal pleasure, an intimate pastoral between father and daughter, thrown into stark relief by the father's death:

> *All the harvest has come down the valley: shelves*
> *Protesting under bushel baskets, barn after barn.*
> *The staghorn sumac rears its bloody hooves against*
> *The ell where grapevine bickers with its shadow self.*
> *Ceremonious maples don the cardinal robes of kings*
> *While the dowager dogwood embroiders her taffeta cape.*

Hexameter is notoriously troublesome in English, and here a slight prosy slackness is the sacrifice necessary to maintain it. Green accepts such risks as an entanglement complementary to her subjects. The four sequences that compose this book, all governed by seasons or chronology, by the fated and fatal swerve of lives, take their griefs within the shelter of family. In one sequence, the speaker prowls among the detritus in the family attic ("damaged stores / from sundered marriages, a wall-eyed moose / surveying the debris") to reinvent the lost childhood of her tyrannical grandmother; in another, her brother's restoration of an old house calls forth the lives of the original builder and his widow. None of the sequences conjures up emotion or argument; their griefs are excuses for the formal possibilities of language:

> *Old mother May has put her burden down.*
> *Her heavy-headed poppies drowse where flags*
> *and epaulettes of crepe across the stones*
> *still will us to our bandaged dead, those flocks*
> *of innocents eternally ordained*
> *to die.* And all of them were captains, stained
> by circumstance.

A young poet's subjects often afford such excuses, and that is their narrow imposition. Addicted to slant rhymes, Green claims the legacy of Wilfred Owen ("my lover, Wilfred Owen, threads the maze") and Auden as well, for whom play was equivalent to purpose. If none of these poems seems deeply felt, or deeply purposeful, it is not due to any lack of seriousness—their tone falls all too easily into elegy—but to the hazy invocations of history, the dreamy and even dreamed lives that drift past, pale as ghosts. It is no wonder these poems are giddy with personification, and that the personifications shiver with more substance than some of these lives: "Where fox-glove in her petticoat has crowned the hill—/ An indolent cotillion girl who tosses gold / From her shoulders, and proudly rustles yards of crinoline." The whole book is steeped in the mood of Keats's ode "To Autumn."

> *I heard the apples softly letting go*
> *at summer's end, and knew abundance drowsed*
> *beside me in the field, her freckled arm*
> *flung wide above her headscarf, while a dream*
> *of cider filled the Nonesuch cheeks with rust.*

Indolence, drowsing, dream: her states of grace all approach sleep, the state of an imagination intoxicated with language. Not all her debts are to the dead. In large measure, Green owes the terms of her allegiance to form and family to Gjertrud Schnackenberg, who has mastered some of the forms (rhymed triplets, for instance)

Green is still apprentice to, and whose own first book was founded on an elegiac sequence for her father and a sequence conjuring up the past occupants of an old house in New England. Despite these obligations to a poet somewhat more gifted and sophisticated, Green has ambitions to match her art, and a passion for language that has restored the fading beauties of northern landscape.

Timothy Steele

In *Sapphics against Anger,* Timothy Steele seem to have leapt fully formed from the brow of Yvor Winters, believing form in poetry is a moral imperative. Like other young poets, he takes from form the stricture, and structure, contemporary free verse so obviously lacks. Unfortunately, he handles his meters like a mannequin:

> *Those who refuse to hunger for event*
> *And who accept the wisely-unbegun,*
> *Just wishing decently to get through life*
> *And trying not to injure anyone.*

And again:

> *If asked why such small lives so fascinate,*
> *Why I observe them, I can't really tell.*
> *But a responsive impulse moves my gaze,*
> *An impulse I can see in them as well.*

The first passage refers to people void of ambition, the second to insects, but neither carries the conviction of its clumsiness. The people might be insects, the insects people, for all the character such sunny generalizations confer. Steele's passions are domestic, his sorrows what the suburban tract-house inspires; but even the raptures of property-owning could not repair these mawkish couplets for a mockingbird: "Erratically, tirelessly, in song, / He does his imitations all day long. / Appropriating every voice he hears, / Astonishingly shifting vocal gears." No mockingbird would dare sing like this; no mockingbird would dare *write* like this.

Every vice has its coincident virtues, however, and Steele has not learned his meters without consulting his masters. The title poem of *Sapphics against Anger* shows a less-than-Sapphic influence (though it is a good example of why quantitative verse is a failure in English):

> *Angered, may I be near a glass of water;*
> *May my first impulse be to think of Silence,*
> *Its deities (who are they? do, in fact, they*
>   *Exist? etc.).*
>
> *May I recall what Aristotle says of*
> *The subject: to give vent to rage is not to*
> *Release it but to be increasingly prone*
>   *To its incursions.*

Wherever the comforting voice of Auden is heard, describing a mountain view or a trick of perspective ("where his own sons will descend / To fertile, river-led perspectives"), in a shiver of syntax adapted to form, Steele briefly seems a poet of more cunning and wit (though mimicking Auden's voice is not the same as having Auden's ear).

When under the influence, Steele has a historical imagination the domestic virtues cannot provide. A poem for Dora Spenlow and David Copperfield, though scored for strings, fashions a necessary ligature between life and literature. For Luther, in hiding after the Diet of Worms, every landscape is the allegory of his anxiety:

> *The garden where he broods is like a riddle.*
>   *The circle of the gravel walk,*
> *The sundial which is stationed in the middle,*
>   *A poppy on its hairy stalk:*
> *These are like clues from which may be inferred*
> *Imperatives of the Almighty's Word.*

In such lines the moral intelligence almost justifies the bland simplicities, the addiction to the alcohol of abstraction, that elsewhere afflict Steele's work. I hardly know how to criticize a poet who believes of the poor that "What they are survives / The limpid vacancies of air," he has criticized himself so well already.

Chronicle
at Home
and Abroad

James Tate

Disaster looms large in James Tate's work, perhaps because all comedy must court or marry calamity before warding it off:

Where the wife is scouring the frying pan
and the husband is leaning up against the barn.
Where the boychild is pumping water into a bucket
and the girl is chasing a spotted dog.

And the sky churns on the horizon.
A town by the name of Pleasantville has disappeared.
And now the horses begin to shift and whinny,
and the chickens roost, keep looking this way and that.
At this moment something is not quite right.

As long as the catastrophe remains unspecified, this is an eerie and suggestive rural nightmare; but let the title ("Land of Little Sticks, 1945") begin to corrode the reader's uncertainty, and the ambition of the poem quickly dwarfs its tiny effects with images of Hiroshima and Nagasaki. Death in war lent substance to the title poem of *The Lost Pilot* (1967), published seventeen years ago. That Tate is now barely forty, and that in *Constant Defender* he can handle so ill a theme once handled so well, reminds us how long a career he has already had and how difficult it has been to sustain his successes.

Tate is a wily and resourceful poet. He can take a bizarre premise and mock dignified anthropologists (and, incidentally, Truffaut and Rousseau): "A head of cheese raised by wolves / or mushrooms / recently rolled into / the village, it / could neither talk nor / walk upright." He can turn a meditation on an old photograph of himself into an Icelandic saga. He is not a surrealist but an absurdist, and his relation to John Ashbery has probably been insufficiently explored. He shares with Ashbery a sublime self-indulgence; a cool shuffling of dictions and tones; an appreciation for, even an obsession with, the ridiculous; and a refusal to allow most poems a central or defensible meaning.

Ashbery, at least on occasion, toys with large and important concerns; but Tate usually settles for the hollow laugh or frivolous act (a better poet would know how to make his frivolity pointed). He defeats his own better designs. Not even Ashbery allows himself such lame wordplay ("She is lumbering through the lumberyard / like a titmouse with goosebumps") or dreary invention ("that moment a gourd drifted / down the chimney on the pretext / of weeding a peninsula"). Tate is proud of his carelessness, of his unwillingness to favor the Imagination in a kingdom ruled by Fancy.

Tate's poems ramble on, and on—the lines are so standoffish, you feel they haven't been formally introduced. Invention without control, ingenuity without purpose, they end in a crash of irrelevant simile:

I'm feeling naughty and falter
like an enormous filing cabinet
in an ashen center field.
And, like an entangled puppet

wriggling at the hairdresser,
I chatter before abrupt sleep.

His least irritating work has a firm subject or an ingeniously silly proposition: interruptions, say, or a mink farm's failure, or a detective specializing in gardens. The man who has "The Dream of Returning to School and Facing the Oral Exam" finds himself "wearing huge antlers / which have sprouted overnight." At such moments Tate's whimsicality begins to frame the awkward posture of the psyche. It is a task he assiduously avoids. How often has the reader been confronted by Tate's "improvising / of waste, of a kind of heroic / negligence that life does not / appreciate"? As in his other books, here Tate tests himself too little and congratulates himself too much. No one else can make painting a house into an absurdist drama more fit for Keaton than Kafka; but there is all too much Keaton in Tate's work, and hardly any Kafka at all.

Alice Fulton

Alice Fulton is giddy and effervescent. The poems in *Dance Script with Electric Ballerina* whiz along, having a motion more than a manner, polishing their surfaces until they glare like ice:

> *I'll take a getup*
> *functional as light:*
> *feet bright and precise as eggbeaters,*
> *fingers quick as switch-*
> *blades and a miner's lamp for my tiara.*

She reaches into a grab bag of simile and pulls out whatever's handy. Fulton works from a wildness of association reminiscent of Jorie Graham's wayward charm, the abstractions tossed carelessly in, the metaphors whipped into pure froth. The lines hurtle on, and we can tell they're poetry because they're so violently enjambed. The drama of enjambment ought to be a pleasure, but much of Fulton's is so hammy it hurts (as in "I didn't create this pain-/ ful grace").

For Fulton, imagery is intended to distract, so its meanings or implications never cohere—they scintillate like subatomic particles after collision. However contrived or curious, her images have little precision, relying on our trust in a fancy that reaches the equivocal more often than the complex. This conception of the trope as merely the shimmering ornamentation of a poem may corrupt the poem itself. A rape is an opportunity for fanciful images ("He is a squeezed tube / spurting words that knife / and twine like eels / under ice") rather than a chance to render the violation of the flesh imaginable or horrible, or horrible because imaginable. In her scene there is no feeling at all, only chattering metaphors.

Such amiable, lighthearted, and even light-headed verse could be over-criticized. Fulton has the courage of the experimenter. She doesn't seem to care what she writes about—any old thing will do; yet the more personal subjects (her father's death, the machinations of various lovers) are a relief from the transient frissons of this high-wire act. A sestina for Janis Joplin, of all people, shows how easily a high-spirited imagination can master form by being mastered by it. Fulton's occasional leaps of invention (the "calm / quantum" of dust) and her ravenous vocabulary ("ballon," "melisma," "corm," "dalmatics," "taphephobia," "nyctophobia" [she suffers from phobophilia]) suggest that underneath the glittering surfaces a mind operates. There are still only glimpses of that mind. "It's true," she says, "I've dispensed with some conventions." This book doesn't so much dispense with conventions as prove itself ignorant of their purpose.

Albert Goldbarth

Many poets know one big thing, but Albert Goldbarth knows many little things. *Original Light* is a selection of shorter work, drawn from six of the fifteen volumes he has published in the past decade. To these have been added, by infuriating convention, a number of new poems. It dishonors the gesture a whole book of new work would make to have a group of the author's recent poems tacked on like an afterthought or, as here, infiltrated like spies. Who, after all, would want to read only *old* poems?

Goldbarth's huge outpouring is suspect in a time that legislates spareness. His imagination teems with Aristotelian possibility, and he clearly hates to let any opportunity go to waste:

> *What encourages our belief in the screw as a diagram*
> *of a tornado, is: it's rusty. These sienna clots*
> *in spirals up its threads are exactly the color of Kansas*
> *in miniature, barnsfull of it, funneling up*
> *an early twister's rapid dismantling turns.*

This is reminiscent of the opening of Pound's Canto XVI, but Goldbarth feels obliged to turn the screw one thread deeper: "If it / happened in April, a drillbit frightens you in May, // or a lazy chickenhawk descending its invisible / conch of air."

The poem has nowhere to get to but its metaphors. The mechanistic metaphor distinguishes Goldbarth's work—he's as infatuated with science as a fourteen-year-old just introduced to physics. Few poets, perhaps unfortunately, find science quite as irresistible as Goldbarth does, and I think none retains quite his innocent awe in the face of it:

> *Up in a corner, a spider's spinning this*
> *real web that enters your world*
> *as a word, "web," on a page, "this" page, then*
> *light through a window*
> *lifts the spider as light lifts everything*
> *seeable and brings it, at the same speed*
> *it was just now brought to my eyes,*
> *to the stars.*

It's as if to say, "Gee, Pop, the light takes this image, see, and then, and then . . ." And then, in this poem at least, come science fiction, quasar travel, planet hops. The poem must also juggle—admittedly, it's a long poem—two early Greek artists, an anecdote about Dürer, a short biography of Michelangelo, various spiders, a lover both real and imagined, the nature of time, a print by Saul Steinberg, and an asterisk. Goldbarth doesn't explain topics; he's too busy exploiting them.

His hodgepodge organization demands too many facts and not enough flesh (I can imagine his dog-eared *Britannica,* his tattered textbooks); but the ideas are skeletons or chandeliers, gorgeous structure without significance. He cannot fuse the image and the information, and his poems are forced to violent juxtaposition: a Norse voyage to Vinland in 1120 and the lover leaving the poet at 11:20. When the violence works, Goldbarth creates something wholly individual. Unfortunately, it usually doesn't work—a longish poem about St. Augustine and pianos ends with the saint at a urinal, "tinkling" like a piano.

Goldbarth's poems maintain a uniform voice, a uniform depth, a straight line on the oscilloscope (he has the one method, accumulation, and the one gabby voice). Even in the poems drawn from childhood or from his father's death, the symbols are coldly manipulated. The better poems are dramatic monologues, where he stops being Albert Goldbarth for a moment. His poems are strongest when most resolute in their oddity—their fierce science is proof against any easy accommodation with charm.

Norman Dubie

For Norman Dubie, history is its private parties, not its public events; and the obsessive design of his earlier books, gathered in *Selected and New Poems,* has been to provide the local habitations history often fails to (he makes design a gimmick). Even history cannot satisfy his appetite for names and places, and in the cacophony of voices and veer of incidents the idea of history itself is often lost. Consider the characters collected here: Mayakovsky, Virginia Woolf, Breughel, Czar Nicholas II, Paul Klee, Ovid, Jacob Boehme, Chekhov, Kafka, Hardy, Elizabeth I. He has filled his dance card with the names of the great.

> *The bears are kept by hundreds within fences, are fed cracked*
> *Eggs; the weakest are*
> *Slaughtered and fed to the others after being scented*
> *With the blood of deer brought to the pastures by Elizabeth's*

Men—the blood spills from deep pails with bottoms of slate.

The balding Queen had bear gardens in London and in the country.
The bear is baited: the nostrils
Are blown full with pepper, the Irish wolf dogs
Are starved, then, emptied, made crazy with fermented barley.

Violent in circumstance, laden not just with the visual but with the pepper and ferment of other senses, his most instinctive poems enact another world on its own terms, appropriating the images that will gather the great to their inferiors—the bears that eat cracked eggs for their eggshell-faced queen. Czar Nicholas II, imprisoned in a barn in the Urals, teaches his children decreasing fractions—a lesson for those whose hours are shrinking by halves. Such images work from psychological violence toward a moral particular, even if the violence is literary and the moral mere morality play.

The half-dozen or dozen poems of this fashion find purposes beyond the mere thrust of narrative. Unfortunately, Dubie is imitated for his weaknesses as much as his strengths. His visual compositions strain for the composure of the picturesque. Even his violent scenes are well-mannered, the etiquette of his visions that of the drawing room, not the abattoir. Further, his exotic lines ("All the dead are eating little yellow peas / Off knives under the wing of an owl"—like bad Chagall!) and Escher-like transformations ("the geese / Broke from the shadows like handkerchiefs / Out of the sleeves of black dresses // At a burial") place high value on cold artifice. His imaginations have all too much control and all too little content. It is not often necessary for Dubie to worry about anything but how things look, and he keeps up appearances in order to keep down what lurks beneath them.

Dubie's images are often precious, distanced from the scenes they derive from; but on occasion the distance mirrors some alienation in character or—and this is adroit—some alienation he wishes upon the reader. The message of his serial images might be, as he says after describing a worm in the heart of a linnet (the linnet is held in a black glove, the glove is worn by a prince, the prince is on a chestnut horse that is shitting into the surf on the coast of Scotland, and around the prince are chieftains on horseback, dressed in furs, drunk and laughing at the linnet), "This is a world set apart from ours. It is not!"

Similar exclamations riddle the poems (at least 120 in the fifty-nine poems collected here)—the coercions of punctuation accompany his hothouse images. Dubie's new poems are more personal but less ambitious and less intertwined than his earlier work. Their locale may be domestic, but their actions are denatured and pale as partially developed photographs, exhibits in reluctant transition toward a new style. The new poems employing literary or historical figures (Penelope, Jerome, Francis of Assisi) use them in an even more perfunctory manner than usual, as though the author could no longer be bothered with the most elementary attempt to make of their lives an art, of their art a life. Too many of his poems already seem, as costume dramas eventually do, very much of this time, not the times their elaborate fashions mean to call forth.

Yehuda Amichai

Yehuda Amichai's reputation as Israel's greatest modern poet is no service to *Great Tranquillity: Questions and Answers.* The reader can make little allowance for poems that suffer in translation, but who doesn't feel sorry for them when they read like this?

> *The air hostess said put out all smoking material,*
> *but she didn't specify, cigarette, cigar or pipe.*
> *I said to her in my heart: you have beautiful love material,*
> *and I didn't specify either.*

However this sounds in Hebrew, it could hardly be more fulsome than in English. Sensibility, like tone, is the translator's burden, but it is not necessarily the translator's *fault*. Encounters with women, memories of women, memories of his father, musings on the young— Amichai gives himself over to subjects that encourage these vain moonings. There are parables: an Arab goatherd searches for a kid on Mount Zion while the Israeli speaker searches nearby for his son. There are walks through ruins ("Even thorns are tired of hurt-ing and want to console") and reunions of veterans ("And you, my few friends, go now / Each of you to lead his herd of memories / To pastures / Where there is no memory"). There are poems about the Lost and Found and love, about flowers and love, about history and love, about guns and love. They are variously infected by mumpish reverie, cloying sentiment (all tears and lard), appeals to nostalgia, blurry description, and inapposite metaphor:

Caution! Nostalgic area!

. . . .

Rest in peace. Your soul is returned
Like a surprise gift. You improved it a lot
Since it was given to you, you improved it without knowing
And angels will open the beautiful wrapping
Crying out in wonder to each other.

. . . .

There will be many smiles left on time
There will be many tears smeared on life
Like on a good towel.

. . . .

And no one knows what the cooking will do to him:
Will he get soft or harder and harder
Like an egg?
That's the thing about cooking.

. . . .

God's in the eye business and the fruit business
I'm in the worry business.

These are not the most egregious examples. About the best that can be said is that Amichai mistakes affect for effect, and hopes by tone to pursue what he cannot by language. The poems have a simplistic, storybook quality, as if the teller believed himself very humble and yet very wise.

These comments apply only to Amichai's poems as rendered into English. I offer, for balance, a few differing opinions: "[The poems] are profound, and delicate, and moving. . . . The world I live in and wander through will never quite be the same."—Gerald Stern; "Amichai has entered that small, accidental, permanent company of poets—Hikmet, Milosz, Vallejo—who speak for each of us and all of us by redefining our nobility, by speaking to us in his voice of many selves."—Stephen Berg; "Yehuda Amichai begins to look more and more like a truly major poet—in the strict sense of the term. . . . Who else is dipping his bucket into such a full river of experience and paid-for feeling?"—Ted Hughes. What delights have been lost or supplied in translation I have no way of knowing; but neither, I suspect, do the poets who provided the encomia on the dust jacket. Amichai should get better translators—or his translators a better Amichai.

Michael Hofmann

Michael Hofmann has brought a sense of history to the banal and domestic, and the miniature scenarios played out in his first book refine an urban post-political alienation. *Nights in the Iron Hotel* is awash with ellipses, those marks of omission and fatigue, and they indicate a world where connection and continuity have vanished, where all that can be had is contiguity, one body lying next to another. When nature intrudes, it is an awkward exterior for interior romances:

> *Birds, feathers, a few leaves, flakes of soot—*
> *things start to fall. The stubble has been burned,*
> *and the fields are striped in black and gold.*
> *Elsewhere, the hay is still drying on long racks:*
> *bulky men prancing about on slender hooves,*
> *unconvincing as pantomime cattle . . . A hedgehog*
> *lies rolled over on its side like a broken castor.*

Even the dead hedgehog is reminiscent of a part of furniture.

Though born in Germany, Hofmann is very much an English poet; and his settings shift between the rough trade of Britain, its socialism collapsed into harsh Tory conservatism, and the prosperous post-terrorist Germany. As cold voyeur he records the politics of dissatisfaction and dissent, the arbitrary borders and failed social experiments. This is a sour, cellar sort of poetry, full of the rising damp, not so much disheartened as past heartening.

What reclaims it from the dark is Hofmann's corrosive irony. He is a bitter and witty observer of "The underdog's leather jacket" and the baby "dressed like His Satanic Majesty in a red romper suit: / a gleeful crustacean, executing pincer movements." Nothing has a future, but everything has a past:

> *Fused with your car, a modern centaur,*
> *you commute to work like the Tartar hordes*
> *who swept across Europe, drinking their mares' milk.*
>
> *Half the week in a neighbouring country,*
> *then, laden with spoils, home to your smoky tents.*
> *Your sulky children, long-haired and murderous,*
>
> *help you unpack. Crates of soda water,*
> *plastic sacks of meat . . . A hard currency buys*
> *the cheap produce of the paper economies.*

This juggling of history with history is reminiscent of Lowell, and indeed Hofmann can sound too often that murderous Lowellian note: "Every day I swam further out of my depth, / but always, miserably, crawled back to safety." It may be no coincidence the first poem in this collection is titled "Looking at You (Caroline)."

Haunted by history, haunted by poets, or by one poet in particular, Hofmann nevertheless manages to seem completely individual, even isolated, in his art. Partly the doom-ridden tone is responsible, partly the violent images ("A gymnast swings like a hooked fish," "his knuckle cocked / against the small of her back like a trigger"), partly the enthusiasm for sexual suggestion and sexual failure, from the homosexual English teacher to the homely sex shop that seems to combine "a health-food store / and a DIY Centre" (a do-it-yourself store). This is a poet who believes the world is past salvaging but not past witnessing; and for such a poet, as for many readers, cynicism is a form of hope.

James Fenton

Without Auden there could have been no James Fenton. The cadences, the insouciant employment of ballad and song, the schoolboy honesty in political drag—all these have been learned by apprenticeship to the master. The forms in *Children in Exile* can therefore seem alien even when the contents are rudely up to date. The pleasures of form have rarely seemed so pleasant of late, however:

> *A nasty surprise in a sandwich,*
> *A drawing-pin caught in your sock,*
> *The limpest of shakes from a hand which*
> *You'd thought would be firm as a rock,*
>
> *A serious mistake in a nightie,*
> *A grave disappointment all round*
> *Is all that you'll get from th'Almighty,*
> *Is all that you'll get underground.*

If this sort of jeu d'esprit were all of Fenton, it might be enough; but he has taken certain tendencies in Auden and forged them into a harsher voice that ranges from the political to the absurd (or the absurdly political to the politically absurd). The most striking poems in this collection derive from Fenton's experience as a war correspondent in Cambodia. "In a Notebook," "Dead Soldiers," and "Children in Exile" have a specificity of vision and horror of moral consequence mostly lacking in Carolyn Forché's picturesquely grim versions of El Salvador.

After his work in Indochina, Fenton was for a time a foreign correspondent in Germany (he is currently on leave as drama critic for *The* [London] *Sunday Times* and last year spent most of two months in the interior of Borneo—this is not a poet who takes place lightly). "A German Requiem" echoes Eliot's displaced or suppressed narratives, and in the wasteland of postwar Germany discovers the counterparts of Mr. Eugenides. During the war, the dead had to be buried too quickly for headstones, so "They unscrewed the name-plates from the shattered doorways / And carried them away with the coffins":

"Doctor Gliedschirm, skin specialist, surgeries 14–16 hours or by appointment."
Professor Sargnagel was buried with four degrees, two associate memberships
And instructions to tradesmen to use the back entrance.

The modern scene may not require the present exhaustions of free verse, and a poet like Fenton finds among earlier influences more instructive models. This is free verse following Eliot, or form not postmodern but post-Auden.

The most accomplished section in Fenton's book contains neither politics nor nonsense (his light verse is not light at all), but domestic dramas, if the households can include a revolutionary in exile, a nest of vampires, a Staffordshire murderer, and the kingdom of Chosun. Fenton is interested not just in other times and other arenas, but in the social organizations that make them distinct. Almost every poem explores the postures, public or private, foreign or local, ancient or modern, that make a time of a time. It is the relations between people as social entities that appall him, and for him problems are essentially societal and not personal. In "The Skip," a man who takes his "life" and throws it on a skip (a dumpster), as if it were a disposable article of clothing, is making public a private futility. Not having a "life" makes no difference—the beer at his pub is still awful. Worse, when he looks in the skip again, someone has left another "life" in place of his. The parable is rather dry, and its criticism is social. For Fenton the personal problems that motivate such action are distant and unmentionable.

The personal notes in *Children in Exile* almost always come obliquely, and even a recent song called "Nothing" is so formal its anguish is less revelation than concession. Some critics may dislike a poet of so many exteriors, but in our too personal a time they are the last challenge. Fenton's weaknesses are elsewhere—some of his lines are insufficiently imagined and do not overcome their influences. His rhyming and metrical practice are not always sure. A section of found poems is embarrassingly weak, though the poems incorporating found material (a very literary vampirism) show an aggressive eloquence in making mute texts speak through context. He is not afraid of clichés, though perhaps he ought to be. What Fenton has is the ability to make poetry matter:

> *He trod cautiously over the dead in the Campo Santo*
> *And saw the fading punishments of Hell*

> *And asked whether it is true that the unjust will be tormented*
> *And whether those who suffer will be saved.*
> *There are so many martyrdoms in the beautiful galleries.*
> *He was a connoisseur among the graves.*

To find the last English poet of whom that could be said, you'd have to return to Geoffrey Hill. If the politics of anguish are not to be merely poetical, they cannot be merely political.

Natural
Selections

The Muses are cruel devils, and never crueler than when they whisper, "Why haven't we read *your* Selected Poems?" They offer the only contract they know, the one they offered Faust. No poet who chooses his own work believes he will betray it.

A book of selected poems is a monument to middle age. It may revive a flagging career or embalm an overvalued one. As a sign of respectability, or a device to return to print poems long out of it, a selected poems is an unendurable temptation for poets who have not received their due (and even great poets fear they have not received their due). Though a clever poet can obscure his old sins or alter his alliances (early Yeats, in our standard texts, is often late Yeats in sheep's clothing), revising with a liver-spotted hand the radical errors of youth, these monumental designs usually falter, like those of public statuary, between ingratiation and ingratitude. Most poets should rest on their laurels or their old reviews.

W. D. Snodgrass has given few hostages to ingratiation, and fewer than ever in *Selected Poems, 1957–1987*. Of the important poets of his generation, none except James Merrill has pursued such eccentric obsessions, and none has suffered so peculiar a history of publication. The obsessions are not entirely responsible for the difficulties of his career. Among our contemporaries, Snodgrass is the shining—or tarnished—example of a poet whose gifts, lavishly bestowed and then prodigally dissipated, have only rarely consoled him. The cloak of invisibility has under other conditions become Nessus's toxic shirt.

Heart's Needle (1959) is a work of imaginative maturity, of concentrated and informed feeling rare in any poet and particularly rare in a first book. It is still one of the half dozen distinguished books of the period, another way station in the progress of private feeling: *The Less Deceived* (1955), *Poems: North & South—A Cold Spring* (1955), *Life Studies* (1959), and *Ariel* (1965) are the others. (The Beats and Black Mountain poets formed a different and largely separatist stemma of descent—more given to rant than reflection, the miasma of Blake or the barbaric yawp of Whitman; but hotter, irritated into idiom, closer to song, unappeasable, and finally a curiosity of culture or antique survival, like a whirling dervish.)

Force in poetry is often the force of repetition. In their stringent focus Snodgrass's early poems offer two movements, from ignorance outward to knowledge and experience, and from observation inward to revelation. The first usually moves from sleep to the shock of consciousness; the second from the mirror of nature to the shock of recognition. The symbolic range of the first is spiritual; the second, psychological. From these mechanisms of argument, so obviously complementary, *Heart's Needle* derives its unity and governing momentum, also its constriction. Snodgrass is not a poet who can take any joy in a mastering knowledge, or even in the humbling that attends a look deep in the mirror. He would not describe himself, as Newton did, as a child picking up seashells. In the early poems there are always horrors to be woken to, and recognitions that become afflictions:

Observe the cautious toadstools
  still on the lawn today
though they grow over-evening;
  sun shrinks them away.
Pale and proper and rootless,
  they righteously extort
their living from the living.
  I have been their sort.

("Song")

Even mushrooms serve a scathing self-denunciation, but then no symbol is innocent to the psychological eye. The repetitions are not just mental but formal. Snodgrass is one of the midcentury masters of formal verse, and as restless as Hardy: every poem throws on a new verse form like a new suit. Restless as Hardy, he is more calculating in his clumsiness, drawn to wandering rhythms and impure rhymes. Singly, these poems have the virtues of their responsibilities, but the concentration of those responsibilities comes only in the notorious title sequence.

Though the poems of "Heart's Needle" may now form a rusty piece of stage machinery, one more exhibit in the museum devoted to the conflict between free verse and form, they retain the original pathos, the pathos of a violated tenderness. In ten sections of a verse always decorous but often distraught, the poet addresses his young daughter, from whom he is divided by marital separation and then divorce. Verse so formally elaborate rarely gives the impression of such simplicity:

Child of my winter, born
When the new fallen soldiers froze
In Asia's steep ravines and fouled the snows,
When I was torn

By love I could not still,
By fear that silenced my cramped mind
To that cold war where, lost, I could not find
My peace in my will,

All those days we could keep
Your mind a landscape of new snow
Where the chilled tenant-farmer finds, below,
His fields asleep.

("Heart's Needle" 1)

This labyrinthine and remotely balanced rhetoric, extending over half a dozen stanzas in one sinuous sentence, argues the poet's high claims but also his self-absorption. That the rhetoric is not *fully* mastered (the precise adverbial function of *All those days* is obscure without emphasis on *those*) suggests how much can be concealed by such elaborations. The construction is involute, but the diction has been willed into monosyllables, a mouthful of monosyllables. Snodgrass's innovation was to borrow the battery of formal method from Lowell, Wilbur, and the poets of the early fifties, but not the encrustations of manner. Upon their intricate stanzas he imposed a direct and even blunt emotional statement that comes perilously close to prose.

In the poet's self-involvement, the Korean War provides no more than a symbolic gratification, a landscape littered with dead fetal figures, for the "cold war" in himself. After this apostrophe invoking the winter of the child's birth, the sequence properly begins in the spring before the couple's estrangement, when the child is three, and advances season by season for two years, until another winter finally yields to spring. Each season is primly commemorated with a poem. By reference to the end of the war, the seasons can be dated from spring 1953 to spring 1955.

The symbolic climate of these seasons marks the poems' strict management, and the progress of seasons forms a motif as studied as the recurring references to poems written and unwritten. The poems have a phrasing deceptively easy and depend on incidents absurdly commonplace: the child planting seeds, or sweating with fever, or masquerading as a fox one Halloween. The normal incidents have abnormal force: the poet imposes on the child's simplest gesture a metaphysical burden (Donne may be the ghostly presence behind those intricate stanzas). For her father, every sign is a sign of loss:

> *Here in the scuffled dust*
> *   is our ground of play.*
> *I lift you on your swing and must*
> *   shove you away,*
> *see you return again,*
> *   drive you off again, then*
>
> *stand quiet till you come.*
> *   You, though you climb*
> *higher, farther from me, longer,*
> *   will fall back to me stronger.*
> *Bad penny, pendulum,*
> *   you keep my constant time*
>
> *to bob in blue July*
> *   where fat goldfinches fly*
> *over the glittering, fecund*
> *   reach of our growing lands.*
> *Once more now, this second,*
> *   I hold you in my hands.*

("Heart's Needle" 7)

The colloquial manner, stripped of most claims upon figurative language, often marries its rhythms barely within a meter, acknowledging but never quite cooperating with the severity such form demands. The sentences maintain their tenuous dignity only by adhering to the scaffolding of form. As prose all their suppressed mawkishness would leak out.

In what does Snodgrass's formality lie? Chiefly in a highly modulated iambic line that subsides, by subtle degrees, from carefully crafted monotony to a superbly varied and flexible instrument that takes advantage of liberal substitutions and inversions, and that finally slips into accentual verse. Much of his poetry (including the passages just quoted) approaches the condition, if not the conviction, of pure accentuals, though he never quite finds the rhythms of hesitation, or of conscience, in Yeats's "Easter 1916." It's not easy to be certain of Snodgrass's convictions, or even his intents, since he permits himself small formal deviations—when composing syllabics (which he does less often than many critics think) he counts about as accurately as Marianne Moore. That may be as much to say, he will not spoil the line for the sake of fulfilling the form, he will not let meter get in the way of the meaning.

Snodgrass is heavily dependent on rhyme for his formal architecture: most poets take rhythm as architecture and rhyme as adornment, not flying buttress. It unites his disparate rhythms, dispels (for the most part) the threat of prose. He can be quite unfaithful, nevertheless; he will adjust patterns stanza by stanza, corrupt a pure rhyme or correct an impure one. He is, in other words, wholly shameless in exploiting formal possibilities, though the poems are not deeply enough dyed by their variety, and the forms they acquire risk seeming merely miscellaneous.

In "Heart's Needle," each poem moves from turmoil toward some fixed position ("I hold you in my hands"), however temporary, in the poet's stages of grief. That position, that settling into the quiet rage of recognition, is often announced by an abrupt rhetorical shift unprepared by the logic of argument:

> *If I loved you, they said I'd leave*
> *and find my own affairs.*
> *Well, once again this April, we've*
> *come around to the bears;*

> *punished and cared for, behind bars,*
> *the coons on bread and water*
> *stretch thin black fingers after ours.*
> *And you are still my daughter.*

("Heart's Needle" 10)

Quotation is unfair to such a moment: the sudden desperate possession in that final line (and possession is not simply possessiveness)

follows a sequence of incidents suggesting easy union between father and daughter—and how superbly placed is the yearning of those
caged raccoons! Snodgrass would not have to write the last line
unless it were in most senses untrue. The structural organization
is repetitive, even compulsive. In such formal and affecting ways,
"Heart's Needle" employed its limited means to express—by nar-
rowness of method alone—the psychological exaction and exhaustion of loss.

The decorum of Snodgrass's early verse signifies the emotion
withheld; the power of emotion is measured by the formal bonds
that restrain it. How much brutality lies behind this feeling! In one
poem, a tug of possession dislocates the child's wrist (the incident is
less innocent than it's meant to be). What masquerades as sorrow in
Snodgrass is often self-regard, and his love hides more than a little
loathing. Such a mixed issue is resonant if unrecognized; but a reader
might be forgiven for flinching, or wanting the child to flinch, from
such attentions.

The poems diagnose a man wrapped in his own embrace: other
people (apart from the daughter, the poor daughter) are seldom
mentioned, and if mentioned scarcely disclosed. That claustrophobic fascination with the self made *Heart's Needle* so radically different
from other books of the period, and so corrosively influential.

Heart's Needle was the determining twin of *Life Studies*. Older
poets are so rarely influenced by younger it's easy to forget the re-
vivifying nature of such reversal—the effect of the young Ezra
Pound on W. B. Yeats was surely less dangerous than the monkey
glands or vasectomy Yeats experimented with. Lowell's *Life Studies*
and Snodgrass's *Heart's Needle* appeared within days of each other in
April 1959, the cruellest month in postwar poetry. The next year
they divided the awards between them, Lowell receiving the National Book Award and Snodgrass the Pulitzer Prize. Snodgrass had
been Lowell's student at Iowa in 1950 and 1953. Some critics praised
the teacher for the directness of feeling common to both books, but
Lowell was not so sure: "[Snodgrass] did these things before I did,
though he's younger than I am and had been my student. He may

have influenced me, though people have suggested the opposite."
(*Paris Review* no. 25, winter-spring 1961). There was of course a
reciprocal influence. After meeting Snodgrass at a writers' confer-
ence in 1951, Randall Jarrell had written Lowell: "I had a boy last
summer at Colorado who was good . . . and most of his poems were
excellent though unconscious imitations of you. You'd had him in a
class at Iowa, I think—De Witt Snodgrass, poor ill-named one!"
The letters and reminiscences of the period have now made plain,
however, the *emotional* innovation was entirely Snodgrass's.

Snodgrass found, in the inner life and the broken family, a poetry
of great pathos and formal character that insulated itself in its period. Lowell, in his concern for heritage, literary posture, and political indisposition, is our acid contemporary—it is not the aptitudes
but the attitudes that are fresh, and freshening. Snodgrass takes the
conventions of the time to their conclusion, gaining force but not a
value; Lowell's disruptive intelligence is bleaker, more damaged, and
less susceptible to the solicitudes of pity.

What has dated Snodgrass's early poems is their diction, not their
delineations. They sound now like the outpourings of a man heart-
broken, but a little vain and priggish, even overweening ("I taught
myself to name my name, / . . . To ease my woman so she came," he
says in "April Inventory"). Poems that so knowingly and so eagerly
take advantage of the rueful idiom could not have these manners
without the example of Eliot. They are Prufrock *after experience*,
after a bite of the peach. Snodgrass is often too calculating, too fond
of the well-made, symbolically governed poem—the careful roughness can't conceal it. But in the aftermath of that school so conde-
scendingly called confessional, the simple declaratives of Snodgrass
were more imitated than Lowell's gaudy mannerism. We have lived
through three decades of prose in consequence.

Not all confessions are meant to be overheard. Snodgrass once
claimed to have been deeply influenced by the poet S. S. Gardons,
who in the early sixties published a few poems in *Hudson Review* and
in the second selection of *New Poets of England and America*. They
seemed to draw uncannily from, or weirdly to prefigure, the rhythms

and stanzas of *Heart's Needle*. Gardons was given an implausible biography in the anthology ("Works as a gas station attendant in Fort
Worth"), and it was not until 1970 that eight poems ascribed to him
were published in the elegant limited edition titled *Remains*.

Among poets their real authorship was an open secret, though it
was discreetly concealed until the death of the poet's parents. The
pseudonym ("Snodgrass spelled sideways," the poet once remarked)
protected him from the consequences of his rage:

> *She stands in the dead center like a star;*
> *They form around her like her satellites*
> *Taking her energies, her heat, light*
> *And massive attraction on their paths, however far.*
>
> *Born of her own flesh; still, she feels them drawn*
> *Into the outer cold by dark forces;*
> *They are in love with suffering and perversion,*
> *With the community of pain. Thinking them gone,*
>
> *Out of her reach, she is consoled by evil*
> *In neighbors, children, the world she cannot change,*
> *That lightless universe where they range*
> *Out of the comforts of her disapproval.*

("The Mother")

The transparent contributor's notes in *Hudson Review* admitted
Gardons was a pseudonym. "Vuillard: 'The Mother and Sister of the
Artist,'" one of the poems appearing there under the name, later
resurfaced in *After Experience*. It is hard not to find this all very odd
psychologically, perhaps odder than it really is: the guilty concealment of the poems (how difficult to claim what is already ours), the
judgments masked by formal dispassion and a formulary sympathy.
The spleen is contained, controlled, and even denied by the dignity
of the diction that channels it, and is the more shocking for that.
Wound within a metaphysical conceit, the anger invites the division
of self that does not violate Snodgrass's most uneasy work, but is its

very heart (how often in his poems he speaks as "we" and addresses "you").

Remains is a ghoulish title, or could be thought so (the innocence is an innocence assumed). Trailing after *Heart's Needle* like a bitter epilogue, the poems are some of his most bitterly accomplished. Most of them refer to the aftermath of his sister's death, and as a group they compose a family pathology:

> *Flowers like a gangster's funeral;*
> * Eyeshadow like a whore.*
> *They all say isn't she beautiful.*
> * She, who never wore*
>
> *Lipstick or such a dress,*
> * Never got taken out,*
> *Was scarcely looked at, much less*
> * Wanted or talked about;*
>
> *Who, gray as a mouse, crept*
> * The dark halls at her mother's*
> *Or snuggled, soft, and slept*
> * Alone in the dim bedcovers.*
>
> *Today at last she holds*
> * All eyes and a place of honor*
> *Till the obscene red folds*
> * Of satin close down on her.*

("Viewing the Body")

The grotesque masquerade (mocking the grotesque mask of Gardons) savages the usual proprieties of death, the proprieties poets observe in their elegies. This cold autopsy, so empty of the expected comforts and petty compassions, does not allow the reader to avert his gaze. The reader is that all-too-unwilling voyeur, but the poet a little too much relishes the abrogation of decency. Snodgrass's moral understandings derive a purity of observation from an impure response. The modestly optimistic note that ends a final poem to his daughter ("I tell you love is possible. / We have to try") is betrayed by the failures of compassion evident elsewhere, but it is those failures that have made confession necessary.

After Experience (1968) lacks the thematic compression, the gravity of an obsession, of *Heart's Needle*. Since unity of impulse is part of Romantic preference, the poems have been undervalued if not ignored. Their subjects are frequently trivial without triumphing over triviality—Snodgrass finds few Grecian urns in the wreckage of household and marriage. The most consuming poems take their rhetorical effects, and their marital pressures, from the provisional comprehensions of *Heart's Needle:*

> Once we'd packed up your clothes
>   It was something to talk about:
> The full moon, how it rose
>   Red, went pale, then went out
>
> As that slow shadow crossed—
>   The way Time might erase
> Its blackboard: one cheek lost,
>   The eyes, most of the face. . . .
>
> . . . .
>
> We wished it all blank, bereft.
>   But no; the mists drifted on;
> Something, one glint was left.
>   Next morning you had gone.

("Partial Eclipse")

The title of these poems has perhaps unfairly bankrupted them into belatedness. The effects at times seem drained, as the simple phrases weaken to nursery rhythms ("This fall, we left your Grandma's / And had to leave your plant behind; / You said if no one watered it / And it would die, you didn't mind") or fall to prose:

> Sorting out letters and piles of my old Canceled checks, old clippings,
> and yellow note cards That meant something once, I happened to find

Your picture. That picture. I stopped there cold, Like a man raking
piles of dead leaves in his yard Who has turned up a severed hand.
("Mementos, 1")

What was I looking for today? All that poking under the rugs, Peer-
ing under the lamps and chairs, Or going from room to room that
way, Forever up and down the stairs Like someone stupid with sleep
or drugs.
("Looking")

Snodgrass makes much, perhaps too much, of being such an ordinary fellow (recall his working-class alter ego), but these lines em-
phasize the tedium over the terror. The rhymes and initial capitals
should let the reader reconstruct the original sestets, if he cares to.
Both poems seem to be searching the suburbs for something.

The selection from *After Experience* (twenty-three of the original
forty poems, not counting the translations, which have been excluded) seriously misrepresents the quality of the book, a less stirring but also less restricted performance than *Heart's Needle*. Many
of the poems of marital discord have been discarded in favor of
alkaline subjects given alkaline treatments ("Looking," "The Lovers
Go Fly a Kite," "Regraduating the Lute") or poems symbolically
fantastic or overwrought ("The Examination," "Flash Flood"). If
Selected Poems had no other flaw, it would be suspect for the omission
of "Leaving Ithaca," "Takeoff," "The Platform Man," "Autumn
Scene," "Point Pelee in March," "Edmund to Gloucester," "A Visi-
tation," and "The Men's Room in the College Chapel." Compare
the lead-footed accents of the stanzas just quoted to the radiant exhaustion of these:

In the public gardens they are walking.
The skies appear correct and glum.
Their heels click drily; they are talking.
Behind their backs, the elms repeat some shocking
News of what's to come.

> *Otherwise, the lawns like quiet.*
> *The beds are vacant, spaded, formal,*
> *Where sparrows peck out a lean diet.*
> *After July's sun-scattering splash and riot,*
> *It's back to gray and normal.*

("Autumn Scene")

Or with the passionate despair displayed here:

> *We slant off toward the bay*
> *Miles and miles above you.*
> *How soon things shrink away.*
> *I don't know whether I love you*
> *Or what I need to say.*
> *. . . . .*
> *Suppose our loves did cross,*
> *Who knows where this could finish,*
> *What cravings we could cause?*
> *Still, who would dare diminish*
> *The loveliness or the loss?*

("Takeoff")

The most astringent poems of *After Experience*, so many of them now missing, moderate the earlier angers into a wryness and moral suspicion reminiscent of Larkin's, though without his smug and sour resignation. If this strain in Snodgrass had been developed, the poetry of the last two decades might have been different. Whatever blinded him to its potential then has apparently blinded him since. Included in this selection instead are the poems after paintings by Manet, Monet, Matisse, Vuillard, and Van Gogh. These are artfully contrived, each poem with its different rhythm and method of attack (a set of instructions for a visit, a lyric effusion), and each utterly parasitical on its visual inspiration. Only the Manet achieves a dramatic Impressionism on its own terms. Elizabeth Bishop wrote two unusual poems about paintings; but they were bad paintings, and as elsewhere in her work the observer became the subject of the thing observed. Snodgrass's observations are utterly impersonal. These suppressions of personality, and the search for adventitious inspiration from visual art or foreign poetry, shadow some philosophical argument with the self over the name and nature of poetry. In the grandiose projects of his maturity that argument was not won or lost: it turned into melodrama.

The Fuehrer Banker (1977) appeared a decade ago over the subtitle "A Cycle of Poems in Progress." The cycle is still in progress, and though Snodgrass released a score of poems initially and has added to them in two limited editions, fewer than half the seventy composed have been published. The cycle is a series of dramatic monologues by most of the major Nazis and a flock of the minor ones, limited to the last month of Adolf Hitler's life, when he had entered the bunker in Berlin. Each character in this Götterdämmerung claims a different poetic form: Goebbels speaks in tetrameter couplets, Himmler in alphabetical acrostics written out on graph paper, Hitler in prosaic free verse. When Göring fattens on his own riddles, or Goebbels plays the leering poseur, the monologues swell with operatic viciousness:

> Stand back, make way, you mindless scum,
> Squire Voland the Seducer's come—
> Old Bock from Babelsberg whose tower
> Falls silent now, whose shrunken power
> For lies or lays comes hobbling home
> Into this concrete catacomb.
>
> Here's Runty Joe, the cunt collector
> Who grew to greatness, first erector
> Of myths and missions, fibs and fables,
> Who pulled the wool then turned the tables:
> He piped the tunes and called the dance
> Where shirtless countries lost their pants.

("Dr. Joseph Goebbels—22 April 1945")

Half a dozen poems might have consumed this absurdist, immature strain of invention; half a dozen dozen creates a tyranny. The monologues neither humanize this gang of assassins nor offer insight into their particular derangements. It may be of service to know, or to imagine, that in private Hitler was a coprophage; but no poetic invention can make eating human shit more malign than death camps, or the malignity of mass slaughter more comprehensible. The poems instead turn the Nazis into stand-up comedians, closer to pratfall than politics. Only the women's voices deserve their measure of pathetic sympathy, and in Magda Goebbels the poet has created a voice and a verse form that perhaps fulfill his intentions:

> *This is the needle that we give*
> *Soldiers and children when they live*
> *Near the front in primitive*
> > *Conditions or real dangers;*
> *This is the spoon we use to feed*
> *Men trapped in trouble or in need,*
> *When weakness or bad luck might lead*
> > *Them to the hands of strangers.*

("Magda Goebbels—30 April 1945")

The cycle is otherwise preposterous and interminable, vitiated by its crude psychology, fulsome irony, and irrelevant fiction. Bad men are rarely good poets.

The Fuehrer Bunker makes me think kindly—I would have thought it impossible—of Hardy's attempt to versify the Napoleonic Wars. Poets resent having to repeat their successes, perhaps even resent having successes to repeat. I can spare no more charitable thought for a poet who has found a way—an ugly, dispiriting, ingenious way—of squandering the complications of his talent in crackpot material. Hearing that Bobby Fischer lives in California flophouses poring over anti-Semitic tracts is just as disheartening.

Snodgrass's other recent project, *Kinder Capers* (1986), is no less driven or deranged: a cycle of poems related to, and frequently borrowing their titles from, the paintings of Deloss McGraw (which sounds like another pseudonym for this poet of masks). The paintings, if one produced on the jacket of *Selected Poems* is representative, are colorful and childlike, by Miró out of Mickey Mouse, and frequently portray the antics of a cartoonlike figure named W. D. The inter-referentiality of this folie à deux is obvious, and the poems encourage in Snodgrass an infantile strain that has rarely been allowed to surface (the most grating poem in *Heart's Needle* used the refrain, "Snodgrass is walking through the universe"). The poems range from nursery rhyme (via Wordsworth):

My hat leaps up when I behold
  A rhino in the sky;
When crocodiles upon the wing
Perch on my windowsill to sing
All my loose ends turn blue and cold;
  I don't know why.

("W. D., Don't Fear That Animal")

to political satire:

The Brutish are coming; the Brutish;
The Rude-Coats with snares and bum-drumming!
  The Skittish and Prudish
  The Brattish and Crude
  Who'll check on your morals
  And find your song's lewd.

("W. D. Tries to Warn Cock Robin")

A vague narrative concerns "The Death of Cock Robin," the title of the cycle's first section. The buffoonish figure of W. D. ("Hot on my track still, / But I tricked 'em; / Now who's your criminal; / Where's your victim? / *Dee-flee-a-beadle-tweedle-free!*") oversees an anthology of clumsy effects and witless humor. If Snodgrass's Goebbels had written for children, he would have written these poems.

Both *Kinder Capers* and *The Fuehrer Bunker* retreat from the unendurable tensions of the early poems, as if those tensions could be avoided only by childish fantasy or deformed monologue, a hyperventilation of personality or a suppression of it. They are the dream poems of a fascist Disneyland. One of the strongest poets of the period has thus been reduced to writing in a manner poisonous to his talent. As Hazlitt said of Shelley, he has a maggot in his brain.

Amid the confused welter of *Kinder Capers* lies one delicate lullaby, its subtlety at odds with its surroundings. Beyond these claustrophobic cycles, there have been a dozen or more poems in the old style, collected here from the two limited editions in which almost all of them appeared, *If Birds Build with Your Hair* (1979) and *A Locked House* (1986). Though the methods of warding off the pain of the early poems affect even some of these, half a dozen requite the old Roman restraint in the face of loss.

> *I'd known them, each one—weighed in hand,*
> *Rubbed, bargained, and then with my love,*
> *Pinned each one on for her, to stand*
> *In fickle times for emblems of*
>
> *What lasts—just as they must have once*
> *For someone long dead. Love that dies*
> *Can still be wrung out for quick funds;*
> *No doubt someone would pay the price.*

("Old Jewelry")

The graceless rhythms here and elsewhere betray a talent too long in disuse; but "Cherry Saplings," "Owls," "An Elm Tree," and "Coming Down from the Acropolis" rank in their autumnal passion among the better, if not the best, of his work. On the other hand, "D. D. Byrde Callyng Jennie Wrenn" is written in Middle English baby talk.

Selected Poems distorts the achievement of a poet who has deserved his sublimity as well as his ridicule. I do not value—I cannot find the means of valuing—his recent work; but his early poetry is a distinctive and sometimes brilliant elaboration of a condition, the condition of introspection within suffering. Snodgrass has so frequently relied on small publishers, or resorted to them, the present volume is necessary if not sufficient. It is a fitting irony that a poet whose work has been marred by egregious lapses of taste has been so poorly served: *Selected Poems* lacks a proper table of contents and has been printed in a Garamond so stolid and unforgiving it ought to be used for funeral notices. The ingratitude of publishers cannot affect the gratitude of readers: poets, unlike tyrants, inter the worst with their careers. The good outlives them.

The
Middle
Generation

Adrienne Rich

Adrienne Rich was a poet before she became a polemicist, but even in her polemics there survives some of the lyric impulse that distinguished her earliest work. Returning to the sources of her poetry in *Your Native Land, Your Life*, she finds in the landscape of childhood a nature gloriously unchanged:

> *the face of milkweed blooming,*
> *brookwater pleating over slanted granite,*
> *boletus under pine, the half-composted needles*
> *it broke through patterned on its skin.*
> *Shape of queen anne's lace, with the drop of blood.*

The nature of the self *has* changed, however, and though a rapprochement with her dead father identifies beneath "the power and arrogance of the male" something deeper—"the suffering of the

Jew, the alien stamp you bore"—she inflicts upon the past the moral certitudes of the present: "These upland farms are the farms / of invaders, these villages // white with rectitude and death / are built on stolen ground." It is not the politics I object to but the banality of their expression, the rhythm that becomes a rant.

Earnestness can be the most subtle form of deception. When a poet's every detail arrives with its political subtext, its ideological tremor, the world comes to seem its own allegory ("walking in the street I found my / themes cut out for me"), and no event is pure of its politic interpretation. In a world so infected, mere poetry has little use—and Rich has little use for it. Whether aligning her own life with the life of Ellen Glasgow or lamenting the limitations of language, she allows what once was an instrument in her hands to become just a blunt instrument. I sense in her the wish, almost devout and certainly despairing, to integrate the realms of her experience—poetry and politics, art and activism. The more she tries to fuse them, the more deeply they remain divided; in her work what is poetry isn't political, and what is political isn't poetry.

Reading through her collected poems, I notice how eager Rich has been to adopt a period style, in the decorous early pieces indebted to Auden, in the looser confessions in thrall to Lowell and Plath, in the then hallowed, now hollow, antiwar rhetoric of the late sixties. The gnawing insecurity only gradually becomes apparent, in this book feeding the return to family conflicts (conflicts that never leave Rich in the wrong) and the descent into a verse diary full of contradiction. Such pulse-taking requires the courage Rich has never been at a loss for, and her self-absorption often serves an absorption in others. She speaks most eloquently, and also most sentimentally, about the circumstance of women:

> *how the women say*
>
> *in more than one language*   You have struck a rock—
> *prepare to meet the unplanned*
>
> *the ignored*   *the unforeseen*   *that which breaks*
> *despair*   *which has always travelled*

> *underground   or in the spaces*
> *between the fixed stars*
>
> *gazing full-faced   wild*
> *and calm   on the Revolution*

No reader can ignore the anger or the hope in such poetry, which is like the pasted-together words of a ransom note, the letters cut from newspaper headlines. Despite the clumsy reportage of events that could interest no one but the author, the rage against the cowardice of capitalism and the American rush to luxury ("frozen tongues licking the luxury meat / or the pizza-crust"), the helter-skelter language and the trivializing of love into politics, there remains a poet whose feelings are deeper and more divisive than those of almost any of her peers. Her loss to literature has been a depressing one.

Donald Hall

Now a country mouse, Donald Hall began his career as a city mouse, as befitted a man educated at Harvard and Oxford. *The Happy Man* is his first book of poems since *Kicking the Leaves* (1978), which celebrated his return to the family farm. The new poems continue that New Hampshire pastoral, though in a landscape of reversion and collapse:

> *The fox pausing for scent cuts holes in hoarfrost.*
> *Quail scream in the fisher's jaw; then the fisher dotes.*
> *The coy-dog howls, raising puppies that breed more puppies*
> *to rip the throats of rickety deer in March.*

The threats of the surrounding country ennoble the passions of the barnyard; he calls the cows "Sweet bellowers enormous and interchangeable," "big-eyed calf-makers, bone-rafters for leather, / awkward arks, cud-chewing lethargic mooers." Although the moos become "dolorous ululations" and a dolorous ululation itself becomes the most peculiar line in recent poetry, "mm-mmm-mmmmm-mmmmmmmmm-ugghwanchhh," even the poet's self-mocking invocations cannot hide his anxiety or nervous dread. Indeed, the tone of these poems veers wildly between mania and depression, from woolly Whitmanian yawp to the plainest of plain speech.

The better of Hall's new poems have the virtues of prose. If those are not quite the virtues of poetry, the fault lies less in the terms of pastoral than in the prosaic tenor of his imagination. Much of his dogged earnestness has been in the prose of criticism and reminiscence, and in the acts of sympathy those require (like his prose, his poetry is best when deferring to his elders—it is professional in some of the best ways and most of the worst). Living through and living out a heritage of house-holding, he is haunted by the ghosts of family and the familiarity of aging. A long poem meant to be the first section of an autobiographical work registers the desperation of routine with a dutiful plainness, and even a dutiful dullness—one can scarcely imagine how Hall will sustain a work three times as long. When his mother speaks, however, he experiences what he elsewhere calls "the ecstasy of my concealment," and emotion otherwise muted or suppressed rises up in her voice:

> "*The year after my father burned in the wrecked car,*
> *my mother came home early from the job she hated*
> *teaching bookkeeping at the secretarial college.*
> *Sometimes she wept because she had flunked someone*
> *she caught cheating. Each day I comforted her.*"

His mother about *her* mother—there is nothing special about such lines, nothing except the tranquillity of reflection he is denied. Hall's authentic voice is the voice of others. There he quietly combines the recollection and regret that have so often provided the reciprocal actions of his poetry. Hall still loves his fancies—poems about baseball, recipes for stew, instructions for scythe sharpening—but they are doomed to dandyism. The most symbolic moment in these poems occurs during just such a fancy—the marriage of Emily Dickinson to Walt Whitman:

> *When we guide her back to the altar, we find the groom*
> *in his slouch hat, open shirt, and untended beard*
> *withdrawn to the belltower with the healthy young sexton*
> *from whose comradeship we detach him with difficulty.*

Such a marriage, however ludicrous or impossible, would unite the literary and the demotic, the private and the public, the two strains of American passion. Hall's poetry draws from both, and neither— *his* is the poetry of the dull, healthy young sexton.

Charles Wright

Every poet is tempted by the lineaments of his life, and some make careers converting their prosaic fates to lines of poetry. Though Charles Wright has often turned to his past for the coarse particulars of his poems, *Zone Journals* is no Wordsworthian project of autobiography and sensibility. It attempts to swell a daily journal into a form more substantial, one that will convey the poet's least shift of mood and the landscape's last shimmer of light:

—Noon like cicada wings,
translucence remembered, half-sheets
Of light over light on the black stones
Of the crescent walk and bodices of the rhododendron,
Red eye of the whirring sun—

The half-constructed sentences suggest the style of this notation, the tourist's hurried pencil rather than the artist's finished oil. The sketchy quality of these journals confirms Wright's fidelity to the ephemeral and evanescent, to the inner restlessness that sends him off to England and Italy. Wright was born in backcountry Tennessee, and he retains a schoolboy awe of Europe and Literature. The continual tension between country and city (the book is dedicated to Merle Travis and Glenn Gould), between American coarseness and European culture, perhaps explains his long fascination with Ezra Pound, whom he stalked through the streets of Venice, not daring to approach. If Wright had once spoken to that pale, grizzled figure, turned the myth into a man, he might have been spared the long homage to Pound's style his work has become:

Waves, and the sea-slack, sunset,
Tide's bolt shot and turned for the night,

> *The dark coming in,*
> > *dark like the dogfish coming in*
> *Under the island's eyelid, under and down.*

Pound's images (especially those of light), rhythms, compounds, literary allusions (especially to Dante), rhetorical questions, and dropped lines: all have been resurrected in Wright's manner, in ghostly devotion to the master. *Zone Journals* often reads like *The Cantos* without the politics, and with Wright's own peculiar admixture of metaphysical assertion ("No matter what things we scrape aside—/ God is an abstract noun") and basso profundity ("everything eats or is eaten," "We must be good to each other").

The most ambitious poem in *Zone Journals*, "A Journal of the Year of the Ox," is fifty pages of a book of days. The smaller journals that flank it, as short as a page or two, have a lyric compression and sometimes even the glimpse of a subject rather than the glance of a sensibility. "A Journal of the Year of the Ox," however, rambles interminably from week to week, month to month, its images shreds without coherence, the themes of death, loss of memory, absence, and negation recurring with little passion and less purpose. The small focus provided by an occasional subject—the Cherokees and their defeat, a summer month in Italy, the poet's fiftieth birthday, visits to the homes of Poe and Dickinson and Petrarch—is not equal to the project's scale or its centrifugal dissolution. A little factual journey in a flatboat, torn from the pages of some encyclopedia, is worth twenty pages of musing:

> *Over the thirty miles of Muscle Shoals,*
> *Loss of the pox-carrying boat and its twenty-eight people*
> *Which followed behind in quarantine and was cut off,*
> *Intercepted, and all its occupants*
> > *butchered or taken prisoner*
> Their cries distinctly heard by those boats in the rear.

Some of Wright's critics would make him a visionary, for which his talent is ill-suited. His most dominating work has always been founded in hard-edged fact, not the gauze of metaphysics. The disappointment of these journals, so laggardly and lacking in life, should not detract from Wright's individuality and seriousness, his gorgeous images and taste for experiment. For twenty years he has written to a consistently high and exacting standard, though he has never managed to write the one book that would lift his reputation over that of his peers. *Zone Journals* may be slave to that ambition, and in it what earlier seemed serious gifts have become merely talent straining for effect.

C. K. Williams

Nothing human is alien to C. K. Williams: a boy shitting his pants ("I can't believe you did that," says his father), a whore rubbing herself in a bar, a man whispering filthy things to a woman in a subway car. In *Flesh and Blood*, as in his last two books, *With Ignorance* (1977) and *Tar* (1983), Williams uses a long line, sometimes subtly rhythmical and sometimes as bare-faced as prose, that takes its passion from the recital of anecdotes and from a boundless sense that the world is there to be observed in its least nuance:

> *They were so exceptionally well got-up for an ordinary Sunday after-*
> *noon stop-in at Deux Magots,*
> *she in very chic deep black, he in a business suit, and they were so*
> *evidently just out of bed*
> *but with very little to say to one another, much gazing off, elaborate*
> *lightings of her cigarettes,*
> *she more proper than was to be believed, sipping with a flourished*
> *pinky at her Pimm's Cup,*
> *that it occurred to me I was finally seeing one of those intriguing* Her-
> ald Tribune *classifieds.*

That euphoric interest in details has now been constrained, even violated, by Williams's decision to write strictly in a form consisting of eight of these elongated, elephantine lines. Poem follows poem— 147 of them—like pickets on a picket fence. Though he has borrowed the burden of the long line from Whitman, and with it a fascination with everything the body can suffer or acquire, *Flesh and*

Blood most resembles *Notebook*, Robert Lowell's failed attempt to cram the stuff of days into a blank fourteen-line stanza. Whereas the most life-soiled of Williams's previous work faced outward, toward emblems of behavior or minor tragedies, many of these octaves turn resolutely inward:

> *How much we've had to pay, though, and how dearly had to suffer for*
> * our liberating dialectics.*
> *The only field still left to us to situate our anguish and uncertainty is*
> * in the single heart,*
> *and how it swells, the heart, to bear the cries with which we troubled*
> * the startled heavens.*
> *Now we have the air, transparent, and the lucid psyche, and gazing*
> * inward, always inward, to the wound.*

These lines come from the book's final sequence, a moving but insufferably mannered elegy for the poet Paul Zweig; they represent the bad prose and bathos that infect too many of these short poems. Given to lists and tiresome repetitions, to posing and to baring his breast, Williams falls victim to a maudlin self-regard verging on self-pity, to an infantilism more appropriate to "About Men" columns: "In how many of the miserable little life dramas I play out in my mind am I unforgivable, / despicable, with everything, love, kin, companionship, negotiable, marketable, for sale." Like most poets who find their own voices attractive, he is his own worst subject.

The most troubling of Williams's poems have always been voyeuristic, the observer attracted to the repellent and thrilled when he cannot avert his gaze. Where length gave his earlier poems time to explore an ambivalent reaction, the new poems are brief and brutal. The trashy and sensationally vulgar stories in *Flesh and Blood* threaten to make him poetry's answer to the *National Enquirer*. It is easy to be sensational. Only when he ignores a self with the soul of a bookkeeper and the taste of a Hollywood producer in order to capture the uncomfortable detail (the gesture of a racist butcher in Paris, a mother's shocked admission that she adores her baby's genitals, an epileptic seizure in the Métro) does he achieve the small immoral triumphs of imagination.

Chronicle
of the
Late
Eighties

Nicholas Christopher

When poets stoop to reconquer their lost audience, a task no more difficult than halting an army of lemmings, they are tempted into those watery genres in which the lemmings are drowning themselves, like science fiction or the novel of manners. In *Desperate Characters*, Nicholas Christopher has had the wit to conceive a detective novella in verse and set it in a surreal version of Chandler's Los Angeles. His unnamed private eye, addressed in the relentlessly immediate second person (perhaps in mistaken homage to Jay McInerney's recent *Bright Lights, Big City*), is threatened by a mysterious woman who carries "steel suitcases / stamped BEDLAM in red." Guarded by the equally mysterious Stella ("her third name / in as many days"), he is driven around a city whose very streets and landmarks have become unstable. The characters seem to have fled from a Hollywood costume party: important clues come from a theosophist undercover cop, who "carries / a paintbrush and a cluster /

of scallions in his back pocket" and is in turn chasing a pair of Romanian opera singers, charlatans pretending to be a mute couple in search of the ghost of Thomas Jefferson, "last seen (they said) sticking up / a savings & loan in Denver."

Christopher unfortunately has no gift for narrative, and his distinctly affectless and soft-boiled private eye can only stumble from one bizarre scene to another without a hint of conviction or character. The poet has let his imagination run not wild but woolly; and all the glitzy detail of stolen begemmed pineapples and "female / impersonators speaking in tongues" cannot conceal a story utterly dead at its center, a dream phantasmagoria more given to Dada than drama. Christopher's overactive fancy, much in evidence in his two earlier collections and in shorter poems filling out this volume, slides too easily into camp and kitsch (he's a whole souvenir shop of kitsch). A few poems with less literary mugging hint at a poetic intelligence more sentimentally humane and now mostly suppressed. Christopher's novella in verse (a verse that is only a lazy prose snipped into short lines) has none of the unforgiving clarity that makes the subrealism of detective novels bearable. Genre fiction, even in verse, is too sophisticated for an author who wishes to remain an amateur.

James Lasdun

There are few things Britain has left to teach us except civility, a sensible attitude toward coinage and firearms, and the importance of a decent railway system. The social lessons of one country are usually lost on another, and the small countercurrents of literature are rarely corrective. James Lasdun, who now lives in New York, is a member of the younger generation of British poets, a generation that includes James Fenton, Craig Raine, Michael Hofmann, and Tony Harrison, most of whom have not been published wisely or well in this country. It is a generation still unembarrassed by intellect or the tradition of form; and in his very gifted first book, *A Jump Start*, Lasdun writes in highly ornate fashion of the glittering decadence of late capitalism, the clubs and restaurants that are our parody of culture.

Though his baroque style is most suited to the night world where the pearls may be precious or paste, Lasdun moves easily from one culture to another, from New York to London to Portugal to Rome, and from the damp maladies of the city to the deep maliciousness of the animal world. In a world where nothing but the surface has value, the depths are likely to be brutal with desire:

Then watch those crayfish in the bubbling tank,
Curled peach-fire torsos peppered like your wrist,
Splayed samurai tails, the stripped-flex feelers
Beckoning what the body must resist;

More intimacy than nature will allow—
Look at them grope, and probe, and interlace
Through drifts of snapped antennae, severed limbs,
Love fused to violence in the one embrace.

Lasdun's poems often have a striking organization, sidling toward their prey in an unexpected way. The charade of elegance can be merely charade, or can seem callous when more serious matters are referred to. There is a moral insensitivity or cold-bloodedness working deep in the manner as well as the material, and despite the broken, brilliant blooms of language the emotional colors approach monotone. A decorative style may not conceal a frigid emptiness, though it may distract the reader from realizing that despite the attractive variety of his subjects Lasdun has a limited rhetorical understanding. Nevertheless, a sensual love of language is not the worst recommendation of a poet's gifts. Lasdun, who has also written a highly praised collection of short stories, shows that the effervescent shallowness of our culture can still be troubled by the careful shudder of meter or the possession of rhyme.

Lucie Brock-Broido

Lucie Brock-Broido is the poet laureate of *People* magazine and the evening news, with a taste for sensational stories, usually relegated to the headlines, that illustrate character at its most betrayed: the eighteen-month-old girl lost down a well, the insane MOVE cult in Philadelphia, the mad mute British twin girls. Her first book, *A Hunger*, lives in a sea of contemporanea, as up to date as a fax message and as teasing as newspaper filler ("I can't take my eyes // Off the news," she writes). A poem that begins with the exhumation of Josef Mengele may move through the death of Marlene Dietrich, a fire in an English football stadium, and the biological death of half of the Rhine before settling into the narrator's narcissistic address to her lover.

It would require a powerful intelligence to bring this heap of broken images into coherence; and Brock-Broido prefers to write a poetry of wavering incoherence, her images all ajumble, her sentences wandering off into confusion. Her poems are rarely able to concentrate for a stanza on the show at hand: she's as bad as a television junkie with a hot remote control. And yet in the midst of all her preening mannerism, there are two or three real poems, particularly "Edward VI on the Seventh Day," which retells the story of Henry VIII's tragic little son, whose death made possible the Age of Elizabeth. Limited to the boy's point of view, it attends to character with a precision that does not allow sentiment and yet retains the oddity of its historical moment.

Her other poems do not escape, but cannot benefit from, her Tudor disregard for punctuation and syntax. Her voices, when she indulges in persona, are strained and tainted by a self-conscious artlessness—or worse, artiness. In a poet so given to antics (like having an eighteen-month-old girl say, "I am born into the dark / rococo teratogenic rooms of the underground"), form finally gives way to performance. It is difficult to sympathize with a poet who so enjoys her own frivolousness and so overestimates the interest of haute-couture vulgarity. If Brock-Broido lacks the vulnerability that might make her set poses telling, she nevertheless has a delightful confidence, and even overconfidence, in her imaginative realm. Her attention to the headlines cannot wholly corrupt her verve and occasional humor ("Dogs bark because they always do in pastorals"). She seems to know what she's doing even when it's not worth doing well.

Molly Peacock

The last thirty years of American poetry have been a love affair
with the committed sins of confession, with the life lived as the
subject earned. The mass of poets now reaching mid-career may
often be distinguished only by their technical variations on a common theme, though technique is rare when poets prefer force of
personality. Poets who intermittently display the vice of character
respond divergently to the impulse to provide a formal psychology
of the middle class.

Molly Peacock's poetry is fraught with anxiety, frazzled with
artifice—the anxiety is purely literary, the artifice pure artifice. *Take
Heart* continues the wounded reflections that marked her last book,
where she discovered the perverse technique she has raised to formal consideration—the use of rhyme without meter. She turns to
her themes like an injured animal: abortion, the loneliness of sex, a
childhood with an alcoholic father ("What happened earlier I'm not
sure of. / Of course he was drunk, but often he was. / His face looked
like a ham on a hook").

"Angry, / dense and mulish" in her own estimation, Peacock seeks
out the unlovely ways of her character. Rhyme is her idiosyncrasy, a
private restraint that permits a public order (without meter, or at
least an ear for rhythm, rhymes are like the red shoes in *The Red
Shoes*, pretty but lethal). Though she employs rhyme only when
convenient, and seldom precisely, she finds it a stimulus to the imaginative dumb-show, and in its small adherences a permission for the
release of repressed feeling: in this, rhyme is a Rorschach. She is not
immune to the brutality, the craving to shock or sicken, that confession easily succumbs to; but such shock gives her writing an electric
vividness it otherwise lacks:

A curette has the shape of a grapefruit spoon.
They dilate the cervix, then clean out the womb
with the jagged prow, just like separating
the grapefruit from its skin, although the softening
yellow rind won't bear another fruit.

Peacock's strength is the stateliness of her self-hatred; she loathes her wish to be the perfect patient. Her poetry is not in the submersion in carnality or the adolescent delight in anatomical detail ("a sweet white discharge / coats the vaginal lips"), but in minor betrayals of character. When she buys a fake fur she cannot afford, she is alive to all the implications of being false and buying false. Peacock's narratives are nervier than her meditations: she doesn't have the verbal gifts to make arresting observations, and her bright notions are neatly fatuous ("What we don't forget is what we don't say," "The ocean's great to look at / because there's enough of it"). Even so, she is sometimes able to capture the complications and clumsiness, the fine moral messiness, of a life anxious to its edges.

Edward Hirsch

Edward Hirsch's poems argue for a sentimental transcendence where "We will be lifted up and carried a far distance / On invisible wings." *The Night Parade* undertakes the suffering exploration of memory begun in his earlier work, but with greater concentration and conviction. Though a few of his poems live in the realm of history, including a savagely long-winded and secondhand evocation of the Black Death, he always returns to the substrate of family, to his grandparents' emigration from eastern Europe and his own childhood in a weepily memorialized Chicago.

Like most poets of sentiment, Hirsch is drawn to the ripeness of death, and his elegies live in the prurience of unconscious seduction, their images ambiguously lush ("cancer feasted on their ripe bodies / From the inside"). He writes limpidly, if often limply; because he has little interest in the formal arrangement of language or even the various subsidizing strategies of free verse, his poems rely on prose for rhythm and anecdote for structure (much of the book might fall under the title of one long poem, "Family Stories"). The tales of his grandmother's Murphy bed, or his sister's Little League triumph, or his moment of rapture on Parents Day in 1963 are well enough rehearsed, but might have been left in the snapshot album. Only occasionally do the images demand art rather than fidelity to memory, as during a hotel-room abortion when the doctor's "girlfriend fiddled with the radio / And lounged against the door in her spiked heels."

Though as a younger poet he has been richly and repeatedly honored, Hirsch relies too much on a solicitude that can be oleaginous, and on those recurring images of transcendence ("Though in a moment I was lifted up / and transported") that invoke the sentimental grotesque. He is capable of language less avidly self-rewarding:

> *There are two purple welts on the horizon*
> *And a thimble of yellow dye*
> > *spilled in the ironwoods*
> *And the fleshy chrysanthemums*
> > *growing out of the hips*
> *Of the Japanese cemetery by the ocean.*

If he were more frequently unfaithful to his furies, the Chekhovian pathos his poems aspire to might be more easily granted, since not so eagerly sought.

Mary Jo Salter

Mary Jo Salter resurrects a world of interiors whose moral and meaning are measured by windows, mirrors, and the self-informing life of paintings and objets d'art. She has not received as much attention as some of her peers, though *Unfinished Painting* is the Lamont Poetry Selection for 1988. The chilly formal manner of its twenty or so poems, including long elegies for her mother and a Japanese friend, is hedged by rare technical regard. Even in the most intimate situations she is closely bound and detached, observing but never implicated, never breaching the artistic distance.

The decorum of this world is the decorum of claustrophobia. If nature is invoked, it is the nature painted on a Chinese fan: "cow-licked shoots of rice // rising up from honey- / combed terraces."

That severe inspection of the artist's delicate stroke requires Coleridge's armed vision, and when turned on the living it creates images of frigid beauty, as in the spectacle of a Japanese bride:

> *to see that snow*
> *mountain of kimono*
>
> *and, falling from the pinnacle*
> *of her lacquered wig, the fog of silk*
> *over a face too shy, too proud*
> *to lift. Who'd made her up?—the natural*
> *milk of her skin absorbed in chalk,*
> *a slope of powder*
>
> *down to her collar.*

Even life can be made into art, into the apparition of Mt. Fuji rising from snow, fog, and powdered slope. "Who'd made her up?" is a question with a double bind, and behind its admission of fictional contrivance lies the complicity and coiling Salter's lines surrender to.

A poet so primly attentive to art is, unsurprisingly, attracted deeply and disturbingly to Emily Dickinson, who also found philosophy in hermitage. Salter has none of her mentor's ease in forming the simple language of feeling, and is too eager to draw a lesson or round a revelation from already constricted means. She might seem too tight-lipped to take advantage of the liberating virtues of her technique; but the personal, unaffected voice she discovers in "Armistice Day" and "Dead Letters," poems tinged with death and the ironies of death, finally overcomes her domestic mordancy and promises a manner equal to her technical mastery. Her unassuming composure cannot mask the ambition of her grace and intelligence, or her demand—still a little too careful, a little too tentative—on the chain of artistic influence and imitation we call tradition.

Sandra McPherson

Sandra McPherson is a charming, translucent, delicately indelicate, even artfully artless poet (I might have said she is artlessly artful, which she is on occasion). Her early books were praised for their striking images, though the images were often cool and detached, like a fleet of icebergs. She has become, quietly and almost unassumingly, a more intense and affecting poet. Of the poets under review here, she is the least prepossessing and the least obviously ambitious.

McPherson's poetry derives from happenstance, from troubled domestic incident, from the observation of wildflowers. She can toy with the trivial without distorting it and face the terror of aging with a calm matter-of-factness. Her poems often remind me of an artist's sketchbook, with their rapid pencil shadings and utterly confident command of line, even while reducing a busy landscape to small weedy scribbles and a few notations of color. That casual manner makes *Streamers* a deceptive and spirited performance, where even plain events may be rendered in phrases as rich as redemption:

> *O his bare travelogues!—*
> *grim for me, intoxicating for you,*
> *in our attic apartment with waiting crib.*
>
> *Spore prints, rashes as baby-talc white*
> *as the paint crinkling off the drying-plank,*
> *spawned unseen; all veils pulled back*
>
> *for a kiss.*

That kiss may be the kiss of death. McPherson has Robert Lowell's sense of the creepily accurate symbolic detail, but unlike Lowell she lives in the still center of her contradictions. Her most unsettling poems—she has a gift for unsettling the settled arrangements of love—expose her conflicting passions as wife and mother: "you're young but you're scary," she says to her daughter, who doesn't find it easy to be her daughter ("I want you to run to me with your kiss. / Still you brood in the lake like wild rice").

The movement of McPherson's poems may be colloquial, their arguments personal and a little unstructured; but, when she sees her daughter's "double new ignited breasts" or discovers in a creek bank "brush as gold / and scratched as an old wedding ring," the eyecatching precision of her language has a more than metaphorical resource. Her descriptions of wildflowers (half the book is what amounts to a field guide to California wildflowers) have the exuberance of botanical illustration:

Wild radish and jointed charlock fly from a gray glass,

propeller-shaped flowers white with blue veins, yellow with coils of subsurface green like wires in an electric blanket.

Their purposes are not merely pretty, however, and their presence serves her themes of nurturing and failures to nurture, of the fragility of life, of the crooked recessions of authority, of the moment where the seamless web of nature catches the human breakdown. She is still a poet more likely to make startling associations than to take advantage of her moments of vision, but she has slowly developed the sensitivity to moral complication that gives her poems a design beyond their details. The passages of intransigent loveliness now entertain the tensions of her best work.

McPherson writes of a realm that "doesn't promise too much," and she refuses to accept easy resolution, leaving her readers off balance, unsatisfied, unappeased. Her recent work has been overlooked in favor of poets with a brighter sense of fashion and none of her awkward glamour, poets so concerned with raw somethings they would have no idea how to make poems out of these "fancy nothings." No one should be fooled by her glowing surfaces. Her recognition of the darkness in the shape of circumstance makes her a very ambitious poet indeed.

At the
Heart of
Grandeur

Anthony Hecht is a poet of classical unreason and classical violence. The ancient world survives, not in the bleached bare ribs of the Parthenon or the still, polluted air of Athens, but in the pagan polychrome the temple was dressed in, the jellied gore of Oedipus' eyes, the hot deaths at Thermopylae, betrayals vanished from all but language. In the late witness of our century, no poet has been more austere in his imaginative engagements than Hecht, or purer in his sense of pacing and weight—his poetry at times approaches the condition of sculpture. Even in nature, to which other poets would withdraw for solace, Hecht can find only the solace of decay, the still life anything but still:

> *The lichens, like a gorgeous, soft disease*
> > *In rust and gold rosette*
> *Emboss the bouldered wall, and creepers seize*
> > *In their cup-footed fret,*

Ravelled and bare, such purchase as affords.
   The sap-tide slides to ebb,
And leafstems, like the drumsticks of small birds,
   Lie snagged in a spiderweb.

Some poets are saved by grace, others by will. Hecht began as a poet of convenience and charm, of brutal form and baroque extravagance, of rhetoric as rheumatic and gouty as the Romans he described bathing in the hot springs at Ischia. His first poems, a selection of them gathered in *Collected Earlier Poems*, smell of powder and the parlor and seem to have come out of Richard Wilbur's overcoat (as Randall Jarrell once said) and Wallace Stevens's vest pocket. That is their veneer, but underneath is a spiritual disease. The Stevens in him titles a poem "Le Masseur de ma soeur," and begins it, "My demoiselle . . . ," but there is no Stevens in "Upstanding nipples under a sheer blouse," or "The fishy slime" of Argus's eyes, or "The Man-in-the-Moon's microcephalic grin."

Those ruptures in a manner so stiff and proper—like that of a man sentenced to life in a morning coat—could not predict the deepening, the darkening of a willed burden, in the thirteen years that separated his first book, *A Summoning of Stones* (1954), from his second, *The Hard Hours* (1967), which won the Pulitzer Prize. A style that had been overelaborate, fussy though on occasion graceful, became elegantly severe, charged with moral authority and an almost helpless despondency, losing all the sleights of expression that divide "letting fall / Lamplight upon her dress till every small / Motion made visible seemed no mere endeavor / Of body to articulate its offer" from

It was the sentence. He was to be flayed alive,
As slowly as possible, to drag out the pain.
And we were made to watch. The king's personal doctor,
The one who had tended his back,
Came forward with a tray of surgical knives.
They began at the feet.

It was as if Osric had taken off his hat and turned into Hamlet.

Scarred by a history whose lessons will be ignored, and whose lessons will murder us, Hecht has become our only poet able to horrify. He has afflicted the modern with its own images, the muscles "Clean as a Calder," the all-night service station where "Andy Warhol's primary colors shine." In "The Cost," a couple on a Vespa wheel carelessly around Trajan's column, but stanza by stanza their innocence is shadowed by the column's spiraling figures, the thousands of raw recruits for the emperor's Dacian Wars, wars long cast into irrelevance. The ending delicately modulates its anger and ambivalence:

> *And why should they take thought*
> *Of all that ancient pain,*
> *The Danube winters, the nameless young who fought,*
> *The blood's uncertain lease?*
> *Or remember that that fifteen-year campaign*
> *Won seven years of peace?*

That poem is haunted by Vietnam; but Hecht, who was present at the liberation of a concentration camp, has been haunted by the longer memory of the Holocaust. The beauty of his language—and no poet can be more beautiful when he wishes to be—is stilled by the horror of knowledge, and that infection redeems many poems that would have been perfumed into prettiness. He uses the beautiful in a cool, calculating way. A poem neutrally titled "Persistences" may begin "The leafless trees are feathery, / A foxed, Victorian lace," but it ends with "The burning, voiceless Jews."

In *The Hard Hours* and the books that have followed, *Millions of Strange Shadows* (1977), *Venetian Vespers* (1979), and now, after another long lapse, *The Transparent Man*, Hecht's value as a poet of accusation has been sharpened by poems, rarely straightforward or plainspoken, of personal affliction. The grimness at the heart of grandeur prevents his work from settling into the isolations of technique, or into what he called in an interview "the matured and mellowed residue of what in childhood had been a poisonous brew of fear, hatred, self-loathing, impotence, and deep discouragement." No poem will chasten such a *horror vacui*. Drawn toward their merciless epiphanies, his strongest poems have refused the solicitudes of postwar poetry.

Every poetic advantage has its corresponding limitation. Hecht has achieved most in the brevity and intensity of the lyric, in poems that can be brought to perfection. He is weaker at narrative, and his long dramatic monologues lack the stress of structure—they are dignified, gorgeous in patches, but rambling and never fully rendered. When he writes in the voice of a chambermaid at an Alpine resort; or about a pillowy alcoholic, Shirley Carson, and her husband, "Kit"; or, in the title poem of his new book, as a woman dying of leukemia, he cannot for all his sympathies escape an undertone of condescension. *The Transparent Man* includes a masque for four voices, the lovers from *A Midsummer Night's Dream* cast as the four instruments of a Haydn string quartet—the resulting play of voice is lovely, but as a poem it is not successful except as an overdetermined, high-arty, sweetly nutty idea. He is addicted to wretched puns— "*Mens sana* in men's sauna" (*echt* Hecht, you might say) was about as bad as it got in previous volumes, but the new book includes "Whirled without end," "somewhat the worse for where," and, amazingly, "Between post oak and propter oak."

The Transparent Man is a strange, gorgeously moody, occasionally imperfect (even Hecht can be left-handed) collection lit by Vermeer or de la Tour. It returns to the concerns that have troubled this troubled poet—death in Venice, the woe that is in marriage, elegies at the core of happiness, and the Holocaust. The subjects are not unusual (who isn't afraid of a poet with unusual subjects?), but the conviction and darkening conscience contribute to the pressure that blooms into style.

"The Book of Yolek" is the most terrifying sestina I know—it is perhaps the most unbearable in the language, yet composed of events as plain as a meal of brook trout, a lost day of childhood, an incident in the war. Its effect depends on the quiet accretions of style, and a few lines would not do it justice. Nor can I quote—I would like to quote—a complex little nature poem like "Curriculum Vitae," whose five stanzas mesh like silver cogs. Each reading proves it more despairing. A few lines cannot suggest the graveness, chased with charm, that animates his elegy for David Kalstone, an elegy that begins, "Lime-and-mint mayonnaise and salsa verde." Instead, I will quote a meal from "See Naples and Die," a lunch that might have been served at Tiffany's:

> *Slowly our eyes*
> *Make out his pyramids of delicacies—*
> *The Celtic coils and curves of primrose shrimp,*
> *A speckled gleam of opalescent squid,*
> *The mussel's pearl-blue niches, as unearthly*
> *As Brazilian butterflies, and the grey turbot,*
> *Like a Picasso lady with both eyes*
> *On one side of her face.*

When someone offers you lines like that, he must be Mephistopheles and you must be Faust—you know you shouldn't succumb to such language, but you succumb.

The Transparent Man has a respect for the reader's perception that has almost been lost from contemporary poetry, with all its prosy ease and selfish concern. From an early age Hecht has spoken like a biblical patriarch—when he thunders, you feel you're to blame for the evil that is the world. That may seem a negative virtue, but his dry and melancholy authority has been a brilliant counterirritant to the wastage of our language. The poems of *The Transparent Man* join the difficult majesties of *Collected Earlier Poems* in elegance, in cold pity, in the harsh, unamenable, cruel condition of life.

c h a p t e r   1 4

The
Midnight
of Nostalgia

And what a dreadful disease Nostalgia
must be on the banks of the Missouri!

SYDNEY SMITH

We have heard the chimes at midnight,
Master Shallow.

FALSTAFF

You don't have to be religious to succumb to nostalgia, though in
some people nostalgia may supplant the religious instinct. The
Christian present pursues its balance between the past of grace freely
bestowed, fall, redemption through blood and the future of redemption in death, rise from sin, grace everlasting. As pure philosophy it
is progressive, though I don't believe the angels will wear togas or
holy tunics to protect their modesty. In practice, and in its daily
injunctions, it tends to be backward-looking, and in its regressive-
ness to resemble the common operations of nostalgia.

We think of nostalgia as the vice of maturity, a disease of age; but
you don't have to pass forty for nostalgia to press into a life, and even

the very young may show its effect. In *The Oxford Book of Literary Anecdotes*, Ronald Knox is recorded as saying, during a bout of insomnia at age four, "I lie awake and think about the past." As a literary theme (rather than transient concern or rhetorical figure), nostalgia required a notion of the self perhaps impossible before Rousseau. Once the trivial incidents of a life had gained the authority of the poetic lyric, nostalgia became another vehicle for certain ancient, governing anxieties: the loss of the past (especially the perfected or romanticized past, an Eden), the forfeit of opportunity and the regret for actions taken or mistaken, the corrupted potential or relative poverty of the present.

There was a feeling before the feeling found a name. When Shallow boasts, in *Henry IV, Part II*, "Jesu, Jesu, the mad days that I have spent! And to see how many of my old acquaintance are dead!", he mingles regret with the consolation of reminiscence, measuring the present on the terms of the past. And Falstaff, later, detects how reminiscence overwhelms the thin particulars: "I do see the bottom of Justice Shallow. Lord, Lord, how subject we old men are to this vice of lying!" (echoing his exclamation in *Part I* when Prince Hal claims the slaughter of Hotspur: "Lord, Lord, how this world is given to lying!").

The burdens of nostalgia aren't just an old man's quarrels with truth—for seeing the past, for saying the past, as better than it was. In an unsparing and sensible book called *The Burden of the Past and the English Poet*, Walter Jackson Bate reminds us that the pressures of the past have been felt since antiquity: an Egyptian scribe of 2000 B.C. named Khakheperresenb lamented, "Would I had phrases that are not known, utterances that are strange, in new language that has not been used, free from repetition, not an utterance which has grown stale, which men of old have spoken." The burdens fell differently on Shallow and Khakheperresenb, the literary construction and the literary scribe, but were jointly derived from and jointly determined by the belief that compared to a past of vital originality, the present was a withering or falling away.

The word *nostalgia* is a learned neologism of the late Renaissance. According to one scholar, it can be traced to an obscure 1688 medical tract, by the Swiss physician Johannes Hofer, describing a disorder found among Swiss mercenaries serving abroad in the armies of Europe. Their symptoms included melancholy, despondency, weeping, anorexia, and attempted suicide. They were, in short, desperately homesick. The first use in English isn't recorded until almost a century later, and before the present century all *Oxford English Dictionary* citations retain the sense of the cobbled-up Greek: *nostos*, a return home, and *algos*, pain.

Even used figuratively, the word remained within the pathology of homesickness: "That pond has . . . about half-a-dozen trouts, if indeed they have not sickened and died of Nostalgia" (1842). The first citation in the *OED* for our modern sense, for the "regret or sorrowful longing *for* the conditions of a past age; regretful or wistful memory or recall of an earlier time," doesn't occur until 1920, in D. H. Lawrence's *The Lost Girl*. No doubt a deeper trawl of literature would drag up earlier examples, but the shift from pathology to *pathétique* comes remarkably late.

It is widely supposed that nostalgia in literature is immitigably bad, that it protects what ought to be examined, falsifies what should be exposed, defends what must be attacked. The nostalgic impulse is thought to derive from the complacency of denial and therefore to exist wholly within the precincts of sentimentality, of the unexamined indulgence in emotional forms. But nostalgia isn't necessarily a wish to return to the past; it is the wish to be privileged to recall it, and to the extent that nostalgia is the admission of a practice, is aware of limit in the character of its longing, it is a gesture of counter-sentiment. Nostalgia is the refuge of poets for whom the current modes of reminiscence have been irremediably stained with sentiment.

The sentimentalities to which our poetry is susceptible contaminate the treatment of private life. The modern poet is an adept of the material or moral condition of his life—even love takes a poor second to the versification of domestic anecdote. When the allocating sentiment raises the trivial to the virtues of symbol, it is not the literature but the life that seems wanting. What is commonly thought to represent "risk" in contemporary poetry, the revelation

of private affairs, employs an attitude to experience smug and calculating when it isn't corrupt, shameless, and insincere. From this,
nostalgia can represent an escape and the radical of a reformation. It
is also, of course, peculiarly permeable to sentiment; and every example of nostalgia in its reforming character may be countered by a
dozen of sentimental misuse.

I have entertained these general notes before coming to the individual case because I am interested in nostalgia only as anti-senti-
ment, as the canker within sentiment. Given the rarity of a nostalgia
of this condition, the subject of this essay might more usefully have
been "The Abuse of Nostalgia," but that would have eliminated
consideration of the reforming instance.

The method of Donald Justice's later poetry accepts nostalgia, a
nostalgia with little of the emotional consolation of submission and
more of the religious desolation of confession. In his arching dark
ironies, Justice has long proved an irritant to the simpler taxonomies
of American poetry, which find it convenient to ignore whatever lies
beyond the margin of immediate comprehension. Justice almost
never uses the self as the location of drama, for the great tragedy
moving through the little event. In his detachment he is a modern
(his most obvious forebears Williams and Stevens) at a time when
the sharper reliefs of modernism have been eroded. Modernism's
respect for history, for a culture that spans millennia and not just
months, has been superseded no less than its cool outward presen-
tation of subject. No longer is modernism's "impersonality" recognized as a matter of tension and tone: when fully employed, tension
and tone don't require the outward display of emotion (Eliot's poems, to me at least, are frighteningly emotional).

The poetry of Pound and Eliot threw out grappling hooks in all
directions; the poetry of Williams and Stevens was, in the main, self-
sufficient. Most of Donald Justice's poems are similarly occlusive;
they are the horizon of their own reference. They have practiced
various strategies of impersonality, and without a side-glancing title
or guarded note the reader would scarcely be aware of a debt to
Vallejo, or Rilke, or Baudelaire. Justice has often made his own what
is most foreign (one might see this strategy as a way of *avoiding* the

burdens of the self)—the foreign landscapes become local, the references to a wider culture turn properly private. His poetry is consequent to its limitations (which is not the same as complacent in them); this may be called its modesty. Within that modesty, however, he has discovered—increasingly in the past decade—a richness and lushness located almost entirely within the remove of the past. In his use of nostalgia, nostalgia can no longer be considered a defensive exhaustion—rather, it has been a recovered plenitude.

Justice's last new collection, *The Sunset Maker* (1987), is a book of assignations with the past, and it is necessary to stand a little aside from the assignatory character to observe the special conditions the artist has made in the fabric of observation. "Nostalgia of the Lakefronts," the poem in which the method most readily implicates the verse technique as well as the verse subject, opens with what seems the destruction of Sodom and Gomorrah: "Cities burn behind us . . ." But the cities burn with lights; these are not the cities of the plain, and the hints of holocaust would be a mild, damning joke if not for certain deepening shadows—of the proper end to wicked pleasures, of the punishment for those who look back.

The poem establishes itself not as a meditation but as a movement through childhood, or through the moment when childhood is "fading to a landscape deep with distance." Neither the moment nor the loss is precise—the poem memorizes, perhaps memorializes, certain summers by a lake, perhaps one certain summer, the summer of 1942, the last before war closed the hotels. The memories have wavered past precision (Justice would have just turned seventeen late in the summer of '42) until what is important isn't their specific outline but their evocative ghostliness, their "indecipherable blurred harmonies"—the loudspeaker, the distant sad piano, the horn over the water.

At such times, wakeful, a child will dream the world,
And this is the world we run to from the world.

But in this blurring (the second line sounds like a blurred quotation of Jarrell, whose favorite word was *world*), the world inwardly dreamed and the world outwardly experienced can't always be kept apart—it is perhaps not the proper burden of the artist to keep them apart:

> *Or the two worlds come together and are one*
> *On dark sweet afternoons of storm and of rain.*

The child dreaming the world may be the artist in his earliest manifestation, but the fiction of the artist is more devouring than the child's mere dreaming. The past has an achieved coherence, though here the subversion of the present by that past lies in the very innocence of its art, the art of a now vanished moment. The lake, for instance, "is famed among painters for its blues":

> *Is their wish not unique—*
> *To anthropomorphize the inanimate*
> *With a love that masquerades as pure technique?*

Here the artist's impersonality is the condition or cost of his feeling—the feeling guaranteed only by the purity of technique. There are two movements from this question, one through subject and one through form. In the poem the question is not answered but overridden, perhaps overwritten:

> *O art and the child are innocent together!*

The remainder of the poem chronicles the loss of that innocence—not the child's but the artist's. "Soon now the war will shutter the grand hotels"—this is the loss or corruption nostalgia expects, even revels in (there would be little point in setting up a stone for something that still existed). But there is a ghostlier, more painful loss in the very concept of artistry. I wouldn't wish to press the suggestion too far, at least not past the point where it is merely suggestive; but in poetry as well as painting a certain innocence (some might prefer to call it sophistication) did not survive much longer. The realism even the Cubists subscribed to, in their way, soon became the province of the amateur only—the line immediately after the exclamation above is "But landscapes grow abstract . . . ," and its bearing on painting (the collapse in value of draftsmanship, the triumph of Abstract Expressionism over line, the later relegation of figure to

THE MIDNIGHT OF NOSTALGIA (DONALD JUSTICE)   159

the cartoon kitsch of Pop Art) isn't wholly compelled by an abstraction of memory. In the final stanza:

And after a time the lakefront disappears
Into the stubborn verses of its exiles
Or a few gifted sketches of old piers.

The verses are stubborn because they *are* verses at a time when metrical verse has long been suspect and "amateur." And those *old piers* sound grimly with the *old peers* whose techniques are vanished issues. I have taken a liberal course with the pun because of the second movement, through form, to which I alluded earlier. The poem's stanzas vary between six and seven lines, but the rhymes are all exact, sometimes a word with itself (*harmonies / harmonies*), but never weaker than a syllable with itself (*cockatoo / 1942, unique / technique, disappears / piers*). The words and syllables rhyme not with something like themselves but with themselves; and this violation of the normal prescription of rhyme isn't just the calculated echo in language of the past's vibration into the present, but the considered deviation in technique that implies, first, that the artist who would respond *to* tradition must respond *within* tradition, and, second, that the history of poetry is the violation of technique, not the abandonment of it. For the artist, "Then we remember, whether we would or no." Nostalgia is not, not necessarily, the parasitic enactment of the past for its emotion, but the enactment of a responsibility by the measurement of loss.

The past is a series of half-forgotten particulars; but in Justice's poetry, to what I think is an unusual degree, the observer stands aside from the force of the particulars, not immune to them (because continually establishing relations between them) but curiously detached from their access. It is as if a poet were permitted every intimacy with a speaker except intimacy itself; that is, all the stoic intimacies of knowledge but few of feeling. This may seem the reverse of what we expect when the speaker is the poet. (The question is, of course, more vexed, but it shouldn't be made needlessly difficult—in other than dramatic monologues, the speaking voice is usually taken for the poet's. That doesn't mean the poem tells the truth.)

The inadequacy of contemporary poetry may lie in its confidence of feeling (even its representation of feeling) and its absence of a knowledge susceptible to anything outside feeling. The determinism of contemporary poetry demands that feelings be enactments of events, perhaps better the performatives of events; that is why the past in most poems is so often on trial. One of the merits of Justice's poetry lies, not in its absence of emotion, but in its withholding of confidence from emotion. The events that suffer this withholding are permitted a range of insinuation more disturbing because less mediated. At a felt distance, the past can't be revealed or reenacted, only rendered (for this reason Justice's exclamations, his mark of exhausted pathos, seem twice lonely). Such a speaker is unreliable because he will not accede to the conventions of sentiment.

The unreliable narrator provides a convenient transition to Jamesian sentiment; that is, a sentiment established and modified by the intimacies of knowing, the intimacies of detail. I don't think it necessary to argue that Henry James was sentimental, as long as I am speaking of the letters, not the literature. It was convenient, and he acceded to it, and whether it was for the sake of his friends or of his mental detachment makes little difference. Justice's poem "American Scenes (1904–1905)" is a variant instance where the use of nostalgia is formal—that is, has formal value (in the structure or the development of structure) beyond the entablature of "meaning." I take it as an example of how a mind that finds longing a kind of failing, a mind both superbly aware and superbly devious, may counter the reactionary gestures of nostalgia even while seeming to observe them. The indulgence is the satisfaction of an urge, while the countering stakes off the grounds of refusal. This is called having it both ways.

The impersonation of James requires a fidelity to external observation, as well as to the internal tones impressed by meter and rhyme (the operations by which poetry establishes its difference from prose, and so the most difficult to set in accord with it). The four sections, the four scenes, that are the emphatic form through which the poem sustains its relation to James's original journey, are mere fragments, shattered recollections of a shattered sensibility: three pairs of quatrains and a sonnet epilogue. This is enough, as a matter of formal responsibility, to create the sensibility intact, or as much of the whole as applies.

Many of the phrases in the poem fall, unencumbered or unelaborated, from James's notebooks and from one of the saddest books of American travel, *The American Scene.*

Cambridge in Winter

Immense pale houses! Sunshine just now and snow
Light up and pauperize the whole brave show—
Each fanlight, each veranda, each good address,
All a mere paint and pasteboard paltriness!

These winter sunsets are the one fine thing:
Blood on the snow, one last impassioned fling,
The wild frankness and sadness of surrender—
As if our cities ever could be tender!

From James's *Notebooks* (borrowed phrases in italics):

The snow, the sunshine, light up and pauperize all the wooden surfaces, *all the mere paint and pasteboard paltriness. The one fine thing are the winter sunsets, the blood on the snow,* the pink crystal of the west, *the wild frankness,* wild *sadness* (?)—so to speak—*of the surrender.*

Borrowing is the artificial shell around which an obligation accrues. Here the very ease with which the pilfered phrases are united in the tone guarantees, seems to guarantee, the fidelity of the poem's exhausted, translucent passion, even though in James the passages are neither as richly evocative nor as exclamatory (the three exclamations create the intimacy of Justice's tone). They are reportorial, professionally engrossed, almost dry—they have leaked into style.

It is the aversion from the original, however, that rescues the richness of feeling beneath James's phrasing. I am reminded of the dramatic placements Shakespeare found for the phrases from Holinshed or North's Plutarch, or of the Elizabeth Bishop poem "From Trollope's Journal" (another version of civil war), funded on a few spare lines from Trollope's *North America*. The reproduction is the supplement to the original, yet it comes to have original force.

James had written to W. D. Howells, before leaving for America, "I *want* to come, quite pathetically and tragically—it is a passion of nostalgia." Here the meaning balances between old and new, in the passion that once was sickly possession, almost ready to detach itself from the pathology of homesickness to become mere yearning for the past. It was the past James came for—he hadn't visited America in twenty years. He had turned sixty. And everywhere among his old haunts were the vastations and devastations of two decades of unrelieved commerce. Some of the ancient streets behind Boston's statehouse had been cleared, but the house of his childhood still stood, rich in its recollections. He looked upon it; and a month later, when he returned to look again, it had vanished completely: "If I had often seen how fast history could be made I had doubtless never so felt that it could be unmade still faster."

I have lingered over these circumstances for their relevance, not to the minor arrangements of the poem, but to the responsibilities such arrangements assume. Any negotiation with the past, it should be clear from James, is either a surrender or a recovery. Each loss of the richness of the past, each triumph of the tawdry or the commercial, freed James from the material aspect of his nostalgia. And yet the very terms of his analysis, of his distaste, were conditioned by a past irretrievably absent. The rage to recover, the "nostalgic rage" as he called it in another context, is thus cruelly limited in its capacities of analysis—that is its pathos. Its triumph is its refusal merely to surrender to the pleasures of recall. The closing lines of the first three sections of Justice's poem mark his wary regard for this temptation, as well as his refusal of its blandishments: "As if our cities ever could be tender!," "Of open gates, of all but bland abysses," "and the South meanwhile / Has only to be tragic to beguile."

In the sonnet epilogue, Justice finally overtakes James:

Epilogue: Coronado Beach, California

In a hotel room by the sea, the Master
Sits brooding on the continent he has crossed.

Not that he foresees immediate disaster,
Only a sort of freshness being lost—
Or should he go on calling it Innocence?
The sad-faced monsters of the plains are gone;
Wall Street controls the wilderness. There's an immense
Novel in all this waiting to be done,
But not, not—sadly enough—by him. His talents,
Such as they may be, want an older theme,
One rather more civilized than this, on balance.
For him now always the consoling dream
Is just the mild dear light of Lamb House falling
Beautifully down the pages of his calling.

Except for the penultimate line (*Notebooks:* "the mild still light of dear old L<amb> H<ouse>"), the phrases are now all the poet's; and yet the impersonation is complete, having shifted to a manner detached no less fondly, or fixedly, than James's own erasure or self-effacement as "this victim," "the strayed amateur," "the ancient contemplative person," and especially "the restless analyst," as he variously styled himself through *The American Scene*. These scenes, this particular book, and this particular author converge in their attractions for a poet himself drawn into the "nostalgic rage." In a poet past sixty, you may read into this epilogue, "sadly enough," a disavowal, perhaps even a farewell, like Prospero's farewell, to certain ambitions (it must be remembered Justice's poetry has been rather liberal in such disavowals since his forties). But it is also a recognition of the subjects proper to such a talent and of the home built in the present, rather than the home surrendered to the past.

The sonnet might also be read as an inversion of "On First Looking into Chapman's Homer." Justice's "strayed amateur" has crossed the continent (the long way, in relative comfort, not the short difficult thrash through an isthmus of jungle and swamp), but he does not stare at the Pacific with a wild surmise—he looks back across the land at what has been lost, and what now cannot be. The discoveries have all been made; the frontier is closed. Keats thought Homer a new realm, and literature a series of lands to be discovered (this was his first great poem—he was feeling like a conquistador); for James the novel will not be written, at least not by him, and certain possibilities have finally and forever vanished. And Justice, too, no longer a young master but an Old Master, finds foreclosure and farewell. It is amusing to think of James as a stout Cortez.

The beauty of the Jamesian epilogue is the manner of its refusal, which may be called the judgment of the observations, while the judgment of the form lies in its deviations from and attachments to tradition. The feminine rhymes, for example, are usually considered a weakness, but here they bind the poem to another modern poem of loss (Bishop's villanelle "One Art," its main rhymes "master" and "disaster") and prepare the gorgeous lambency of the final couplet. Too, it is the subtlety, as well as the frequency, of the metrical reversals and the spondaic or anapestic substitutions that establishes the emphases and delicacies of tone. In these deviations—permissible deviations though they are—the accord with prose described earlier is reached, where, for the poet as well as the novelist, the past is not succumbed to but regarded, not like a yielding but like an availing.

But there, there again, is that register of innocence being lost. James's demonic eye could not help recording the subversions of landscape and manner with the most rectifying precision, even while each notation (at least in the nostalgic landscapes—he hadn't visited the South or West before) drove him further from the fond memories inhabited during his decades in England. Further, or more deeply within them, because however much the past is minutely modified by the present, it is never sufficiently vast to sustain itself as a fiction—those who would pretend otherwise must drive themselves to ever more heroic measures of submission. (What is interesting about the past is not its vastness, but the narrow channel of episodes to which our memories reduce it. We're likely to recall, in our indulgence, only what we have recalled before; in the repetitive traffic of scene and event, we worry the same wounds and the same pleasures.)

The more Justice has made the past his subject, the more richly textured and tonal his vocabulary has become. This purging of earlier dictions is most acutely evident in the long poem "Childhood," which closes his *Selected Poems* (1979) and is dedicated, self-protectively, "to the poets of a mythical childhood—Wordsworth, Rimbaud, Hart Crane, and Alberti."

> *Winter mornings now, my grandfather,*
> *Head bared to the mild sunshine, likes to spread*
> *The Katzenjammers out around a white lawn chair*
> *To catch the stray curls of citrus from his knife.*
> *Chameleons quiver in ambush; wings*
> *Of monarchs beat above bronze turds, feasting.*

It is difficult to recapture a visual innocence, but if something can be recaptured it isn't innocent. The detachment of recollection, which is often illicit, is here explicit in the system of *en face* notes that explain some of the less and most of the more obscure references to Miami in the thirties. The notes create the double world that is the sufficient cause of longing: the modalities of pathos lie in the detachment of the present from the past. The notes are the evidence of the present; but in their admission that a distance exists, and can't be breached, the thwarted wish becomes the pathos and not the longing itself. Here, I would argue, where nostalgia is no longer a succumbing to, it has become a recovery of. The notes are the "smell of ocean longing landward." (In later books reprinting "Childhood," the *en face* notes were removed and Rilke was added to the dedicatory list of poets.)

In a poem that reveals the logic of its longing as a structural design, there are apt to be traces or accidents of that longing in the verbal play. It is not, or not just, that the reader is more attuned to such accidents by the structure; but that the divided attention of composition prepares, elicits, such slips or tremulations of reference. "Already / I know the pleasure of certain solitudes," the poet says, and we would be more certain those pleasures were merely *particular* pleasures if we were not made aware they might also be *assured* pleasures. Similarly, in the "cool arcades" of the shops:

> *O counters of spectacles!—where the bored child first*
> *Scans new perspectives squinting through strange lenses.*

This is "a tray of unsorted eyeglasses"—the notes tell us so. And yet the deposition of the note seems insufficient, in a poem that is one long relation of spectacles, from the world beyond the horizon, the distant world of doomed republics and the nearer one where "Westward now, / The smoky rose of oblivion blooms, hangs" (the Everglades afire), to the circumscribed world of the boy's osteomyelitis: "on my knee a small red sun-glow, setting." (And aren't the readers, to darken and deepen the pun, apostrophized as mere *enumerators* of spectacle, like Romans at the Coliseum?) This world of suffusions— of the globe's "blur of colors," of the "Myriad tiny suns" that "Drown in the deep mahogany polish of the chair-arms," of the "soft glow / Of exit signs," of the horizon afire and the knee's "sun-glow"—suggests the inevitable haze, the partial blur, in which the past exists. It is hardly surprising that when the boy catches sight of himself, he is not quite himself:

> *Often I blink, re-entering*
> *The world—or catch, surprised, in a shop window,*
> *My ghostly image skimming across nude mannequins.*

That blink, that ghostly image shimmering in the divided attention for which the structure has prepared us, is the sign of the present as it imposes itself on the past. There has been in Justice's poetry an increasing recognition—a dawning, perhaps—that there will be no hereby, no chance of alternative, and little of change. In this recognition the character of Justice's work has grown gradually Jamesian: for James, fate was only the accrual of sensibility.

If this withholding is the necessary condition for a nostalgia that eludes sentiment, it acts on itself as a loss of innocence, the loss to which these poems have obsessively returned. Those who have been expelled from the garden of the past are doomed to recall it, and all recollections conditioned by the sin of knowledge must be fictional. What such sinners re-create in the name of the past will be tainted by their own determining circumstance. (This is the retrospective burden: you can't analyze without being afflicted by the past; you can't re-create without being afflicted by the present. The acts of reference and renewal are flawed in their very terms—here literature approaches the uncertainty principle, and criticism may be substantial but must be unscientific.)

If the wilderness can never recall the garden without some acknowledgment, some trace or fleck must betray what has come after. I am reminded of James himself, having escaped in the middle of his journey, having taken refuge from the disaster of his visit to Richmond in the drafty recesses of George Washington Vanderbilt's mansion, Biltmore. *The American Scene* scarcely alludes to this week of "deviation"; but, in a letter to his nephew Harry, James described the misappropriation of energy that attends the attempt to create the past within the present:

> *I arrived at this place, last p.m. in a driving snow storm (the land all buried, and the dreariness and bleakness indescribable), and the first thing that has happened to me, alas, has been to have a sharp explosion of gout in my left foot. But I hope to make this a* short *business . . . ; only the conditions, of vast sequestered remoteness and "form," pompous machinery that doesn't* work, *are unfavourable to it; huge freezing spaces and fantastic immensities of* scale *(from point to point) that have been based on a fundamental ignorance of comfort and wondrous deludedness . . . as to what* can *be the application of a colossal French château to life in this irretrievable niggery wilderness.*

That is what the reinvented Eden will suffer, if created without continual suspicion toward its attraction, even its possibility. The knowledge from which nostalgia must descend is that the substances of the past are always a little tawdry, "Forlorn suburbs, but with golden names!" That is the final line of "Childhood." To go further, and even perhaps too far, nostalgia requires the wish for religious grace compromised by a religious scrutiny.

Chronicle of the Early Nineties

Robert Creeley

Robert Creeley's tense minimalism is unusual in American poetry because his austerity is not religious. Very early in his career he turned away from the open-faced lyric to a style more suitable to his temperament, or to the thin-lipped temperament he wished to project. His early poems show the unsettled absorption of Pound, Williams, and Olson, those gifted harpies who have ruined more poets than Milton or Pope.

If a book called *Selected Poems* is a sedimentary index, the career's deepest layer is a lyric called "Return," which has the unsentimental fabric of a poem by Larkin:

Quiet as is proper for such places;
The street, subdued, half-snow, half-rain,
Endless, but ending in the darkened doors.

Inside, they who will be there always,
Quiet as is proper for such people—
Enough for now to be here, and
To know my door is one of these.

Unsentimental, perhaps, until the fray of the ending. Its declaration of modesty comes a little too eagerly—the small epiphanies that close so many of Larkin's poems are not available to Creeley. For all his submission to silence, Creeley has never been open to the suffering irony or humiliating bitterness that might find such epiphanies properly excoriating.

By breaking and distorting his sentences, by submitting those sentences to the denuded proprieties of prose, Creeley conveys not urgency but an afflicted torsion, Wittgenstein's concern for the bearing of sentences.

Do you think that if
you once take a breath, you're by
that committed to taking the next one
and so on until the very process of
breathing's an endlessly expanding need
almost of its own necessity forever.

Such a style approaches, as a limiting case, the philosophical petulance of Beckett, which would be a comparison highly flattering to Creeley. But Creeley does not have Beckett's hopelessness, much less his morbid genius—Creeley's poems seem dreams of dreams of depression rather than an accommodation with suffering slowly arrived at. The stanza above is no better than—indeed a little worse than—R. D. Laing's now-forgotten psychological conundrums.

Perhaps I am unusual in thinking Creeley indebted to the wounded, withdrawn aestheticism of Dickinson. The staccato perceptions, the severe self-engrossment, the asceticism protectively embraced, and the damp and slightly fussy primness suggest "the existential / terror of New England / countrywoman, Ms. // Dickinson." For all its love affair with the brawling humanity of Whitman, our avant-garde has its roots in the poetry of aesthetes like Eliot and Pound.

Creeley has fled everything that makes Dickinson such a scathing, bleaching poet. If he sometimes seems a poseur, it may be wise to remember what he has given up in his pursuit of a purity of meditative expression. In Creeley we never get a memorable image, a thing seen precisely, a sentence carried as far as thinking will take it. He has eliminated most of the texture of verse, of the pleasurable massing of words. He has at times lost his very taste for sentences and dissolved into the tedium of diary jotting or the Dictaphone. But this stripping down is not the same as stripping away. Instead of "In the gloom, the gold gathers the light against it" or "On the glass tray // a glass pitcher, the tumbler / turned down," we get

> *One forty five afternoon red*
> *car parked left hand side*
> *of street no distinguishing*
> *feature still wet day a bicycle*
> *across the way a green door-*
> *way with arched upper window.*

Nothing replaces this loss of the frivolity of beauty except the quiet squalor of sentiment. Given the amount of time Creeley spends in the subjective mode, it is remarkable how little actual disclosure can be found in his work. By appearing to be a minimalist, an All-American monk with a taste for Charlie Parker, he can indulge in a sentiment that would be unbearable in any more figured art. The personality revealed is not unsympathetic so much as failing in its sympathies. Lines like "All who know me / say, *why* this man's / persistent pain, the scarifying / openness he makes do with?" are not convincing, because his poems are so rarely painful, or scarifying, or really open at all.

What is convincing in Creeley is his send-up of his own manner. "I Know a Man" is a favorite anthology piece, not just because the disjunctive mysteries of the style imply more than the lines can reasonably mean, but because here the ironic regard exposes the limitation of character:

As I sd to my
friend, because I am
always talking,—John, I

sd, which was not his
name, the darkness sur-
rounds us, what

can we do against
it, or else, shall we &
why not, buy a goddamn big car,

drive, he sd, for
christ's sake, look
out where yr going.

The famous turn at the end manages to be witty *and* dangerous (Creeley can almost never afford to be funny) and not to fall into the blind insouciance or bland pomposity that disfigures much of his work. His general pretension, his ignorance of others, his ignorance even of surroundings, lie cruelly exposed and indecent.

A poetry founded on "I Know a Man," "For Love," "Something," "A Tally," "The Finger," and "'The day was gathered on waking . . . ,'" as well as such focused and considered poems as "The Passage," "Talking," "Flaubert's Early Prose," "Song" ("Love has no other friends . . ."), and "Plague," would have been far less susceptible to what is indrawn, self-absorbed, and a little repellent in his work. A hatred of anything like lushness in poetry, of anything that might pardon the language, has produced the vacuous ruminations that are those of a man as a chamber decompresses and the oxygen goes out of his head.

J. D. McClatchy

Until *The Rest of the Way*, J. D. McClatchy was a trusting epigone of the high-tea manners of Auden and Merrill: his poetry was wickedly and wearyingly clever, a little too conscious of the bric-a-brac of its own intelligence, flashingly pretty, at worst guilty of "Frail, cold-hearted / Priggery . . . / Protected by a sneer." He wrote a poetry easier to admire than to like, despite its flaring ambition and sedulous skill. Because he lacked the ability of his masters to transcend the sins of the style, little in his early books prepares the reader for the casual mastery encountered here.

McClatchy has not abandoned his taste for the tour de force, the grand gesture that is often just grandstanding; but his style has been subverted by a new generosity of feeling: he has become a European. Americans are often defensive and mandarin in their uses of a high art Europeans accept as their inheritance, if sometimes a decaying or prescriptive inheritance. McClatchy's chilly aloofness has become a warmly implicated observation.

> *And what I miss goes without saying. Has*
> *The explanation even there been brief as a flame and its ash?*
>
> *I speak to the air that takes these things finally as its own.*
> *Tell me who that is beyond the stairwell's next turning now.*

The transformation unhappily endured (how easily the poem echoes James's "The Jolly Corner") is broodingly mocked by couplets whose endwords are anagrams: *cloud* becoming *could, pages* turning to *gapes.* The fraught mirroring in the surface of language chastens the fantasia of art: McClatchy has become a poet for whom the flimsiness of language darkens toward fatality.

> *We're made to feel*
> *Even she is beyond the spell of speech, the gift*
> *Of fate she gave the others. But a moral starts*
> *To echo. The children's screams. And to each wheel*
> *A body's tied with ribbons, pale and stiff.*
> *The words had made no sense, but the sword was real.*

The play may be only a stage play of *Medea,* but here *words / sword* are the same word, its tempering drawn through the watery surface of the real, the word made flesh, made to rend flesh, made mightier than the sword by becoming the sword.

Coldness in poetry may be acquired, but warmth must be achieved. Consider a visit to ruins in McClatchy's first book, *Scenes from Another Life* (1981):

> *Who can walk today like Byron among Ayasoluk's ruined*
> *Mosques, kicking the heads off yellow tulips and eating*
> *Cold game? Or thinks to envy some crouching Bedouin*
>
> *For whom no city dies when any wall will brace*
> *Against a sand-white wind? Heat rash, the hotel dream,*
> *With luck a pediment's stone egg. . . .*

This is the speech Demosthenes recited with a mouthful of pebbles. The breakneck enjambment, the stumble of syllables, the filigree of details: the style is elegantly punitive, overwrought because overworked.

A poetry of such elective affinities reserves itself for the novitiate; but it lacks the chastening pressure, the moral scruple, that makes a mystery religion of poetry like Anthony Hecht's or Geoffrey Hill's. Compare the ruins of Turkey to these:

> *Here is a country of ruins,*
> *Vine-propped facing stone pushed back to clay,*
> *The dead eating the dead down there,*
> *And up here, where so many paths, so many*
> *Turnings are to be seen that all is in doubt,*
> *The way here and back again, a stair*
> *That rises now into the murderous air.*

Here the details are engraved by the tone, not begemmed in the text; *murderous* rises up like a villainous specter above the ruins of Ireland. Gone, the imposture of rhetorical address; gone, the imposture of a style. This is the difference between possession of language and possession by language.

McClatchy has not completely escaped his old ways, but the chummily affected tone of "An Essay on Friendship" or "Cysts" (I can hardly imagine a subject less opportune) only sharpens the manner of the rest of the book. The informing passion and seriousness of his new poems are haunted by death, by a language that cannot bargain with death. His tortured prettiness is now sometimes a gorgeously gloomy beauty.

Les Murray

Les Murray is the most arresting and angular poet to come out of Australia since A. D. Hope and Judith Wright, and he is similarly free of the geographical constriction of tenor that throws up barriers to the trade between poetry and poetry. He has a burly, somewhat shambling style, excursive and unmethodical, odd and clumsy and hard to categorize, like a platypus, but with an immense appetite for subject: cartoons, the fat ("the Stone Age aristocracy"), sprawl, things that never were, the emu, wearing shorts, a lottery winner's tormented mail, the history of the milk lorry, bats, going deaf ("It's mind over mutter"), yachts. He's like Midas, as Jarrell once said of Conrad Aiken (he also said it of Marianne Moore)—everything he touches turns to poetry.

This plenitude may suggest a certain dissipating scattiness, and indeed some of Murray's poems in *The Rabbiter's Bounty*, his collected poems, seem a drunk man's walk from one page of the encyclopedia to another (his long poem on cows begins with a digression on Sanskrit). He is a poet of thick-browed sensibility and therefore liable to the indifferent organization of sensibility. Such a poet does not need a particular subject, only a moral or geographical center for reflection. Murray's moral center is Christian, though there are few poems of an overtly Christian character; but New South Wales (also the birthplace of Hope and Wright) has provided the homely landscapes and homely figures, as well as the captiousness toward history crucial to his work.

One of the reasons for reading foreign poetry (and poetry in English can be more foreign than poetry in Xhosa or Fortran) is its casual way with the exotic. This is not the only reason, not even finally an important reason; but no photograph will regain the visual suggestiveness of lines like

Bloodwood trees

round there were in such a froth of bloom
their honey dripped on shale and gummed
blady-grass in wigwams and ant-towns.

Bloodwood trees and blady-grass might be perfectly familiar (or at least not estrangingly unfamiliar) in a snapshot, but as pure language they are lost to the alien.

The high moments of character in Murray's poetry have an enviable antagonism to set feeling, to the normal sympathies and conventional sentiment:

That homestead is long gone—man should hae led trumps—
and the times are flattening down. The ringbarked Twenties.

"*Man should hae led trumps*"—such acerbic wryness and suppressed anger are rarely Murray's own; they belong to his farmers and stockmen and timbermen—"*You have to send flooded gum quick. It don't stay flooded*— / *ironbark's a bugger to bark if it comes dry weather.*"

Murray's own character, containing multitudes, is easygoing and Micawberish, generous in a muzzy, unfocused manner, "philosophical" in the most naive and unhappy way. He's addicted to exaggerations of metaphor ("whole branches / of blossom appear on the tree your lives have reached"), timeless immensity ("I go into the earth near the feed shed for thousands of years"), a larval aesthetic musing ("Art is what can't be summarised: / it has joined creation from our side, / entered Nature, become a fact"), and grotesque hyperbole ("The depth in this marriage will heal the twentieth century"). We cannot expect any niceties of control, or of image, in a poet of such consoling breadth—so goes the argument for similar brawny poets, like Whitman. But this will not excuse Murray's mawkish cast, which particularly afflicts *The Boys Who Stole the Funeral*, his verse novel.

This "novel sequence" of 140 sonnets was first published in Australia in 1980. The "sonnets" do run to fourteen lines, but they are novel only in their lack of obligation to meter or rhyme. Two boys steal the corpse of an old man (the distant relative of one of the boys) and drive him, propped up in a Morris Nomad, out to the country, where he'd wanted to be buried. The boys suffer numerous Arthurian adventures, meet various semi-allegorical figures (the Burning Man, the whistle-cock man), and make the evening news. The cautionary design is redolently silly—after the funeral, one of the boys is killed by a policeman and the other wanders into the bush, where he has a mystical vision in the company of two legendary Aboriginal spirits.

I'm not convinced the verse novel is anything but a nonce form, though Murray might have made more out of the thin resonances of his fiction if he weren't continually giving voice to infected grandiosities, ludicrous enough in the mouths of his characters ("*In the New Society, perhaps we won't despise money*"), but weak-minded when delivered by the author ("An understood world is a tuneable receiver"). The old arguments between youth and age, country and city, class and class deserve better than flatulent speeches.

Murray's writing is unusually clumsy for a poet of such intelligent range. He has a pack rat's organization, phrase accruing to phrase without any sense the description is gelid, the metaphors mere costume jewelry:

> *How many metal-bra and trumpet-flaring film extravaganzas underlie the progress of the space shuttle's Ground Transporter Vehicle*
>
> *across macadam-surfaced Florida? Atop oncreeping house-high panzers,*
>
> *towering drydock and ocean-liner decks, there perches a gridiron football*
>
> *field in gradual motion; it is the god-platform; it sustains the bridal skyscraper of liquid Cool, and the rockets borrowed from the Superman.*

The reader can imagine the rest. This is "fine" writing gone wrong. Murray is also tempted by what might charitably be called newspaper verse:

In the acid war the word was Score; rising helicopters cried Smack!
   Smack!
Boys laid a napalm trip on earth and tried to take it back
but the pot boiled over in the rear; fighters tripped on their lines of
   force
and victory went to the supple hard side, eaters of fish sauce.

Thus the war in Vietnam. I cannot think of another poet of such striking extension (or such proud intention) who sinks so often, or so gratefully, into bathos.

Murray's styles, from his clumsy bouts with rhyme and meter to his goofy abstract expressionism, amount to ways of charging his attentions to the subject. The rhetoric is forced and arbitrary, the feeling arbitrary and forced. The reader has to wade through an appalling amount of second-rate poetry to get a few lines of vivid hopelessness (often hard by an equally vivid haplessness).

Murray's poetry is a collection of mannerisms, but the mannerist sentiment is responsive—by a curious inversion—to the poems of bush and outback, least exposed to his appetites because most conventional. In the yarns and tales he shows a superb ear for dialect (which is equally an ear for syntax); the small rehearsals of betrayal and deception have the innocent cunning of Frost and Hardy. The simplicity of such poems is threatening to the modern notion of an author's governance, but they honor the long tradition of Australian yarning—the country's history, without irony or apology, wears into the present like a palimpsest. Poems like "Inverse Ballad" and "Federation Style on the Northern Rivers" draw from conventions of storytelling, but the conventions have more powerful and more courteous forms of organization than the froth of fine writing or elegant perception that are a by-product of the author's push toward "significance."

Grandfather's grandfather rode down from New England
that terrible steep road. One time there, his horse
shat over his shoulder. It's not so steep now.

Anyway he was riding, and two fellows came
out of the brush with revolvers pointed at him.

This has the fastidious simplicity and command of Kipling. It is
perhaps too much to ask a poet to limit himself to what he does
superbly well, when there are so many temptations for him to write
superbly ill.

Christopher Logue

Kings is Christopher Logue's latest essay at the *Iliad:* his version of
Iliad 21 appeared in *Songs* (1959), and his *Patrocleia* and *Pax* (*Iliad* 16
and 19), first published separately, were collected with the intervening books as *War Music* (1987 [UK, 1981]). *Kings* is his "account" of
books 1 and 2, though it runs only halfway through the second book,
stopping short of the catalogue of ships, which some think the most
ancient lines of the poem. Those who have read the earlier translations will know what to expect: *Kings* is a brilliantly deranged, sloppy,
complacently odd, handicapped work, vividly and violently phrased,
frequently "modern" and un-Homeric.

Logue has the significant advantage, for a radical translator, of
knowing no Greek. He is not unaware of the difficulties he has set
himself and his critics, though his edged demurrals (that his, for
example, is "Not . . . a proper translation") are not completely satis-
factory. No translator, however faithful to his text, can entirely avoid
deceit or compromise. Since infidelity is inescapable, we can only
meditate on its degree and design. Like Pound (whose greatest poems are his peculiar translations—"The Seafarer," *Homage to Sextus
Propertius*, and the poems of *Cathay*), Logue has attempted an English equivalent of register and force, of Homer's effect if not his
simple meaning. This has required translation not just by approxi-
mation but by addition and subtraction, and by gross rearrange-
ment.

The *Iliad* begins with plague in the Greek camp, the quarrel between Agamemnon and Achilles, Agamemnon's seizure of the slave
girl Briseis, and Achilles' withdrawal from battle. All this is con-

signed to flashback in *Kings*, framed in its opening section by Achilles' appeal to his mother, the sea goddess Thetis, for revenge against his fellow Greeks. The first book of the *Iliad* is largely a collection of speeches, and Logue has succumbed to the temptation to sharpen these parliamentary reports by dramatically framing and democratizing the dialogue. Consider Agamemnon to the priest Chryses, who has come to ransom his daughter:

> *"If," he continues, "if, priest, if*
> *When I complete the things I am about to say,*
> *I catch you loitering around my Fleet*
> *Ever again, I shall, with you in one,*
> *And in my other hand your mumbo rod,*
> *Thrash you until your eyeballs shoot.*
> > *As for your child:*
> *Bearing by night my body in my bed,*
> *Bearing by day my children on her knee,*
> *Soft in the depths of my ancestral house,*
> *If ever she sees Ilium again*
> *She will have empty gums."*

Compare this with Robert Fagles's recent Whiggish version (1990):

> *"Never again, old man,*
> *let me catch sight of you by the hollow ships!*
> *Not loitering now, not slinking back tomorrow.*
> *The staff and the wreaths of god will never save you then.*
> *The girl—I won't give up the girl. Long before that,*
> *old age will overtake her in my house, in Argos,*
> *far from her fatherland, slaving back and forth*
> *at the loom, forced to share my bed!"*

Or Richmond Lattimore's older Tory account (1951):

> *"Never let me find you again, old sir, near our hollow*
> *ships, neither lingering now nor coming again hereafter,*
> *for fear your staff and the god's ribbons help you no longer.*
> *The girl I will not give back; sooner will old age come upon her*

in my own house, in Argos, far from her own land, going
up and down by the loom and being in my bed as my companion."

Lattimore's lines are closest to the original (his translation is still used as a crib), but they seem tame and insipid for what the Greek characterizes as κρατερὸν μῦζον, harsh words (the virtues of Lattimore are rarely apparent in brief quotation).

Both Fagles and Logue have hit happily on *loitering* (it occurred earlier in Robert Fitzgerald's 1974 translation), which may seem too jaunty, unless you recall that loitering would be far beneath the dignity of a priest of Apollo. Merely to suggest the possibility is slanderous. Not content with an effect so subtle, and in any case someone else's (it must always be remembered that Logue's is based on other translations, and that his virtues are sometimes borrowed), Logue introduces the "mumbo rod" and the threat to "Thrash you until your eyeballs shoot." The failure is not a failure of intention: Logue's ideal is the repartee of comic books, his gore the gore of Hollywood (Homer was himself a genius at violent special effects). I'm not an antagonist of this design—in Logue you find an aggression, a vivacity of experience, beyond the available versions. He has responded to the underlying pulse and tremor of the Greek, its flattening terror. But he goes wrong in his management (the coarse effects too often seem deliberated) and his staging: with Chryses in one hand and the "mumbo rod" in the other, Agamemnon would seem more likely to begin a juggling routine. The anaphora and antithesis of "Bearing by night . . . / Bearing by day . . ." are a rare recognition of the power of mere rhetoric, though its stateliness is oddly positioned between the shooting eyeballs and the deliciously abrupt "She will have empty gums." Nothing in the passage rises to the compressive passion of Pope's "'Till Time shall rifle ev'ry youthful Grace, / And Age dismiss her from my cold Embrace."

Logue is the victim, often at the same instant, of ideas good and ill: every advantage comes ready with disaster. His phrasing is astringent and highly charged, even witty: the enslaved Chryseis is "A gently broken adolescent she." Achilles speaks of his humiliation: as if Agamemnon had "Painted my body with fresh Trojan excrement." Thetis to Zeus: if he refuses her request, "I am a lost bitch barking at a cloud." Hera to Zeus: "From where I sit your city on the hill / Stinks like a brickfield wind." Diomedes of the mass: they "have as gods / Some rotten nonsense from the East." None of this is Homeric. The language is appealingly mordant and bracing (everyone in the *Iliad* has something to complain about), but it is an imposition. In Homer, Thetis only wants to know if she is to be "the most dishonored goddess of all." Reserved, regretful, angry on her son's behalf, she is shrewd in her supplication. Logue's Thetis is brazen and unsympathetic.

The loss of shading, of the subtlety of character, may be an assumed cost; but the miscalculation of effect is beyond subtlety. To have the king of all Greeks say "Ditchmud" to Achilles and to have Achilles shout back "Mouth! King mouth!" drags us into the schoolyard. The intrusion of camera angles ("Reverse the shot," "Cut to") and the trappings of the twentieth century ("Ajax, / Grim underneath his tan as Rommel after 'Alamein," "Atreus is king. What need has he to keep / A helicopter whumphing in the dunes . . . ?") makes me wonder why the Greeks haven't been issued Kalashnikovs.

Logue's excesses are part of his point, even part of his tough charm. In order to turn these books into a "poem in English," he has invented scenes and speeches, imported numerous "atmospheric" details ("The dawn wind pats their hair. / Odysseus gazes at his big left toe"), interpolated parts of books 6 and 7 to give the view inside Troy, and freely altered motivation and character (Agamemnon's famously odd testing of the Greek troops is made smoothly logical—it's all Thersites' fault). If deviation is permitted, he has given himself full latitude.

The *Iliad* can never be an English poem. It must bear a culture and a set of rituals and gods forever alien to us. Its grandeur lies in that opaque mask of the foreign. To simplify the action, to gnarl or burl the language, threatens to cheat the rhythms and seriousness of the Greek, its repetitions and antique formulae, its construction and pacing. (Poor Homer. What did *he* know about telling a story?)

Kings is less an attempt to do *Hamlet* as a Noh play than to stage *Crime and Punishment* as a musical. And yet some of the alien leaks into this alien style. We are unlikely to get a Homer as vigorous, or as rough and tumble—this Homer sounds like a terrorist.

Seamus Heaney

It is almost impossible to dislike a poet as gifted as Seamus Heaney. His later poetry has been so well-mannered and well-marveled, so shapely and infused with the dark instinct of life, so full of respect for the ancients of poetry and for the form itself, so little afflicted by the international bonhomie that grates in the poetry of Brodsky and even Walcott, so moodily decent and eloquently anguished it seems churlish to suggest that much of his new poetry consists of the smile without the Cheshire cat. It seems churlish because *Seeing Things* is a more distinguished book than any of the others under review—indeed, a more distinguished book than most books of the past decade. My difficulty with Heaney is not with what he *can* do (with what he can do perfectly easily, as if it meant nothing at all), but with what he no longer thinks it worth his trouble to do.

Admirers of Heaney divide into those (often Irish or British) who prefer the poetry before *Field Work* (1979), the more rugged and costive volumes from *Death of a Naturalist* (1966) through *North* (1975), and those (often American) who prefer the more leisurely and openhearted (if at times similarly bleak and guilt-laden) style of the later poetry. No doubt this division is an argument of national character, though those who came later to the poetry often prefer the later poetry—Heaney was a phenomenon at home long before he was noticed abroad. The books from *Field Work* to *Seeing Things* now form a second arcana (major or minor according to your disposition), and the transition from a poetry often aroused by the art of writing in the act of writing to a poetry worried about its place in literature is typified by the translations from the *Inferno* that close those two later volumes. The younger Heaney wrote like a man possessed by demons, even when those demons were very literary demons; the older Heaney seems to wonder, bemusedly, what sort of demon he has become himself.

To make the devil's case, I must argue for the graces. The fluent, homespun style Heaney assumes in *Seeing Things* is a style so easy it hardly seems a style at all. In poetry, the pure assumptions of voice are often highly literary (they usually appear so to later generations), but they create for an age the manner of its speech. Heaney's poetry speaks for his age—this flattering age of prose—in the way Eliot's or Auden's or Lowell's did for theirs: it is not a transcription of expression so much as what we wish our expression were, an implement purely responsive to minor acts and desires. Eliot remarked, in "The Music of Poetry," "No poetry, of course, is ever exactly the same speech that the poet talks and hears: but it has to be in such a relation to the speech of his time that the listener or reader can say 'that is how I should talk if I could talk poetry.'" And even if you suspect this is just what Heaney says to himself, he has abandoned the more studied art of language to sustain a way of speaking. Such a poet creates his voice by a set of articulating discoveries.

This voice is rendered responsible by continuous supplication to, and frequent invocation of, the dead: the shades of Heaney's past and the literary figures under whose shadows he writes. The volume begins with the *Aeneid* and ends with the *Inferno*, and both scraps of translation mark voyages to the underworld. The translations are pallidly conversational—they do not aspire to something as unmannerly as style (this criticism might be made of classical translation in general, which is why Christopher Logue's gall may be necessary). There is a certain donnish wit in translating these incidents, the humility of translation not quite concealing the esteem that identification with Aeneas and Dante confers on the poet.

It is not without delicate irony, then, that after the prologue from the *Aeneid* the book begins with the shade of Philip Larkin (whose death has occasioned a number of elegies unusual for their deep affection—as a misanthrope Larkin was an utter failure):

"And not a thing had changed, as rush-hour buses

Bore the drained and laden through the city.
I might have been a wise king setting out
Under the Christmas lights—except that

It felt more like the forewarned journey back
Into the heartland of the ordinary.
Still my old self. Ready to knock one back.

A nine-to-five man who had seen poetry."

A nine-to-five man is of course what Heaney is not (Larkin's order-liness and punctuality of address were just those of a nine-to-five man)—for him the local has permanent access to the mystical. Hallucinations, ghosts, shadings of the past: Heaney has become a poet increasingly at the mercy of seeing things. For a poet of the quotidian, the everyday either embodies the reductive mysteries of the world (as it did for Williams, or Larkin for that matter) or provides the focus of the historical or metaphysical force outside the world. The former ground permits (though it does not entail) the consolation of cynicism, the latter the irritation of faith, or something very like faith. In this Heaney is the proper heir to Yeats.

But Yeats did not like the quotidian; he liked the other world much better. Heaney is mired again in Ireland, and for him part of the burden of seeing things that are not there is seeing things that are. Like other poets of a withdrawing temperament, he is drawn to narrative; but he cannot shape a story with the rude tempo or inevitability of Frost. Narrative requires a poetry more centrally uneasy than the still lifes Heaney still favors. Many of the poems in *Seeing Things* suffer fatally nervous, finicky hoardings of noun and adjective:

Riveted steel, turned timber, burnish, grain,
Smoothness, straightness, roundness, length and sheen.
Sweat-cured, sharpened, balanced, tested, fitted.
The springiness, the clip and dart of it.

This is a pitchfork, but it might as well be a carriage wheel or a demonic pencil. Heaney's portraits and objects (a biretta, a settle bed, the pitchfork, a basket of chestnuts) sometimes have a dusty, passive air, like objects in an abandoned shopfront. But this makes them pliant to a transformation out of the demotic into a realm almost demonic, as in "The Biretta":

Now I turn it upside down and it is a boat—
A paper boat, or the one that wafts into
The first lines of the Purgatorio
As poetry lifts its eyes and clears its throat.

Or maybe that small boat out of the bronze age
Where the oars are needles and the worked gold frail
As the intact half of a hatched-out shell,
Refined beyond the dross into sheer image.

But in the end it's as likely to be the one
In Matthew Lawless's painting, The Sick Call,
Where the scene is out on a river and it's all
Solid, pathetic and Irish Victorian.

In which case, however, his reverence wears a hat.
Undaunting, half domestic, loved in crises,
He sits listening as each long oar dips and rises,
Sad for his worthy life and fit for it.

Heaney is a master of the dazzling mock-religious transfiguration. For all its seeming indolence, his poetry lacks any weedy excess—it is a meditation that is finally a sort of mediation. Much of *Seeing Things* is unfortunately given over to forms too partial to respond to anything like meditation: a second sequence of Glanmore sonnets, not nearly as owl-eyed or willful as the first in *Field Work*, and a long, peculiar series of twelve-line poems called "Squarings," which takes up the second half of the book.

"Squarings" is composed with a very writerly confidence, but the poems have an irresolute, unfinished air: fragments shored against his ruin, they are not backed up in the immaterial realm. The eight or ten that accrue around a kernel of incident point out the losses of attention elsewhere. Many poets would be pleased by—they would award themselves a Pulitzer for—a handful of poems as sincerely exposed (the best are i, vi, vii, viii, xv, xvii, xxvi, xxxiii, xlii, xliv); but against Heaney's better work they seem offhand and a little desperate.

Each recent book by Heaney has made the previous book seem better: this means it is hard to take proper measure of the new work until it is the work of the past, not that Heaney has gradually been getting worse. Most of Heaney's books have been books of transition, if not transformation: by the time the reader adapts to the angle of vision, the chameleon has moved on. However darkly moral and moderating the later Heaney has been, he is sometimes only a compound ghost of his earlier selves. *Seeing Things* includes many achieved and remarkable and individual poems—as would be expected, since Heaney is one of the few masters we have; but the early work, the work before he was writing poems, was better poetry. I'm not sure anyone has been moved by a late Heaney poem—he seems incapable now of writing anything instinctive or marked or passionate. There comes a moment when a man doesn't *want* to write poetry as much as he wants to write poems (perhaps he can do nothing else *but* write them), and it isn't necessarily a change to be discouraged. Poets this good are natural forces, like avalanches. They cannot be argued with—one can only get out of their way.

The
Charity
of the
Mystery of
Geoffrey Hill

There is strategy even in negatives, and when a poet as reverent of reversal as Geoffrey Hill chooses as his subject a poet fallen in battle, and fallen in reputation as well, the resurrection of the dead may require the justification of the living. Hill, after all, collected his early work in *For the Unfallen* (1959), a title that announced its resonant regard for those who stood when the battle was over. To select so late in his career a figure who chose not survival but slaughter may indicate the travails of the intervening quarter century.

It is perhaps more than amusing coincidence that the terms of the prefatory matter to Hill's *Collected Poems* (1985), the publicity flack (itself a term possibly drawn from the flak of air war, though there is James's gossip writer, George Flack, in *The Reverberator*) meant to guard the battlements of a reputation, swelled so long and lovingly on the negative manner of his critics, who have styled his poetry as "unbearable, bullying, intransigent, intolerant, brilliant," "mandarin and rarefied," "toil and artifice," "sick grandeur," "glowering, unlovely egotism." These phrases were presented, in that inversion advertising occasionally resorts to, as badges of honor, not dishonor, the medals of someone who had "disturbed the literary consensus for three decades."

A poet like Hill might well feel wounded by disparagement, and yet perversely honored by it. You don't attract such attention except by virtue of nonconformity, by damaging the icons of whatever religion, or whatever modernism, holds sway. A man displaying his scars of battle honors his enemies, while not ignoring the cost of his opposition. War relies on a metaphysics of hate, war poets on their hatred of metaphysics, at least if they are not mongrels to a cause. The inner conflict, between the mortar shell and the shock of recognition, echoes the conflict without, over which no poet can speak with authority. It is toward this inner conflict, this battle between the poetry of fervor and the morality of doubt, this battle within that survives the battle without, that Hill's long poem about Charles Péguy tends. All war poetry is a metonymy of survival; but the justification for that difference, for standing firm in the face of fire, must come from the recovery and resurrection of the dead, however vexed and inconvenient the operation. The soldiers' memoirs agree: worse than facing the enemy was facing the half-buried, rotting corpses of friends. Toward the corpse a soldier can invoke only the void of black humor, and in black humor there can be no charity. The farce of such tragedy and the tragedy of such farce bracket the work and the torment of a poet whose difficulties must be dissected in almost clinical detail.

Charity is one of the Christian virtues, but parents prefer to name their children Faith and Hope. Hope and faith are convenient abstractions for what are often inconvenient acts, but you can have faith and take hope: charity must be given. When the other virtues are selfish it must remain generous; when they reach in, it must reach out. It is therefore peculiar and peculiarly appropriate, a stricture self-applied, to find charity the subject of a poetry as devious and miserly as that of Geoffrey Hill. The afflictions of the post-Romantic poet allow him to wrestle with his faith or deny his hope, but such self-consciousness cannot provision a charity: in modern poetry the anthologies of faith and hope, even by the faithless and hopeless, casually ignore the difficult lines charity bestows.

What devil has got into Geoffrey Hill? A devil of a responsibility. *The Mystery of the Charity of Charles Péguy* confronts, in a hundred quatrains of bruised pentameter, minor incidents of a major war: an assassination and a death in battle. The assassination is political, the death pointless; the first the work of a madman, the second the work of madmen. Péguy, a French poet never much regarded in English, is a figure ridiculous in his propriety: a peasant with a pince-nez, a bookshop owner whose unsold books were used by his friends as tables and chairs, a squanderer of his in-laws' money. All this in service of his fortnightly notebooks, *Les Cahiers de la Quinzaine*, the ideal of *le journal vrai*, a paper that would tell the truth and would not cheat. All this in the years of la belle époque, the long weekend before the First World War, the years of Dreyfus and the years of euphoria.

Born Orléans 1873, died the Marne 1914. If Péguy seems a slightly ridiculous figure at this distance, with his hot temper and the droning repetitions of his verse, he seemed no less so to his acquaintances: "A little man with square shoulders, squeezed into a skimpy jacket. Enormous hobnailed boots on his feet and a soft hat on his head," "A small brusque man always in a hurry . . . , his glance travelling from the ground upwards like that of a bull," "Short-sighted and bustling, with the obstinate forehead of a peasant shop-keeper," "He wore a hard collar, and from below it hung a badly knotted tie. . . . His voice was incredibly monotonous and its rhythm made it even less attractive for it reminded one of a person dictating." His English biographer Villiers (from whom I have borrowed) has recorded the drama of his details, but has missed the mystery, the mystery that makes an ordinary man, even one of extraordinary gifts, suffer the death of a martyr. That requires the propriety of another poet, one whose own difficulties of faith have been much disciplined by martyrology.

A martyr sins even in his saintliness, and Péguy was no saint. When his young friend Marcel Baudouin died in the army, Péguy set off with a revolver and a group of friends to murder the sergeant he thought responsible. He led his friends into street fights against the anti-Dreyfusards. He called for a death and the death came, and with that act the poem begins:

> Crack of a starting-pistol. Jean Jaurès
> dies in a wine-puddle. Who or what stares
> through the café-window crêped in powder-smoke?
> The bill for the new farce reads Sleepers Awake. (1.1)

The shots that killed the socialist leader Jaurès on the last day of July 1914 were drowned out by the guns of August. Jean Jaurès was a pacifist in an hour when pacifists were easily dishonored. The "new farce" is an old hymn, sung at Advent, and its promises prove as hollow as the harmless starting-pistol's shots prove murderous. The lines play with just those darkening inversions that establish farce: a starting shot starts the poem, as it might start a race, the race not of a few men but of whole cultures careering toward destruction. It echoes the shot that a month earlier killed Archduke Ferdinand in Sarajevo. The café window (it was, farcically, the Café du Croissant) is wreathed in the crêpe of mourning, but the crêpe is the same powder-smoke soon rising from the battlefields of the Marne. Who or what stares through that window? The white-faced assassin (a young man ridiculously named Villain) or only the bill for a farce? Is it a playbill, or an account tendered? The ambiguities are brutal, and beneath them lies the sacrificial body of Jaurès, performing a profane version of transubstantiation, his blood a puddle of wine. This is the farce that history would enact:

> History commands the stage wielding a toy gun,
> rehearsing another scene. It has raged so before,
> countless times; and will do, countless times more,
> in the guise of supreme clown, dire tragedian. (1.2)

To History, that old ham, it little matters how the scene is written. Such scenes are made to be raged through, whether comic or tragic, though as tragedian History may truly be dire. Péguy was suspicious of history, and Hill uses that suspicion, repressing the dross of the details to promote the drama of figurative acts. The poem more than once wreathes the incidents of history in the protections of stage or screen, etching or engraving, providing certain cruelties of judgment in the knowledge that any pain may be usurped and travestied as art, any blood rendered into ink. The Caesar we know is Shakespeare's Caesar, his death a stage death: "In Brutus' name martyr and mountebank / ghost Caesar's ghost, his wounds of air and ink / painlessly spouting." That is all history offers, an existence ever more tenuous, a ghost made into a ghost.

Péguy hated history's taste for the spectacular, the battle and the blood. Clio had become the modern muse, part of the conversion of the old France into which he had been born to the new France into which he had been thrust. The timeless world had become time-ridden. Péguy's crippling exile from the world of his preference, his anxious desire to restore the harmonies of that world in a Harmonious City, comprehends the viciousness of his conflicts. Jaurès had been his hero, then his friend, then his enemy. A year before the assassination, Péguy had been calling for his blood: "Jaurès in a tumbrel and the roll of drums to cover his strong voice." (Hill writes in his biographical note that "By 1914 [Péguy] was calling for his blood . . . ; though a young madman . . . almost immediately shot Jaurès through the head." The crucial quote to which Hill refers, however, was published in "L'Argent suite," a *Cahier* of April 27, 1913. Péguy made other attacks later.) He was not alone, but a lawyer who after the war defended the young assassin believed Péguy's influence had been the most malign. The assassin was acquitted.

> *Did Péguy kill Jaurès? Did he incite*
> *the assassin? Must men stand by what they write*
> *as by their camp-beds or their weaponry*
> *or shell-shocked comrades while they sag and cry? (1.4)*

That is the mystery of his charity. Words written in anger, even in the throes of a patriotism Hill calls "regenerative and sacrificial," may have bloody effect. It was only one death; millions were to follow. Péguy was only "Truth's pedagogue, braving an entrenched class / of fools and scoundrels." It is all absorbed in the mockery of history, the thin and bloodless unreeling of a cartoon:

> *Violent contrariety of men and days; calm*
> *juddery bombardment of a silent film*
> *showing such things: its canvas slashed with rain*
> *and St Elmo's fire. Victory of the machine!*
>
> *The brisk celluloid clatters through the gate;*
> *the cortège of the century dances in the street;*
> *and over and over the jolly cartoon*
> *armies of France go reeling towards Verdun. (1.7–8)*

The film spools reel, the wounded stagger and reel, but the deaths are real and Hill's savage mockery is no less unspeakable—the film, after all, is silent—than Péguy's mocking savagery. No horror so huge could be realized except in the false notes of such comedy, such giddy laughing at the grave. The seriousness is honored by being avoided, avoided in order to be understood. The bleak question remains: "Did Péguy kill Jaurès?" Must a writer, even one caught up in the foolish whirl of events, stand by what he writes, as a soldier would by his bed, or his arms, or his comrades? It is a zeugma yoked to militance, full of honor and adherence.

"Rage and regret are tireless to explain / stratagems of the out-manoeuvred man": Péguy was an educated man, and proud of being a peasant. If he was outmaneuvered by events, by the forces of a history he could not control, anger and disappointment do make tireless explanations of his tactics. They do not explain the mystery. He rises above such explanations as an accusing figure of sacrifice and expiation, one who can't be reconciled with the trivial pilgrim-ages of the tour guide ("'Sieurs-'dames, this is the wall / where he leaned and rested, this is the well // from which he drank") or the posthumous glories of sculpture: "in blank-eyed bronze, brave me-diocre work / of *Niclausse, sculpteur,* cornered in the park // among the stout dogs and lame patriots." Cornered, indeed. The sculpture sits in a park in Orléans, where Péguy grew up in contact with the

old France, his grandmother still wearing the costume of a Bour-
bonnais peasant, his mother a mender of chairs. The moral language
became moral action in defense of country, but the country was the
country of his childhood, the country of his vision.

Péguy fought his first war with words, as if in rehearsal for his
final role: "You know the drill, / raw veteran, . . . defend your first
position to the last word." In his schooldays a sign over the door of
his study was inscribed UTOPIA. He collaborated with his friend
Baudouin on what became *Marcel: Premier Dialogue de la Cité Har-
monieuse* (1898). Only one copy of this vision was sold.

> *Vistas of richness and reward. The cedar*
> *uprears its lawns of black cirrus. You have found*
> *hundred-fold return though in the land*
> *of exile. You are Joseph the Provider;*
>
> *and in the fable this is your proper home;*
> *three sides of a courtyard where the bees thrum*
> *in the crimped hedges and the pigeons flirt*
> *and paddle, and sunlight pierces the heart-*
>
> *shaped shutter-patterns in the afternoon,*
> *shadows of fleurs-de-lys on the stone floors.*
> *Here life is labour and pastime and orison*
> *like something from a simple book of hours. (3.1–3)*

The shadows of the cedars lie cloudlike on the lawns: the shadows of
one world lie across another. The community of old France gave life
a continuity in which all the acts of the household were sacramental.
It was to such a promised land Péguy wished to return; but circumstance, and the circumstance of this poetry, cast him in a different
role, that of Joseph in the land of exile. Joseph was not fated to lead
his people out of exile, only to prophesy the fulfillment of a promise.
Mann wrote *Joseph the Provider* while himself in exile, "under the
serene, Egyptian-like sky of California," as he later put it. Exile calls
to exile, and Péguy's estrangement from the modern world, from
the world of superficial talent that had replaced the world of labor,

from the Egypt of new France, produced this radical reversion. His republican socialism is undermined by this simple society of obligation, where "labour and pastime and orison" mingle like static pictures in a book of hours. Hill's simile is blind neither to the feudalism evoked nor to its status as fable. Like most visionaries, Péguy could not see that his importance lay in fostering the vision, not fulfilling it. He was not a character suited to the utopia he would found.

For Joseph, however, the vistas of richness and reward were in Egypt, in service to the pharaoh. The stanzas shrewdly blur Péguy's utopian vision with a utopian version of his accomplishment. Within certain limitations, he lived precisely the life he would have invented. The courtyard and hedges and pigeons could describe his house in Lozère, where he moved in 1908, with its front garden filled with flowers and its back lawn leading to the park of a neighboring château. The relics Hill pictures on a desk, "bits of ivory quartz / and dented snuffbox won at Austerlitz," could be the stuff of homely fact, not hectoring fable, though the snuffbox is redolent of Napoléon's defeat. Péguy was proud his life combined the purifying labors of the intellect with the practical chores of bookshop and printing press: in these the socialism and the static society found equal terms. His proper home was among the proof sheets of the *Cahiers:* "Here is the archive / of your stewardship; here is your true domaine, / its fields of discourse ripening to the Marne." Joseph was a steward, and the domain of a steward can be encompassing:

> *Chateau de Trie is yours, Chartres is yours,*
> *and the carved knight of Gisors with the hound;*
> *Colombey-les-deux-Eglises; St Cyr's*
> *cadres and echelons are yours to command. (3.6)*

These sites are particular, however, and of particular significance to Péguy: they mingle the past and the prophecy, the personal and the public. Napoléon founded the national military academy at St. Cyr. De Gaulle, one of its graduates and later one of its teachers, retired from his services to France to Colombey-les-deux-Églises, where he died and was buried. Péguy was often invited to Château de Trie by the young actress Simone Casimir-Périer. On one of his visits, they went to see the cathedral of Gisors, a few miles away, and paused in front of the tomb with the knight and his greyhound. It was Chartres, however, that Péguy considered *his* cathedral. Though it rose from the flat plain of the Beauce he had walked as a child, he did not see it until he was an adult. He made pilgrimage to it when his son recovered from typhoid, and for it wrote "Présentation de la Beauce à Notre Dame de Chartres." He possessed these things and did not possess them—if he arrived at the château when his hosts were away, he would act at home and begin to write. He possessed them by virtue of a vision, the dream of the cadres and echelons at St. Cyr, or indeed the dream all these places embodied:

> *Yours is their dream of France, militant-pastoral:*
> *musky red gillyvors, the wicker bark*
> *of clematis braided across old brick*
> *and the slow chain that cranks into the well*
>
> *morning and evening. It is Domrémy*
> *restored; the mystic strategy of Foch*
> *and Bergson with its time-scent, dour panache*
> *deserving of martyrdom. (3.7–8)*

The France into which Péguy was born had suffered defeat and disaster, humiliated by the German troops at Mars-la-Tour and Sedan. Alsace-Lorraine had been lost, Strasbourg had been lost, and the myth of the invincible French army, that corrupt core of French pride, had been forfeit. The losses of the Franco-Prussian War prepared the Third Republic, but they also conceived the nervous anxiety and sour morale that later affected French military strategy and were in part responsible for the Dreyfus Affair. The dream fortified by these sites of Péguy's stewardship was earlier and more powerful, the dream of the militant-pastoral army of Joan of Arc. Her attractions affected him even as a radical student, a freethinker and revolutionary socialist. He traveled to Domrémy, where she was born and where she found her vocation, to research the manuscript he kept secret in a box, the trilogy of plays titled *Jeanne d'Arc* (1897).

She has served her country as a figure of complex regard, but the young Péguy was uninterested in the response of her holiness. Only after he had recovered his faith, a decade later, could he transform and expand the first acts of *Jeanne d'Arc*, his socialist Joan, into the work that offers Hill his title, *Le Mystère de la Charité de Jeanne d'Arc* (1910). The opening play of the trilogy was *Domrémy*, and in a number of entangled senses this Domrémy of birth and vocation was restored in dream and in drama. It was significant to Péguy that the girl of Domrémy became the Maid of Orléans.

One dream negotiated by another, one time imposed upon another, one meaning measured against another: the controlling strategy of this poem requires these intricate focusings. They are Hill's method, to be sure, the argument by ambiguity and anachronism; but where, in *Mercian Hymns* (1971), for example, they are comic impositions upon a sullen subject, here they rise out of the competing temperament of the poem itself. Offa was there a figure proposed, but Joan is here a figure disposed, even if outside the direct mention of the poem. Joan provided an animating spirit for Péguy's dream; but the warrant for Hill's direction, and his indirection, lies elsewhere, in the philosophy of Henri Bergson. It was to Bergson, whose lectures he avidly attended, that Péguy stood not as student but disciple. The endurance of l'élan vital, the vital impulse that is the past within the present, sanctions the shifting and superimposed planes within this deliberate construction, a construction that extends to the slanting rhymes that work various changes on the quatrain. Bergson's intuitions of knowledge were elsewhere enacted in the digressions and repetitious variations Péguy practiced to numbing effect: Bergson once said Péguy often articulated what he himself had only secretly felt. The militant counterpart to Bergson's élan is the panache of Marshal Foch, that tenacity of will he preached first in the classroom and then with devastating effect at the front. They are the dual impulses of Péguy's reckless and doomed behavior in battle.

There is danger in such dreams ("Such dreams portend, the dreamer prophesies, / is this not true?"). Joseph, dreamer and interpreter of dreams, found riches and provision; Péguy will discover only that the world does not recognize such stewardship:

This world is different, belongs to them—
the lords of limit and of contumely.
It matters little whether you go tamely
or with rage and defiance to your doom. (*4.1*)

What is dreamt in one section is awoken from in another. The lords of limit govern this world, and by a fine irony they inhabit, through Auden, the title for Hill's prose. Péguy occupied that dream within limits, but the limits were narrow. The land and landmarks belonged to different masters: "This is your enemies' country which they took / in the small hours an age before you woke." Péguy did not possess those places, any more than he possessed a grand manor where a servant could protect him from wisdom at the door:

This is no old Beauce manoir that you keep
but the rue de la Sorbonne, the cramped shop,
its unsold Cahiers *built like barricades,*
its fierce disciples, disciplines and feuds. (*4.5*)

In the fierce world the light that would illuminate the Boutique des Cahiers is cut off by the Sorbonne. In this world actions have bloody effect. The days expect not the rectifying labors of the book of hours, the water taken from the well morning and evening, but street fights and broken glass ("all through your life the sound of broken glass"). One violence begets another, and in such an economy "So much" may signify shrugging dismissal or financial reckoning:

So much for Jaurès murdered in cold pique
by some vexed shadow of the belle époque,

some guignol strutting at the window-frame. (*4.6–7*)

A *guignol* in English is Mr. Punch. Here and elsewhere in the poem, the French absorbed into the English disconcerts it, one culture grating against the other. The mock horror at the café window reckons the real horror inside. The French repays the real horrors of the Hundred Years' War. Péguy claimed that in the street fights no one behaved dishonorably: they seem boyish tangles. Years later he was calling for blood, and the blood came. The poem turns to this indictment, this fatal calculation; but the indictment goes further and deeper, from the forgivable error to the unforgivable act: when Péguy was told of the assassination, he was savagely exultant. The reaction is bestial, but the questioning is almost mild: "But what of you, Péguy, who came to 'exult,' / to be called 'wolfish' by your friends?"

What of Péguy? Five weeks after Jaurès was shot, Péguy was leading a battalion across a field of beetroots toward a line of German machine guns. With the other officers he stood upright under fire. For half an hour, miraculously, none of them was hit, then the two captains and the other lieutenant were killed in quick succession. Still Péguy refused to lie down. He was shot through the forehead and the rest of the battalion was slaughtered. This is the shape of his martyrdom, a reckless disregard, a "dour panache." A death forgives a death, and the poem treats these deaths as bare matters of fact. It is not the words but their form that makes a judgment:

> *Jaurès was killed blindly, yet with reason:*
> *"let us have drums to beat down his great voice."*
> *So you spoke to the blood. So, you have risen*
> *above all that and fallen flat on your face*
>
> 5
>
> *among the beetroots, where we are constrained*
> *to leave you sleeping and to step aside. (4.8–5.1)*

The enjambment hurtles across the sections, as reckless as Péguy; but the rupture records, silently and eloquently, that fatal change of status, that transition from live man to dead figure (and to fall "flat on your face" is to fail comically and humiliatingly). The debt of blood has been repaid in blood, and Péguy has "risen / above all that" only to fall, from life into death, from a section of rude awakening to a section of deathly sleep. He does not ascend into Heaven. He falls to the ground, where the Christian argument is roughly subverted and returned to the soil of its origins.

Péguy is left sleeping in order to consider the vision of France afresh, this time not as the external domain of social obligation but as the internal one of religious act. The forward look of utopian prophecy gives way to the backward glance at religious descent and the operations of "the radical soul" in response, "waking / into the foreboding of its inheritance." Péguy's radical soul ("instinct, intelligence, / memory, call it what you will") darkens here into its etymology, its agricultural *root*. The vision shimmers and reforms, revised and reviewed through a different lens, where the landscape discloses its religious heritage. Magi march across Artois to Bethlehem. The workers, the hedgers and ditchers (different lords of limit), even the country priests, are transformed in this "bleak visionary instant" into seraphim gazing at Chartres. The cathedral is itself transfigured into an agricultural shrine, with its

> *spired sheaves,*
> *stone-thronged annunciations, winged ogives*
> *uplifted and uplifting from the winter-gleaned*
> *furrows of that criss-cross-trodden ground. (5.5)*

The Passion has collapsed into the Nativity, those *annunciations* rising from the *cross* in *criss-cross-trodden ground* (and it can be no unhappy accident the cross splits what would have been the Christ in that word). This world is older than the Christian myth: we are deep in the seasonal ritual of the vegetable god, sacrificed after his annual reign to bring forth the crops, Osiris torn limb from limb to fertilize the soil with his blood. The fertilizing imagery recalls Péguy's "Présentation de la Beauce à Notre Dame de Chartres": "here is your Beauceron Tower, / The hardest ear of corn."

The Christian past rises from an even more distant past where the Pentecost blooms in the "coagulate magnified flowers" of a hawthorn tree, a tree with its own suggestive burden of thorns. Here the "Landscape is like revelation," God's disclosure of Himself and His will to His creatures. The "Cloud-shadows of seasons revisit the earth," like the cloud-shadows that invoked the earlier vision, now not a vista of richness but an annual ritual of death and rebirth. Part of this continuing and renewing order, the soldiers go down to their bloody deaths in the fields:

> *Happy are they who, under the gaze of God,*
> *die for the "terre charnelle," marry her blood*
> *to theirs, and, in strange Christian hope, go down*
> *into the darkness of resurrection,*
>
> *into sap, ragwort, melancholy thistle,*
> *almondy meadowsweet, the freshet-brook*
> *rising and running through small wilds of oak,*
> *past the elder-tump that is the child's castle. (5.8–9)*

The carnal earth. "Heureux ceux qui sont morts pour la terre char-nelle, / Mais pourvu que ce fût dans une juste guerre": *Happy are those who die for the carnal earth, / As long as it is in a just war.* The lines are from Péguy's "Eve," an interminable chant of eight thousand alexandrines ("bound to the alexandrine as to the *Code // Napoléon*") afflicted with his monotonous repetitions and variations. The lines form and reform, like the lines of soldiers, dying only to be reborn. The section that forms around "Heureux ceux qui . . ." is now Péguy's anthology piece. Hill's lines suggest the childish innocence of a chilling idea, however harrowing and Horatian (*dulce et decorum est*).

The hope is strange, strangely pagan, the resurrection not in body but in freshet-brook, the life of the world to come that of the rag-wort and thistle. The Christian hope has been redefined, but this is no more than to take literally what men die for figuratively: they die for their country. One of Péguy's men was killed in his own garden. The vision of innocent courage infuses even the children's tin sol-diers: "winds drumming the fame / of the tin legions lost in haystack and stream! / Here the lost are blest, the scarred most sacred." (In *Collected Poems* that exclamation has been tempered to a full stop, the only textual change made in *Péguy*.) The legions stand for their adult

models, whose own scars are sacred. Such a vision makes its sentimental assumptions and is particularly susceptible to

> *solitary bookish ecstasies, proud tears,*
> *proud tears, for the forlorn hope, the guerdon*
> *of Sedan, "oh les braves gens!," English Gordon*
> *stepping down sedately into the spears. (5.13)*

The pathos allowed is crude and disgusting, the stuff of penny patriotism. It denies any knowledge of men in their death spasms or
the cries of the wounded. Here again the English is scraped against
the French, Gordon's death in the Sudan at the siege of Khartoum
grimly mirroring the defeat of Sedan. Gordon became, perhaps
undeservedly, the martyred warrior-saint such a vision requires; indeed, just the sort Péguy became for so many, in posthumous
fulfillment of his worship of St. Joan.

The vision will not hold, especially after a humiliation like that at
Sedan. Sedan produced no such heroes, and the defeat was bitter.
The religious must wait for the Second Coming, the soldiers for
their second chance; but both ask for patience, and patience is a
failing virtue after the Germans have held Alsace-Lorraine for two
generations.

> *Patience hardens to a pittance, courage*
> *unflinchingly declines into sour rage,*
> *the cobweb-banners, the shrill bugle-bands*
> *and the bronze warriors resting on their wounds. (5.14)*

Resting on their wounds instead of their laurels. The scarred tin
soldiers become impotent bronze statues; the militant ideal declines
into its thwarted courage and ruined banners. The *pittance* remaining is a petrifaction of *patience*. It is a fine stroke of Freudian wordplay to say such *courage* shrinks into *rage* (such declines are also falls),
that the *rage* (even "sour rage") persists when the *courage* does not.
The honorable virtue becomes dishonorable anger: the high ideals
become low concern for "familial debts and dreads, / keepers of old
scores." The religious militance that encouraged a militant vision is
also corrupted, the property not of those who believe in religion's

vital mystique, but of "the child-eyed crones // who guard the votive candles and the faint / invalid's night-light of the sacrament." This is the sickly and superstitious Catholicism Péguy fled from and was never reconciled with. He recovered his faith, but was never to take the sacrament. He was forced to find salvation elsewhere, in a devotion that ignored the truth and justice the Catholic myth offered; he cleaved instead "to a kind of truth, / a justice hard to justify." The religious past provided a vision no more secure than the utopian future.

Péguy worked closely with his printers, and *justify* trembles not just with the usual meanings but with a printer's justification. Péguy's justice is difficult, and difficult to set exactly to the required margin. Like all justice it is tenuous and contingent:

> *To dispense, with justice; or, to dispense*
> *with justice. Thus the catholic god of France,*
> *with honours all even, honours all, even*
> *the damned in the brazen Invalides of Heaven. (6.1)*

Justice requires fine distinction, and fine distinctions; but here a lowly comma dismantles it, separating service to an honorable standard ("To dispense, with justice") from the betrayal of standards ("to dispense / with justice"). Péguy, that "meticulous reader of proof" (as Hill describes him in the biographical note), would have noticed and corrected the error. Only that hesitating comma separates the utopian notion from the rule of the mob. There is great power in typography: a catholic god is very different from a Catholic God. The "catholic god of France" can aspire to a justice greater than the Catholic God's, can honor even the damned, treat them as crippled soldiers in one Heaven, as they would not be in another.

The Invalides was built for crippled soldiers, but it houses the tombs of Napoléon and Foch and is therefore central to any notion of France militant. To its associations with those who dispensed, with justice, must be added memories of those who dispensed with justice. In the cobbled courtyard, the Cour d'Honneur, Dreyfus was degraded.

Dreyfus with his buttons off, chalk-faced
but standing to attention, the school prig
caught in some act and properly disgraced.
A puffy satrap prances on one leg

to snap the traitor's sword, his ordered rage
bursting with "cran et gloire" and gouts of rouge. (6.3–4)

Gouts of rouge, not gouts of blood. Courage and glory, "cran et gloire," better pursued in battle than betrayal. The rage is orderly, but it has been ordered by those who prefer a miscarriage of justice to the admission of error. Order must be maintained, the one sacrificed for the many. The horses at the scene are more agitated by this outrage than the soldiers or the powers of Heaven: "no stir / in the drawn ranks, among the hosts of the air." The disgrace of Dreyfus was the disgrace of France: for Péguy it divided, as neatly as that comma, those who defended *mystique*, devotion to the values of the spirit, from those fatally soiled with *politique*. All *politiques* originally issue from a *mystique*, but a *politique* that does not remain infused with *mystique* degenerates into mere expedience and reasons of state.

Those ranks, drawn up, drawn and haggard, or merely drawn as an artist would draw them, are "draped and gathered by the weird storm-light / cheap wood-engravings cast," subject to the same artistic distancing suffered by the "jolly cartoon / armies." Such distancing reduces all acts to artistry, rendering equal, as in the pages of a pulp magazine, the men at Mars-la-Tour and Sedan and those "in the world-famous stories of Jules Verne // or nailed at Golgotha." History, fictional prophecy, religious myth: the examples duplicate the substance of those ruined visions, artistic constructions falsely tempting, temptingly false. The mob may howl for Dreyfus's blood, "A mort le Juif! Le Juif / à la lanterne!" (echoing the cry of the Revolution, "Les aristos à la lanterne!"—*The aristocrats from the lamppost!*), but its howls are rendered serene by the silence of art: "silent mouthings hammered into scrolls // torn from *Apocalypse*." Those are the silent mouthings and scrolls of generations of political cartoons.

The function of art is not to bury but to resurrect, yet these distancings are false ennoblings, these caricatures the creatures of our indignation. Here art mediates and rouses by the failure of its mediation. The false equivalences provoke equivalent rages. The artistries shake us from our silence, shake until we tremble with a righteous anger: "No wonder why / we fall to violence out of apathy, / redeemed by falling and restored to grace." Péguy and Dreyfus were both redeemed by falling, restored to grace like the damned in the brazen Invalides. But who are "we," falling into violence and suffering such redemption, "heroes or knaves as Clio shall decide"?

> *"We" are crucified Pilate, Caiaphas*
> *in his thin soutane and Judas with the face*
> *of a man who has drunk wormwood. We come*
> *back empty-handed from Jerusalem*
>
> *counting our blessings, honestly admire*
> *the wrath of the peacemakers, for example*
> *Christ driving the money-changers from the temple,*
> *applaud the Roman steadiness under fire. (6.9–10)*

The self-judgment is brutal, and brutalizing. We are the judge overruled by the mob and crucified by history. We are each of the judges of Christ, Roman and Jew and disciple, each condemned by his judgment. We are those who return empty from Jerusalem, counting our blessings like coins, or blessed we have not been involved. We are those who admire equally "the wrath of the peacemakers" and "the Roman steadiness under fire," as if there were no moral choices to be made. Bystanders, we stand by our innocence as others stand by their words. Judges, we judge wrongly and judge ourselves: "We are the occasional just men who sit / in gaunt self-judgment on their self-defeat." This is a public confession of a public failure, a self-mortification harsh and hardening. But it is also a confession made and a mortification endured, acts that prepare us, even if only to realize the nature of our role:

> *We are "embusqués," having no wounds to show*
> *save from the thorns, ecstatic at such pain.*

Once more the truth advances; and again
the metaphors of blood begin to flow. (6.12)

Like *embusqués,* soldiers who shirk their duty at the front, we are subject only to self-inflicted wounds and self-afflicted crucifixions. There is nevertheless something almost saintly in that, a truth that advances truth, advances like the soldiers who *are* at the front. Even if we are dishonored by our avoidance and mock infliction, we honor such pain by repeating it, understand such blood by metaphors of blood. That self-recognition is chastening and even perhaps redeeming, all the redemption we can expect. We find our ground in imitation of those like Péguy; and the poem, halted for this long section of self-analysis in despair, moves forward to blood by its blood metaphors.

If we are among the judges of Christ, bystanders at his blessings and his rage, imitators of his Passion, how are we judged by Him (if you care to divide the earthly man from the Catholic God)?

Salute us all, Christus with your iron
garlands of poppies and ripe carrion.
No, sleep where you stand; let some boy-officer
take up your vigil with your dungfork spear. (7.1)

Christ cannot return our salute, a sentry standing asleep amid the iron garlands, the poppies, the rotting bodies ready for the military graveyard. Only a sleeping Christ could allow such slaughter between two "Christian" armies. The boy-officer who will assume Christ's vigil with a "dungfork spear" displays the symbol of a militant-pastoral army, like that of the French Revolution. The dungfork spear reduces the honored dead to mere manure. The reduction is savage, but it is also sanctified as that marriage of blood with the carnal earth, that resurrection in the ragwort. As if to remind us, Péguy's line "Heureux ceux qui sont morts" is resurrected, still read and read "dutifully," which may compose the duties of irony or those of transcendent fulfillment. Or, as would be proper in a poem of such compressed identifications, fulfillment collapsed into irony.

The Christian myth charges this scene with unconsoling certitudes, or consoling incertitudes. A "relic fumbled with such care / by

mittened fingers in dugout or bomb-/ tattered, jangling estaminet's
upper room" turns out to be only "incense from a treasured tabatière," no doubt gambled for by the "watchmen at the Passion"
for whom it is identified. Yet what is that room but the upper room
of the Last Supper, now a bombed-out ruin? An *estaminet* is a bistro
or café, another example of the French infiltrating the English
line—but when did *estaminet* last trouble English poetry? In "Ger-
ontion," which might supply many an epigraph. ("After such knowledge, what forgiveness?") What is the incense in that *tabatière*, that
snuff box, but the frankincense and myrrh of the Magi? Here the
Nativity rises again within the Passion, images of the past carried
into the ruins of the present, that vital impulse that endures. The
snuffbox has appeared before: the "dented snuffbox won at Austerlitz."

"Drawn on the past / these presences endure": not merely the
Christian images or the Horatian lines of Péguy, but the presences
who have endured through this poem, the soldiers about to die.
"What vigil is this, then, among the polled / willows . . . ?" the poem
has asked, and through these images of battered grace arrived at the
vigil of the soldiers the night before their deaths. Péguy quartered
his men in an old convent the night before the fatal battle, an appropriate site for such a devotional watch. The soldiers of the poem
crouch in the hail, "like labourers of their own memorial // or those
who worship at its marble rote," merged with those who, like the
embusqués, live in secondary relation, dependent on their example,
erecting or worshipping at the war monument on which their names
are engraved,

> *their many names one name, the common "dur"*
> *built into duration, the endurance of war;*
> *blind Vigil herself, helpless and obdurate. (7.6)*

Dur: hard, tough, unyielding, obdurate, harsh, merciless, unkind,
hard-hearted, unfeeling, hardy, courageous, austere, painful, labori-
ous, difficult. The French provides the name for this poetry, the
poetry of *dur.* The many names of the dead merge into this one
name; but it is also the *dur* in Bergson's duration, the inner form of

all outward matter, the endurance that establishes human freedom by overthrowing the narrow conception of time on which scientific determinism depends. This central insight, the basis of the whole of Bergson's process philosophy, gives their deaths a continuing presence and Péguy a continuing role. Their vigil has been personified as blind Vigil, who cannot see the future, their many names also its one.

Though the future is blindly withheld, there have been adequate revelations and recognitions in the past:

And yet what sights: Saul groping in the dust
for his broken glasses, or the men far-gone
on the road to Emmaus who saw the ghost. (7.7)

Saul confronted by Christ on the road to Damascus, the two disciples approached on the road to Emmaus: these Christian presences may endure into the present, as Saul's broken glasses prochronistically suggest; but their comforts are uncertain (as are the jokes: the "sight" of a man groping for his glasses, the disciples gone far along the road, or merely far-gone into madness or the madness of belief). They seem to mock the soldiers, who will not enjoy such revelations during their vigil, who will blindly join the line of battle: "The line // falters, reforms, vanishes into the smoke / of its own unknowing." The line is not less lethal for being a line of poetry as well. Péguy said history was a man remembering, and these men become mere memory ("Commit all this to memory"), atomized in a shell-burst, names upon marble, all "'pour la patrie,' according to the book." According to the book of history, which remembers and endures, and in the approved manner, by the book.

They represent an impulse that deserves attention and address:

Dear lords of life, stump-toothed, with ragged breath,
throng after throng cast out upon the earth,
flesh into dust, who slowly come to use
dreams of oblivion in lieu of paradise,

push on, push on! (8.1–2)

These wretches embody l'élan vital at its most basic and bestial, knaves as Clio shall decide, embracing dreams of oblivion because paradise is beyond reach. In their hopeless infirmity, however, these beggars who beggar description offer a version of life more vital, because more tenuous and more tenacious, than the lords of limit whose title theirs ridicules. Hill urges them onward, through conditions increasingly degrading ("through berserk fear, / laughing, howling") to their inevitable doom, "in nameless gobbets thrown / up by the blast." Those nameless gobbets savage the names afterward engraved on marble. Mere word made rotting flesh, they recall the critical feast of Hill's "Annunciations," where men "flavour their decent mouths / With gobbets of the sweetest sacrifice."

Against these horrific images, Hill reassures the common soldiers of their common place; but the assurances are hollow:

> *Death does you proud,*
> *every heroic commonplace, "Amor,"*
> *"Fidelitas," polished like old armour,*
> *stamped forever into the featureless mud. (8.4)*

These are the heroes, as Clio shall decide (with their "skins of silver, steel and hide")—their end is the same. So much for the old armor of love for a country, faithfulness to an ideal. Something featureless may indeed have a commemorating image stamped upon it; but when the rare medallion is the common mud, the stamping of feet obliterates any feature that might honor *amor* or *fidelitas*. The poet channels his fury on behalf of rather than against the common soldiers and junior officers, the *poilus* and *sous-officiers* ordered to their orderly deaths. That fierceness is softened by the expectations of these soldiers, who went to war with the cheerful certainty of their sacrifice, "expecting nothing but the grace of France, / drawn to her arms, her august plenitude." Drawn into the carnal earth of their country, into an august plenitude ravaged by the guns of August. The poet rudely chronicles their end, the mind extinct in the very leap for salvation, the last thoughts, snagged on barbed wire, a contagious eruption on the furrows of the *terre charnelle*. The meditation on the dead and the nature of their heroism admits the haunting presence, confirmed by some of the incidental imagery, of a poem that has much affected Hill, Allen Tate's "Ode to the Confederate Dead."

"En avant, Péguy!": Péguy too is urged forward to his death. If Bergson's duration confirmed the demands of freedom against those of determinism, these deaths are not fated but freely chosen ("it is not / fate, to our knowledge"). That liberating choice, a choice that is also a charity, contains its ironies, particularly and most persuasively "The irony of advancement." The philosophy advances a freedom, the soldiers advance upon an objective, yet what awaits them is not progress but putrefaction. To those who will lose everything in such service, the poet's advice is rueful: "Say 'we / possess nothing; try to hold on to that.'" To hold on to that is to give up everything else.

That is the force of their charity, and their deaths contrast severely with the lives of those who have different notions of sacrifice, who have appropriated the vision of France and employed it for purposes radically different, or conservatively suspect:

> *There is an ancient landscape of green branches—*
> *true tempérament de droite, you have your wish—*
> *crosshatching twigs and light, goldfinches*
> *among the peppery lilac, the small fish*
>
> *pencilled into the stream. Ah, such a land*
> *the Ile de France once was. Virelai and horn*
> *wind through the meadows, the dawn-masses sound*
> *fresh triumphs for our Saviour crowned with scorn. (9.1–2)*

The phrase *tempérament de droite* is Jacques Maritain's, later used by a biographer to describe the novelist Georges Bernanos, as Hill fastidiously notes. Bernanos was of a political persuasion so inimical to Péguy's their undeniable similarities afford a resonant contrast and resistant comparison. Catholic royalist, anti-Dreyfusard, member of *les camelots du roi* ("the camelot-cry of 'sticks!'"): Bernanos represented that reactionary sensibility still alive among the aristocrats, gentry, and upper-middle class and ignited among the bourgeois in the aftermath of the Commune. The rage for order fed a return to the church. The antidemocratic *tempérament de droite* indulged in a corrosive nostalgia for the ancient landscape of monarchy and faith. This was not a landscape to which Péguy was entirely immune, as that earlier vision of life and labor in the simple community of a book of hours will suggest. The contradictions of Péguy's temperament in part attended the contradictions of his early education, divided between *curés* who thought modern France a moral darkness and masters for whom it was filled with republican light. Though 1789 was a sunset to one and a sunrise to the other, their students responded to such refractory myths with a complete and charitable acceptance of both. The young Péguy admitted that to bring the Republican and reactionary within him into harmony he'd taken to shouting, on alternate days, "Vive la République!" and "Montjoie et Saint Denis!"

Bernanos, according to his biographer Speaight, shared Péguy's mystical inclination and sense of prophetic endowment. They were equally attracted to the glamour of ancient France and equally "unjust in their pursuit of justice." Péguy believed people of opposing *mystiques* were closer in temperament than those of a *mystique* could ever be to those of any *politique*. (*Mystiques* are attractive. Bernanos married a "descendant" of Jeanne d'Arc *named* Jeanne d'Arc. But how could she have been a direct descendant?) Both Péguy and Bernanos were capable of scathing attacks upon the expedience of their own sides, and the meticulous integrity of which this was a sign extended to Bernanos insisting a forgotten waitress be tipped by post and Péguy giving to beggars his last worthless sou. What was contradiction in Péguy was continuity in Bernanos, and Péguy devoted much prose attempting to recover for the left the aggressive patriotism long monopolized by the right.

The poem's return to the ancient landscape, arrogated by "the lords of limit and of contumely," heightens the *mystère* central to this moral drama. The "crosshatching twigs and light," the "small fish // pencilled into the stream," the sigh of senile regret: all confirm the vision is an artistic convenience and retrospective falsification. The lines are an indictment not merely of that vision, however lusciously contrived, but also of the "Good governors and captains" who pursue and protect it: "you also were sore-wounded but those wars / are ended." Whether those wars were the Crusades, the Hundred Years' War, or the late disaster of the Franco-Prussian War (and Péguy's vision of old France was chronologically insecure), such men and their *politique* exist in a chronic aftermath:

> *Iron men who bell the hours,*
> *marshals of porte-cochère and carriage-drive,*
>
> *this is indeed perfection, this is the heart*
> *of the mystère. Yet one would not suppose*
> *Péguy's "defeat," "affliction," your lost cause. (9.3–4)*

Indeed, it was not. Péguy fought out of charity for that vision, such men for the protection of its advantages. The *mystère* is the impulse behind the action, here as selfless on one side as it is venal on the other. Just as any *mystique* may be devoured by the *politique* to which it gave birth, so even poets may be compromised by a vision to which they have contributed, their scars profaned by the "Old Bourbons" who "dream of warrior-poets and the Meuse / flowing so sweetly; the androgynous Muse" who is both mistress and priest.

That lesson is not lost on Hill, whose poetry rises most luxuriantly to the occasion of such landscapes. He has responded bitterly to accusations of nostalgia, claiming in an interview with John Haffenden that he has been "offering a diagnosis," not "exhibiting a symptom." Even so, his descriptions from nature indulge an affection that nearly becomes affliction, a line-by-line attraction that must always be resisted in argument. The first sonnet of "An Apology for the Revival of Christian Architecture in England" provides the English prevision of this French vision: "lords of unquiet or of quiet sojourn" against "lords of limit and of contumely"; "midge-tormented ghosts" against "wraiths" that appear "when the gnat-swarm spins"; "bloom Linnaean pentecosts" of the lilac bush against the "Pentecost" of the "coagulate magnified flowers" of the hawthorn tree; "sweet carnality" against "terre charnelle"; "hymns of servitude" against "servitude et grandeur"; "the sacred well" against "the slow chain that cranks into the well // morning and evening." If these images constitute a warning as well as a welling-up, it is a warning against their complacent misuse.

As so often, one poet rescues another. The memories of Bismarck and 1870 haunt these lords of landscape ("Bad memories, seigneurs?") even as the storm of the next war gathers: "The chestnut trees begin to thresh and cast / huge canisters of blossom at each gust. / Coup de tonnerre! Bismarck is in the room!" The French means both thunderclap and bombshell. The rain's "night-long vigil" and the "small hours' advance" that precede the morning salient return us to the soldiers waiting for battle while not taking leave of these reactionary lords on the verge of the war they have eagerly prepared. Here another poet, whose life also argued for action, addresses a dire distinction to those *seigneurs*:

> *"Je est un autre," that fatal telegram,*
>
> *floats past you in the darkness, unreceived.*
> *Connoisseurs of obligation, history*
> *stands, a blank instant, awaiting your reply:*
> *"If we but move a finger France is saved!" (9.8–9)*

That reply, the call to action of a militant-pastoral army, cannot be made by "Connoisseurs of obligation" who choose carefully and choose to their own advantage. They never receive Rimbaud's fatal telegram, which in the guise of stating an aesthetic demand precisely delineates the dissociation of self that must determine any act of charity: "The I is another person." That demand also rescues the poet from the consequences of his affliction, and prevents his coercive appropriation by the forces of reaction. History blankly waits "a blank instant" for their reply, and then moves on.

> *Down in the river-garden a grey-gold*
> *dawnlight begins to silhouette the ash.*
> *A rooster wails remotely over the marsh*
> *like Mr Punch mimicking a lost child.*

At Villeroy the copybook lines of men
rise up and are erased. Péguy's cropped skull
dribbles its ichor, its poor thimbleful,
a simple lesion of the complex brain. (10.1–2)

The actual deaths are recorded almost negligently, mere lines erased from a *cahier*, a child's copybook. All the men who quartered with Péguy were killed the following day in the field in sight of Villeroy (but in late afternoon, not at dawn). Péguy's "cropped skull" has been harvested in the field of beetroots; he has entered the *terre charnelle* with the "fraternal root-crops," finally achieving transcendent union with the earth, "at one / with the fritillary and the veined stone." The stone, carrying animating blood or covered with it, may serve equally as local rock or marble monument. Péguy's "ichor" may be the blood of the gods or merely the watery discharge of a wound, a simple lesion. Every grand image is counterpointed with its humbling alternative. The grotesque figure of Mr. Punch rises before the scene, as he rose at the café window at the assassination of Jaurès.

In death Péguy, who chose action over his essays ("Rather the Marne than the *Cahiers*"), has finally "composed his great work, his small body"; and the body does lie composed, "his arm over his face as though in sleep," recalling that first rehearsal of his death, when he was also left sleeping. Though he "leaves a name // for the burial-detail" and "personal effects" whose effect may be far from personal, "he commends us to nothing." The line clarifies the deadly advice, "Say 'we / possess nothing,'" and is central to the charity and atonement of his act. He asks nothing, and expects nothing in return (and it is to nothing, to oblivion, that he commends us). He atones for the death of Jaurès not in dying—he would have seen no reason to atone for the assassination—but in standing by his words in the most difficult of situations. He has sacrificed his life for a *mystique*, in "tribute of his true passion, for Chartres / steadfastly cleaving to the Beauce, for her, / the Virgin of innumerable charities."

Some eighty stanzas earlier the poem recorded a judgment: "Dying, your whole life / fell into place." Though there have been a number of intervening falls, the last fall is into grace, "that grace won by inches, / inched years." Péguy has slogged toward his troubled fulfillment, and the final image of the battlefield lures out the Passion always sleeping in Péguy's "true passion": "The men of sorrows do their stint, / whose golgothas are the moon's trenches, / the sun's blear flare over the salient."

Péguy's fulfillment has been reached, but not the poem's. The poet turns toward those lords of limit and of contumely:

> *J'accuse! j'accuse!—making the silver prance*
> *and curvet, and the dust-motes jig to war*
> *across the shaky vistas of old France,*
> *the gilt-edged maps of Strasbourg and the Saar. (10.9)*

Strasbourg was what had been lost, the Saar what would be gained. This is disputed ground, not just between the French and Germans, but between Péguy and the old enemies who had taken possession of his vision of "the shaky vistas of old France." Those enemies incited a war for the furtherance of a *politique*, and it is appropriate for such anti-Dreyfusards that Hill should appropriate Zola's shout against them. But it could also be a shout against Péguy's bellicose temper and stirring for war. (On the day of his assassination, Jaurès was carrying Péguy's new *Cahier* and speaking kindly of it. "Who was the more Christian of the two?" one of Péguy's friends later asked.) The struggle descends, like the war, like the poem, into "Low tragedy, high farce, fight for command"; but above such farcical tragedy, or tragic farce, stands the charity of Péguy, and Hill pauses to hurl that charity into the breach:

> *Take that for your example! But still mourn,*
> *being so moved: éloge and elegy*
> *so moving on the scene as if to cry*
> *"in memory of those things these words were born." (10.11)*

The French eulogy and the English elegy are set at one, each atoning for the use of the other. The English poet has honored a French sacrifice; and in that final line the past rises into the present, a last instance of Bergson's l'élan vital, Péguy's "battered élan." The poet behind these lines, in both senses, can observe the selfless act only in words, but with his last word can make certain that from this hard-earned death something is born.

The compound rectitudes that contrive this poetry achieve the force of grace, if the ambiguity inherent in that word, the secular partaking of religious form, can properly be allowed. Péguy was a man whose comprehensions were inflicting and afflictive: the conflicts that raged within enlisted him for the conflicts without. A poetry that seeks to do him honor finds certain demands irreducible, and Hill has met them in a language so couched a reader must work through its moral actions to stand on the plain of its understanding. The equality must be won: the poetry fends off false approach. I have the uncomfortable feeling when reading Hill's poetry of having opened, perhaps by mistake, more likely by misapprehension, a private account between a man and his conscience. It is not accidental that Hill has been attracted to a figure who "was at the same time moved by violent emotions and violently afflicted by mischance." The description is Hill's, but the application may be variant and variable: "Like others similarly wounded, he was perhaps smitten by the desirability of suffering."

Péguy's mischance extended beyond the beetroot field. His medals were for years withheld because it was decided the Battle of the Marne had begun on the following day; and his great unrequited love, mysterious l'Innominata, learned of his death from a scrap of newspaper wrapped around a piece of fish. During the next war both the left and the right attempted to claim him. The poetic discipline his adversities require poses an unreasonable question: whether Geoffrey Hill's aesthetic demand, arising from adherence to an external ideal or from an internal clench of the spirit, can impose its purity upon the reader, whether it seeks a position or an imposition. Poets whose imaginations are similarly stunted, who do not have daily or weekly recourse to effusion, are often driven to reflect in style or substance the contrariness of the poetic act. Their idea of vision becomes vacuity, their version of idiom the ideogram. There are enough modern counterexamples, Bishop and Larkin among them, to suggest that ease does not have to be absent from a poetry whose occasions are infrequent. Nevertheless, in the one book where Hill's poetry seems to rush too eagerly onto the page, *Mercian Hymns*, his particular music is lost amid the welter and clatter.

Hill's fears about the propriety of indulgence are perhaps tainted by the sin of pride. His poetry hoards its conclusions, forces the reader to bore toward them or be bored by them. He would present an easier case if his work demanded a reader of rare or arcane intellect, though a wide range of reference or a good library may be an advantage when reading him. His limited and humorously inadequate attempts to explain his work do not deny he is a poet who wishes to be admired and absorbed, but he has never mastered the social skills involved or wished to pay the costs of this gratification. That is to his honor. His charity is to consider the difficult case, like Péguy's, and not flinch from its ambiguous reach or his own ambivalent response. Such charity and integrity adequately reform a poetry that must serve, for poet and Péguy, "the solitary ardours of faith but not the consolations of religious practice." By such prosaic and hardly uncalculated asides, a poet reveals the afflictions of his own mischance, and the terms of his difficult refusals.

The Absolute
Unreason-
ableness of
Geoffrey Hill

I think no one would read Geoffrey Hill's essays for pleasure, any more than one would read for pleasure the political tracts of John Milton. Milton's pamphlets are part of an oeuvre and illuminate transiently, or transversely, a mind that composed great poetry. Hill is not a great poet, at least not a poet as great as Milton (he is not, for example, conveniently dead); but he is often a poet as inconveniently intelligent and as exercised by the eagerness of dogma: an epic poet scaled to the corridors of the country house, an epic poet of cloister or interior.

Even interiors have their bloody philosophies. The critical writings of poets are irritable affairs in a tradition of belles lettres, not scholarship. They range in our century from the exquisite pulse-taking of Eliot to the helter-skelter theorizing of Empson, from the journalistic smash-and-grab of Randall Jarrell to the cranky domesticity of John Crowe Ransom. What unites the varying temperatures of their prose is the degree to which critical method justifies poetic manner. The prose is the unguarded back door to the designs of the poetry. A critic as self-devouring as Geoffrey Hill must realize, when he accedes to another critic's proposal that "Ransom on Milton . . . is also Ransom *as* Milton, or Ransom on Ransom," that such a concession may be turned against him. A critic who gnaws his own entrails may even want it to be.

If poets must create in their prose the taste that will celebrate their poetry, Hill has made every attempt to thwart that celebration. Thick with its own purposes and heavy with apparatus, one hundred and sixty pages of text dragging the slow length of forty pages of notes, the result of twenty-five years of meticulous scholarly practice, *The Lords of Limit: Essays on Literature and Ideas* could be the work of a professor anxious to publish no line not already buttressed by three quotations, able to pass the most stringent inquisition and satisfy the nicest scruple. At their worst Hill's essays parody the academic mien and bring to their subjects none of the élan we expect when a poet takes up the cause of literature. Hill considers his prose, like his poetry, too much a discipline to admit any reaction as fatal as delight; nevertheless, his seriousness is not the seriousness of the professors. These are not professings but deep engagements with the nature of language and literature, the wrestlings of someone fatally enwrapped with the Word.

Most poets approximate the condition of man before the Fall, content to name the beasts as if the beasts had never been named before and to practice the craft in Edenic innocence. There are no real snakes in such imaginary gardens. Hill's opening essay, "Poetry as 'Menace' and 'Atonement,'" reveals how far into the post-Edenic wilderness he has traveled and with what guilts. Justifications are self-justifications, just as criticisms are self-criticisms; and the essay, in establishing poetry as an act of atonement, itself atones for poetic practice. Theologically justification is the divine absolution of guilt for sin: as Hill wittily recognizes, it is enormously difficult to confess a sin if no one but yourself believes a sin has been committed.

That is a transgression typical of Hill: to usurp the prerogatives of religion in a secular atmosphere, borrowing the burdens without making obeisance to the faith. In his prose as in his poetry he drains religion of its fact in order to clothe himself in its fiction, unable to immerse himself in its healing unions, whether transcendent and mystical or formal and baptismal. This would mark him for the damnation of expedience if it were not the mark of a deeper damnation, a self-damnation recognizing that only the faith in which it is impossible to believe provides the myths, and more importantly the acts, that respond metaphorically to his predicament.

Poetry becomes atonement only by the adroit and repentant translation of etymology, which returns atonement to at-one-ment. To Hill language is inertial and coercive, and to overcome that inertia and that coercion in the act of composition is to achieve a momentary sense of fulfillment and concord. That sense is attested to not least by the reader's instinct and Hill's own practice, where the inertias of language, however dominant and determining, are line by line overcome to reach a temporary accord, an agreement or understanding. Reading, though Hill does not acknowledge it, is the act of atonement that recapitulates the act of composition. Not content to trust instinct or practice, Hill finds that moment of fulfillment phrased by two poets more than usually sensitive to the transcendent potential of language: Yeats for whom "a poem comes right with a click like a closing box" and Eliot in his "moment of exhaustion, of appeasement, of absolution, and of something very near annihilation." It may be noted wryly that the mystic's definition is resolutely practical and mundane, while the banker stutters toward a meaning unreliably mystical, one that in failing to reach that moment of fulfillment provides instead, or very nearly, an example of annihilation.

Those two definitions are severely different, as Christopher Ricks has noted, but that does not prevent Hill from imposing on them the silence of reconciliation. If poetry is to atone, it must atone for something, and it cannot be the mere anxiety or guilt that afflicts ordinary mortal existence, for which literature is the troubling and troubled conduit. It must be something harsher and more intractable, "a sense of language itself as a manifestation of empirical guilt." When the unnamed beasts approached, Adam could name them immediately and without reflection, again and again achieving effortlessly the concord that is at-one-ment. As Milton recognized, or as Milton as Adam articulated, that concord is the binding of comprehension: "I named them, as they passed, and understood / Their nature." But what if Adam had gotten their names wrong? Hill can approach the guilt inherent in language only through a shrinking that is not a shrinking from, through the knowledge that you can repent a sin but not a mistake.

It is not the last instance of Hill's mordant humor that the propriety is social, and the aptest quotation Chesterton's: "There are ways of getting absolved for murder; there are no ways of getting absolved for upsetting the soup." Hill can approximate the mortal sins of language, generally acts of omission, of failing to set the words and the things at one, only by cataloguing the venial sins more culpably committed and more easily reproached: *"faux pas*, the perpetration of 'howlers,' grammatical solecisms, misstatements of fact, misquotations, improper attributions." Although these are only minor acts of oversight, of failing to set the words at one with themselves, they are no less reprehensible. They are crucial betrayals of the writer's responsibility, the worse because once set wrong they can never be set right. Retrospective correction never alters the original commission of error or the "empirical guilt" that attends it. To enforce the notion that such error is a matter of ethics, not accident, Hill quotes Simone Weil, another mystic able to exact definition from the mundane: "anybody, no matter who, discovering an avoidable error in a printed text or radio broadcast, would be entitled to bring an action before [special] courts."

I can then imagine, with only the brief flickering of a smile, the writhings to which Hill might be subjected on discovering that in this very essay he has misdated the letter in which Yeats marks the closing click of a poem. It makes no difference to the argument that he wrote the letter to Dorothy Wellesley in 1935, not 1936, though it makes an ethical difference that a critic in quoting Hill has already repeated his faux pas: from such innocent transmissions whole rot-

ting branches of scholarly error derive. The sin lies not in the duplication but in the original transgression: as a symbolic act it represents the disharmony, the unfulfillment, the discord of the words set
against themselves. This is only the shadow of a larger guilt and a
deeper despair, the poet's discovery of the moral darkness of language.

Hill is aware of the disproportion of setting careless proofreading
(Péguy, it will be remembered, was "a meticulous reader of proof")
beside the more monstrous guilts to which language is subject, to
which the world itself is subject. The case of the knitting editor
worried that if he makes a mistake "there are jerseys all over England with one arm longer than the other" is ludicrous and almost
insignificant measured against the life and death of Mandelstam,
against the world of torture and political murder over an idea. In
making the comparison Hill strengthens his argument by seeming
to strangle it. The anxiety over faux pas is only a "comic sub-plot,"
a mimesis of a larger anxiety that must be established in a world of
moral idea and moral scruple: "in the act of 'making' we are necessarily delivered up to judgment." That is not merely the judgment of
critics.

If the "menace" is the poet's discovery that language has a moral
nature, the "atonement" must take place in the satisfaction of moral
demands, in setting at one not just the mean particular with the
mastering plan, the language of feeling with the life of the form, but
even the act said and the act done. In that acknowledgment is the
argument of *The Mystery of the Charity of Charles Péguy* (1984). Hill
honors and atones for that world of moral action by his own private
rectifications, the rectifications in the poetic act: "local vividness"
set at one with the "overall shape," the "sense of language" with the
"feeling for the ways of life," the "density of language" with the
"specific gravity of human nature" are the terms he employs, some
borrowed and some merely brokered. The burdens are the burdens
of language, but they are not what they seem.

Hill must return to Eliot, that figure always lurking beneath the
horizon of his prose and verse, for a phrase that implicates the poetic

act even while it means to implicate something else: "the unmoral nature, suddenly trapped in the inexorable toils of morality." Though the relation is imperfect and accidental, it allows Hill to admit what he would prefer to deny; and in so self-denying a nature the admission must come, as always, through a quotation by someone else, in this case Wallace Stevens: "After one has abandoned a belief in god [sic], poetry is that essence which takes its place as life's redemption." The scrupulous *sic* is Hill's, at once diplomatic to God and undiplomatic to Stevens, the appropriate priority for a poet whose anxiety must be that his "agnostic faith" is indelicate to divinity and overdelicate to poets.

The burdens, then, are accepted in lieu of religion by a nature whose longings cannot master its reason, if "reason" is not too dry and ennobling a term for the sickness of hesitation and the cowardice of irresolution, not presence of mind but absence of will. The judgment is harsh but not harmful. Hill has too many times admitted the desire unfulfilled, the hunger unsatisfied, for there to be any doubt about the tension between possibility and practice; in his interview with John Haffenden: "One is trying to make lyric poetry out of a much more common situation—the sense of *not* being able to grasp true religious experience." Where poetry substitutes for faith, the agnostic, alive to his own disability, his suppurating wound, receives his measure of menace and atonement. But, as Hill has also said, "I would not wish to describe myself as an agnostic."

This leads to an irony and an escape. The irony is that "a man could refuse to accept the evident signs of grace in his own work; that he himself could never move beyond that 'sorrow not mingled with the love of God' even though his own poems might speak to others with the voice of hope and love." Hill's poems are not likely to risk speaking to others with hope and love, but the point holds. No man can be his own reader. A poet is forever foreclosed from the pleasures other readers take from his work, whatever the prickly satisfactions of composition. No man can read innocently what he has guiltily composed. These satisfactions, however, contrive his escape. The poet subject to the guilt of language, the moral dread in the medium he would master, is consequently afflicted with the shame of the "irredeemable error in the very substance and texture of his craft and pride." What he cannot enslave he must be servant to, living with the affliction as a vocation. Adam after the Fall, Philoctetes in his cave: "in the constraint of shame the poet is free to discover both the 'menace' and the atoning power of his own art."

Hill is often engaged not by specific poetries as much as by specific moral acts construed through style. To such men as the martyr and poet Robert Southwell he can stand only in allegorical relation, reasonable in the face of "The Absolute Reasonableness of Robert Southwell." The poet is not a martyr—he is more often the penitent knitting editor than the persecuted Mandelstam—but certain conditions of the poetic act can be more easily comprehended in the martyr's constraint of language. The comparison is grotesque and attractive: most poets would flatter themselves as persecuted or even prosecuted outsiders, sacrificing to bring the black letter, the true Word, to countrymen starved of religion. The pressure on language a sense of moral responsibility occasions, whether fantasized or simply aggrandized, is a tension of style. It is not the only time in these essays that the tension of such relation uncovers some anxiety in Hill's own poetry.

Style is not merely the measure of speech but the manner of silence; and behind Southwell's eloquence, in speech or in silence under torture, lies "violence and coarse preciosity and disgust." What Southwell achieves is an equity, a reasonableness that transfigures the violence ranged against him. Even the possibility of evisceration may be transformed, acknowledged, and accepted by conceit: he writes to a colleague in Rome, "You have 'fishes' there greatly wanted here, which, 'when disembowelled, are good for anointing to the eyes and drive the devils away,' while, if they live, 'they are necessary for useful medicines.'" If poetry makes nothing happen, it need not collude with the violence the world outside it offers. That is the religious vocation Hill would command for poetry: to accept injustice and atrocity and return moderation if not mildness. The martyr understood both the reparations such a course required ("how well verse and vertue sute together") and the cost of such equity in sacrifice. The cost is sacrifice, but the reward is serenity realized through acceptance and transfiguration, "achieved in the full awareness of the realities of spiritual and legal violence."

The poet is often at odds with his time, with the circumstances his time has contrived, and this may be an estrangement felt or a division recognized. It is not as a moralist that Hill, after establishing the guilts inherent in language, speaks of the poet "necessarily bearing his peculiar unnecessary shame in a world growing ever more shameless." Here the estrangement is shamelessly embraced (as the "renewed sense of a vocation"), and no one who has twisted in the coils of Hill's poetry will fail to detect the sinuous self-gratifications in such a remark. Any poet may take pleasure when he has convinced himself what he has said can be said no better; but the pleasure takes a caustic wash of pride when the poet relishes, however thinly, the travails of his difficulty.

Such divisiveness is internal and subjective, however external and objective its effects. Against it must be set the public divisions that may menace the poetry and even the poet himself. Southwell was martyred but not for being a poet. Jonson's thumb was branded for murder, and only benefit of clergy saved him from the scaffold. Still, it is well to remember he almost lost his nose and ears over the libelous statements in *Eastward Ho!* and that he was imprisoned for his share in *The Isle of Dogs.* The question that most deeply afflicts Hill's criticism, the shudder at the heart of much of his poetry, is whether the poet can respond to his time without either compromising with or being compromised by it. The essays on Southwell, Jonson, Shakespeare, and Swift trace the strategies of reaction and restraint used by these poets to moderate different circumstances of menace.

The poet who does not face death may face something worse than inconvenience, and art may serve a public discretion whatever its private serenity. Southwell may have tried to evade capture because evasion was a moral duty, but he was not trying to evade the penalty of his Catholicism. The moderations of his prose and verse were inner notations against an outer threat, a threat whose death sentences no sentences of his could make worse. Jonson and Shakespeare were forced to practice their craft under the dangerously shifting claims of Elizabethan and Jacobean politics. In both dramatists the subversive is voiced, but usually under the restraint of characters evil, corrupted, or betrayed. In a medium hemmed in by official censors, the subversive must be subverted if it is to challenge official myths. The playwrights are allowed the confrontation between ideas without the risk of being called to account for them. The tactfulness of this art ensures that ambiguity is not damned as equivocation; but, as Hill notes, the dramatists "contract out of direct commitment" when the commitment would be to sedition. The compromise is not compromising, unless we believe playwrights should sacrifice their ears and noses to the waywardness of their tongues. The artist can be true to his art without being untrue to himself: Jonson spent a decade composing court masques.

It is a matter of great importance to Hill and to his work that the artist not be confused with the ideas he manipulates. Certain effects and certain understandings may be reached only through artistic detachment. His model is the artist, like Jonson, who "redeems what he can." The reader who believes in the official myth of freedom of speech may find this nonsense, even subversive nonsense. He might study with instruction the libel actions that have been so expensive to *Private Eye* or the official prosecution within the past decade of a "blasphemous" poem. The incidents are English, but in England *Romeo and Juliet* is not censored in secondary schools. In any society there are things that cannot be said and times when an artist like Hill must quote Pisanio: "Wherein I am false, I am honest; not true, to be true."

Swift's problem was different but no less dangerous. There was £300 on his head after *The Public Spirit of the Whigs* and another £300 after *Drapier's Letters*. The printer of *A Proposal for the Universal Use of Irish Manufacture* was prosecuted. For an upholder of public order Swift did his best to undermine it. Hill isolates in him the tension between Tory stoicism and wanton destructiveness, not as ideas the artist contemplates but as contraries his imagination embodies. If Swift enlisted as an artist what he loathed as a moralist, it would explain what Hill defines as his ambiguous attitude to anarchy: "In principle he abhorred all its aspects . . . ; pragmatically he played along with it to some extent; poetically he reacted to it with a kindling of creative delight." You could define in Hill a similarly ambiguous attitude to order.

The artist is often attracted to what might destroy him, whether anarchy or an excess of order; and it is the responsibility of his art to transfigure that destructive element, the element that may be responsible for the art itself. The art must transfigure, not just the warring tendencies of the artist's imagination, but the dissonant divisions of his life. The disorders of the imagination may be discomfiting, perhaps even maddening, an estrangement felt; but the external disorders, or excesses of order, endanger the artist's life with his livelihood. Hill, always alert to the daily conditions of an artist's hazard, locates Swift in the governing class of an Ireland that did not want to be governed. Shakespeare and Jonson among the censors, Southwell among the priest-catchers: the circumstances of difficulty released the creative energies such circumstances were transformed by. In this way defeat (and Swift felt Ireland a defeat) may be converted, just as, in those poems where defeat is the poet's condition, "wit converts the necessary failure into moral and rhetorical victory." Hill aspires to the reactionary poetry of which he has often been accused only in the sense that he uses "reaction" of Swift: not as "a supposedly 'retrograde tendency' in politics or . . . a 'revulsion' of feeling" but "the capacity to be at once resistant and reciprocal." To redeem the time is to redeem yourself.

Hill's essay on "Redeeming the Time" is nominally "An enquiry into the nature of rhythm," the rhythm of speech disrupted in the nineteenth century. Each century requires its concessions, and those who oppose them must adopt methods of resistance in the language itself; these resistances are evident in the poetry and the prose, raw speech and arguments cooked in speech. The essay opens in opposition to an assertion by Iris Murdoch that "the nineteenth century, where the disruptive forces were not only dispossessed and weak, but incoherent, disunited, and speechless, could think itself a single world." Hill thinks this is nonsense, not even seductive nonsense; but the form of his opposition is peculiar and sidling: "Faced with such a statement by so manifestly intelligent a writer one looks nervously for a hidden language-game." To call someone "manifestly intelligent" is to call that intelligence into question. And "nervously," even in a writer as nervous as Geoffrey Hill, offers more than a hint of Uriah Heep squeezing his hands. It is the nervousness of someone about to be caught in the act, for no sooner is the possibility of a language game in Murdoch rejected than language games begin furtively to infiltrate the essay.

Such games are not usually worth notice; but for motives that are only gradually clarified Hill prefers, in this as in the opening essay, to argue through a perversely coiled and indwelling mimesis. It is not for pleasure that the rhetoric prepares to mirror the reason, though pleasure may issue from the small recognitions and reciprocities these games entail. The pleasure, say, when praise of "a brief comic masterstroke in counterpoint" is immediately counterpointed by an example of failure, or when Engels's description of England as "the classic soil of . . . transformation" is transformed to serve a description of an English orator: "The 'classic' oration of a tribune of the people suffers a grotesque 'transformation,' 'soiled' by the outflow of a fractured tradition." The pleasure, say, of a tenuous transition between paragraphs immediately followed by Coleridge's suspicion that *The Spectator* had "innocently contributed to the general taste for unconnected writing" or of the key phrase "recurrent responses" in George Eliot parroted by this attack of recurrent responses in Hill: "'familiar rhythm' is both liturgical and extraliturgical, telling of a rhythm of social duties, rites, ties and obligations from which an individual severs himself or herself at great cost and peril, but implying also the natural sequences of stresses and slacks in the thoughts and acts." I'd be ready to dismiss such appealing torments as, well, tormented appeals, if Hill had not written that "It should not be thought, however, that in referring to the possibility of a 'language-game' one is being lightly dismissive."

The explanation lies in the arguments about rhythm. "Rhythm," Hill writes, "is . . . more than a physiological motor. It is capable of registering, mimetically, deep shocks of recognition." If rhetoric is rhythm, or obtains rhythm, it too is capable of rendering these deep shocks as part of the drama of reason. The "drama of reason" is Coleridge's term for his parentheses, devices that contradict and condition the growth of argument, preventing argument from sliding into the subsidies of self-agreement. Staging that drama requires, as Hill makes clear, the "antiphonal voice of the heckler," the "cross-rhythms and counterpointings which ought, for the sake of proper strategy and of good faith, to be part of the structure of such writing." There is danger in such drama: to take account of such conflicting forces, to allow yourself to be sensitive to the disjunctions of argument and not merely the cozy proprieties of the age, may be "to risk convolution and incommunicability," whatever your admiration for plain speech.

The issue for Hill is a sacrifice, the sacrifice of "a powerful and decent desire, the desire to be immediately understood by 'a common well-educated thoughtful man, of ordinary talents.'" The structure of the style that results is peculiar and peculiarly familiar: "a recognition and a resistance; it is parenthetical, antiphonal, it turns upon itself." It is of course the style of these essays. Hill must turn to Hopkins, that figure of resistance to nineteenth-century rhythmical life, for what may fairly be regarded as a justification of his own long toils in verse and prose, both opaque to the common well-educated thoughtful man:

> Plainly if it is possible to express a sub[t]le and recondite thought on a subtle and recondite subject in a subtle and recondite way and with great felicity and perfection, in the end, something must be sacrificed, with so trying a task, in the process, and this may be the being at once, nay perhaps even the being without explanation at all, intelligible.

Such prose, periodic to the point of Jamesian annoyance, full to satiety with "recurrent responses," coldly smothers its own simplicities. The prose is unfortunate, but the perception is not. The alternative for Hill is a different and more disagreeable sacrifice, the sacrifice to "a certain laxity in the use of language" John Stuart Mill found "must be borne with, if a writer makes himself understood." Although the dichotomy is hardly convincing, it has a convincing application to the critic who asserts it and whose work assents to it. Hill's fear, as critic and poet, is that surrendering to the laxities of the time, to "the very inertia of general taste," would be surrendering the complexities that might redeem it.

Coleridge, Hill believes, "surely foresaw the obligation to enact the drama of reason within the texture of one's own work." *Surely* is surely a plea, and the sly insinuation of *one's* for *his* ought to remind us, if the language games do not, that Hill seizes the obligation as his own. The language games, however frivolous, are the minor mimesis of a major enterprise: the drama of reason the verse and prose are elsewhere attempting. Self-indulging and seemingly irrelevant, they form a template for reinforcing ideas in the identity of a style. They echo in rhetoric the moment of rhythm on which the essay turns: the "change of time-signature" that quickens the opening of the ninth stanza of Wordsworth's "Ode: Intimations of Immortality from Recollections of Early Childhood":

> *O joy! that in our embers*
> *Is something that doth live . . .*

Hopkins thought the change magical; Hill believes it "perhaps the greatest moment in nineteenth-century English poetry." By breaking the rhythm the poem has previously settled upon and settled into, by registering a shock in a change of speech, it acknowledges that disturbance these meditations on an antiphonal, resistant style derive from. The lines respond not just in their rhythm but in their reason to the argument that language must provide these recognitions, whatever the sacrifice. Only through such sacrifices may the time be redeemed.

Or so the poet would like to believe. It is comforting and even consoling to be bound ethically to the very choice your inclination would make. No time can be redeemed through the ethical intuitions or rhythmical grumblings of its poets. To make this redemption a vocation, as Hill claims for Hopkins and as I claim for Hill, is to accept the terms of your own defeat. That defeat may be the poet's reasonable and even acceptable condition is a proposition that might command Hill's assent: "There are triumphs that entrap and defeats that liberate." As poet and as critic, Hill has consistently flinched from the triumphs that entrap, if triumph entails conditioning your language to the taste of others. However, his unctuous and insincere handwringing (the apparition of Uriah Heep appears again) over the sacrifice of that "powerful and decent desire," to be understood by the ordinary reader, reminds us that defeat can be relished all too eagerly.

The subtheme of "Redeeming the Time" is the danger of compromise, and the two companion essays offer cautionary examples in John Crowe Ransom and T. H. Green. Green, the Victorian idealist philosopher, succumbed in the conflict between "writing to be received, and . . . conducting a running battle with the premisses of current receptivity." Because he ignored language *as* moral action in favor of language *about* moral action, his ideas are no longer alive in his language and "his lectures now seem heavy with the diffuseness of paraphrase rather than tense with the bafflements of communication." A less fastidious critic might say Green simply could not write well, but Hill would isolate in that *well* a moral sickness only the precise use of language can cure. The problem is as brutal as its probity: the compromised use of language offends its moral nature. By ministering to the desires and derangements of his audience the writer places himself, or at least his work, beyond redemption, and becomes the negative example of a positive obligation.

The essay on Ransom requires the most exacting formulation of that demand: "the double consequence of a poet's involvement with language is complicity and revelation." When this formula is repeated, however, "double consequence" becomes "double-consequence," suggesting by renovating accident or cunning revision that complicity and revelation may be brought into malignant equilibrium, may even disastrously intermingle, a complicity to revelation, a revelation in complicity. That is the particular and telling failure of John Crowe Ransom: his revelations were purchased at the cost of complicity. Although Hill is never slow to admire a virtue, he will not tolerate a writer's "coy indulgence of the 'humble reader.'" There are errors, even knowledgeable errors, but there can be no forgiveness (not even by the most 'umble person) when a writer, even a writer as uncompromising as Ransom, "has been led . . . to mistake compromise for communication." To indulge the reader out of whatever generous motive or genuine mistake is license, and against this Hill erects the standard of an implicit regard if not an explicit belief: "It is possible for a poet to serve the integrity of thought and language in the exemplary nature of his constraint."

That constraint may be observed wherever the poet is tempted to abandon it, most conveniently in the laboratory of his revisions. There Ransom occasionally found it possible to "clear his meaning," even after a lapse of decades and the failure of intervening experiments. This was the rare fortune in an unfortunate tendency, for otherwise he was "gripped by a 'mania' which drove him . . . to the ruinous rewriting" of earlier work. Hill's own restraint may be measured in the fussy integrity of the small adjustments scattered through his *Collected Poems* (1985). Except to correct some unfortunate hyphenation in the prose stanzas of *Mercian Hymns* (1971) (in one case clearing the ambiguity of certain "male- / factors" who ought to have been more prosaic "mal- / efactors"), he has rarely tampered with his later books. The minor revisions betray an intelligence afflicted with coercive responsibilities, coercions no more evident than in his admission: "I have felt impelled to alter words and phrases here and there. I have changed only those details which have become a burden over the years."

Burdens that impel are not opportunities grasped: the amendments disclose a moral resistance more than an aesthetic renewal

and express belated penitence rather than timely possibility. "Words
and phrases" is perhaps an aggrandizing phrase: of some sixty textual changes only seven concern matters more grave than punctuation or spelling. That is not to take lightly the details that weigh
heavily upon Hill: a small change of punctuation may signify a great
change of heart. Even so, such adjustments mostly modify a rhythm
or remove an eyesore. The separation provided by a parenthesis,
that drama of reason, hardly needs to be reinforced with external
dashes; and a mature directness has chastened whatever youthful
delicacy was responsible by dropping the dashes or removing the
parenthesis. Still, there is a distinction, perhaps even a magnifying
difference, in the detachment that "Shrunken, magnified—(nest,
holocaust)—/ Not half innocent and not half undone" surrenders to
"Shrunken, magnified (nest, holocaust) / Not half innocent and not
half undone" ("Of Commerce and Society"). Dashes are elsewhere
denied, the awkward precision of "From bitter—as from sweet—
grapes bled" becoming the more comfortable blurring of alter-
natives, "From bitter as from sweet grapes bled" ("The Bidden
Guest"). Some gulfs are widened, others narrowed: a dash or a semicolon promoted to a period; a semicolon demoted to a comma. In
"Funeral Music," what was the World becomes the world.

One does not have to admire the individual changes to admire the
meticulous nature that has found them necessary. The sober critic
corrects his youthful indiscretions most stringently by tempering to
dour statements a number of spirited exclamations: "Those varied
dead" are deader now than when they were exulted as "Those varied
dead!" ("Metamorphoses"); "O visited women, possessed sons!" are
more solemnly invoked as "O visited women, possessed sons" ("Annunciations"); the expectation of "Love, oh my love, it will come /
Sure enough!" now adopts the resignation of "Sure enough" ("The
Songbook of Sebastian Arrurruz"). A change of heart.

Elsewhere a change of mind. Lowell might have made seven grave
alterations in one edition and changed them back again in the next.
Hill's nature does not adapt easily to correction because correction
always admits an original mistake. He would shudder at any aes-

thetic practice that eagerly contemplated a shifting range of potential additions and contractions, alterations and corrections. The burdens must impel: the unhappy note of plump vulgarity (or perhaps grim tautology) in "By day I cleansed my pink tongue" must be narrowed and cleansed, must become more nastily vulpine as "my thin tongue" ("Three Baroque Meditations"). The passively functional "railway-sidings" in "An Apology for the Revival of Christian Architecture in England" are exchanged for the more actively dangerous "railway-crossings," resonant with the central crux to which Hill is always attracted (and thereby averting the collision of "lop-sided" and "railway-sidings" in adjacent lines). The submissively leaden "accrued," in a hymn on Offa's coins (*Mercian Hymns* XII), is transmuted into the more visually aggressive "raked up": "I have raked up a golden and stinking blaze." Blazes are rarely accrued. It would not do, in "God's Little Mountain," to have the devil's cloven hoof silently associate with "And yet the sky was cloven." The poem is about the absence of gods, not the presence of devils. The association has already been prepared by "a goat / dislodging stones" and a mountain that "stamped its foot." The sky must therefore be "riven," not "cloven."

The burden of beginnings weighs more heavily. It is perverse and perversely attractive that, of all his poems, Hill has been impelled to alter most severely the one that stands first, the myth of artistic creation, "Genesis." It may be a sensible act of violence to maintain that the "tough pig-headed salmon" are "Ramming the ebb, in the tide's pull." Critics can seldom question confidently a voice so confident in its ambiguity, but the change invites the doubt the salmon were ever sensibly "Curbing the ebb and the tide's pull," unless they were very large salmon. The "glove-winged albatross" has lost its gloves, become the more prosaic "long-winged albatross." Hill may finally have seen an albatross in flight and thought better of his metaphor, or he may have been annoyed to find "glove" in this poem, "cloven" in the next, and "glove" and cleave" in the one after that. The final change is also the first, not amendment but deletion. Where there was once

Against the burly air I strode,
Where the tight ocean heaves its load,
Crying the miracles of God,

there remains

Against the burly air I strode
Crying the miracles of God.

The contraction expels an influence, the Lowell whose "Where the heel-headed dogfish barks its nose" is still archly present in the "tough pig-headed salmon." It expels an influence and accepts for the speaker a deepened isolation, his labor stripped of setting, no longer doubled and dramatized by the ocean's struggle against its own weight. The sea is first brought to bear only in the second stanza, as if the speaker had a hand in its creation. A burden has been removed: the ocean no longer heaves its load. The acknowledging pun does penance for the excision.

The scarcity of these revisions registers a difficulty, not a complacence. That difficulty in turn measures the penitence of an earlier alteration, the reprinting in *King Log* (1968) of a poem from *For the Unfallen* (1959), then out of print. Hill's note read: "I dislike the poem very much, and the publication of this amended version may be regarded as a necessary penitential exercise." The poem was "In Memory of Jane Fraser," and aside from a few trivial changes in punctuation the amendment consisted of altering the final line from "And a few sprinkled leaves unshook" to "Dead cones upon the alder shook."* Some authorial discomfort with the verb "unshook" is understandable, but the wording of the corrective note is odd, even strikingly odd: Hill seems to say he is reprinting the poem *because* he dislikes it, a form of penance for having written it. If this goes too far, "I dislike the poem very much" goes well beyond disagreement with

*There is error even in correction: Peter Robinson in "Reading Geoffrey Hill" unrepentantly renders the line as "Dead leaves upon the alder shook" (Peter Robinson, ed., *Geoffrey Hill: Essays on His Work* [Philadelphia: Open University Press, 1985]).

a line and seems to carry dislike even into the amended version. The new version carried the subtitle "An Attempted Reparation," which may seem to conclude the matter more simply; but the act, whether simple or compound, advertised self-flagellation. Perhaps Hill felt the need to make amends for a bad line, but not at the cost of allowing readers to think he admired the poem. Another poet would have revised the poem and reprinted it without comment. The reparation, its punctuation repaired, is now silently entered in the editions of *For the Unfallen* and *Collected Poems.*

In the great burden he places upon revision, however minute, Hill shows the strength of purpose he would muster against those who cannot take seriously the moral obligations of poetic language. The burden may be no less sharply felt even if such changes are neurotically motivated or dramatized. The epigraph to Hill's final essay, "Our Word Is Our Bond," reads in part: "We can issue an utterance of any kind whatsoever, in the course, for example, of acting a play or making a joke or writing a poem—in which case of course it would not be seriously meant." The philosopher so irresponsibly responsible is J. L. Austin. Hill would rescue poetry from those empiricist philosophers who believe it a parasitic use of language, but to defend poetry against some of its enemies he must protect it from some of its friends. Empiricists like Austin cast poetry beyond the "actual languages" that alone deserve study into the outer dark of the "ideal languages." The bias against poetic language and in favor of plain speech or plain prose unites, Hill argues, even such seventeenth-century philosophical adversaries as Hobbes and the Cambridge Platonists. Poetic language, that infected medium of metaphor, will not serve the philosophers: first, it clouds the supposedly transparent discourse philosophy requires; and second, although it can speak, it cannot enact, cannot mean seriously what it seriously says. It forms easily but imperfectly performs, and for Austin "a performative utterance will . . . be *in a peculiar way* hollow or void if said by an actor on the stage, or if introduced in a poem." The poems cannot stand by their words, cannot say *our word is our bond.*

Against such antagonists, poetry cannot maintain its claims when even its friends are prepared to cede its position. Sidney meant to defend poetry when he said, "Now for the *Poet*, he nothing affirmeth, and therefore never lieth." It is not unreasonable to suggest, though Hill does not suggest it, that a language that cannot lie cannot tell the truth. This would hardly perturb most poets, who have an elastic and expedient regard for truth, though that does not make them politicians, or priests. The retreat may be galling to some, but it is galling to Hill in the intensely personal way that implies the infection of public argument with private motive. We are returned to Stevens: "After one has abandoned a belief in god, poetry is that essence which takes its place as life's redemption." It cannot redeem if it is falsified in its very nature, falsified by not ever being false. It cannot even ransom a poet from the academics, and these essays in part attempt to redeem him on their ground and in their terms.

Sidney's proposition temptingly relieves the poet of responsibility to the world, if not the imagination. The status of poetry is secured, but at the cost of the poet accepting "that his art is a miniature emblem or analogy of res publica rather than a bit of real matter lodged in the body politic." That will not satisfy poets who require redemption from their art, though Hill does not deny that an art acceding to such limitations can be real and responsive. It knows its place, but what he requires is an art that does not, that wrestles with "dark and disputed matter." The views are incompatible and mutually incomprehensible, felicity versus perplexity, cure versus infection, wit's providence versus wit's anarchy. The comedians claim "the undoing of language is . . . the making of it"; the melodramatists mutter "its very making is its undoing."

Hill appreciates that temperament may incline a poet to a certain view and the constraints of a practice, in his case the melodramatic view and practice that "In a poet's involvement with language, above all, there is . . . an element of helplessness, of being at the mercy of accidents, the prey of one's own presumptuous energy." Someone "at the mercy of accidents" (and even a "meticulous reader of proof" may fail to notice the quotation mark inadvertently dropped from *Mercian Hymns* XX in *Collected Poems*) may be unnaturally sensitive to the intent and designs of others. The matter of his defense is the manner of his reconciliation; and in conciliatory manner he notices first that, despite their intentions, the philosophers cannot keep infection from their language. They indulge in "nuanced play," oblige the poetry inherent in prose, and measure their words not precisely to their uses but in excess of them. The infection is inherent in words cooperatively employed, in "ordinary circumstances" and "ordinary language," and so what might have merely been registered must be insisted upon: that there is "'dark and disputed matter' implicated in the nature of language itself." The comedians and the melodramatists realize separate halves of a complex relation: *our word is our bond* as "reciprocity, covenant, fiduciary symbol" versus "shackle, arbitrary constraint, closure of possibility." If language is a reciprocal shackle, an arbitrary covenant, it discovers its possibilities at the very moment it seems closed off from them, though, as Ransom noted, "The density or connotativeness of poetic language reflects the world's density." Where the world is poised against the word, it is poised in the word: it was perhaps by the "mercy of accidents" that in the *Poetry Book Society Bulletin* (autumn 1968) recommending *King Log* the first line of "Annunciations" read, not "The Word has been abroad, is back," but "The World has been abroad, is back."

To recognize a substance is not to recover a status. Poetry can impose no sanction for its statements: they lack the essential "hereby" that converts the words proposed into the act accomplished (the "comic subplot" of the essay is Ezra Pound's entanglements with the verdicts of criticism and the verdicts of courts). If modern poetry is to satisfy its desire for a "sense of identity between saying and doing," a desire no less admirable whether it reflects a general demand or a particular need, it must return to those understandings that implicate verbal obligation with moral necessity, verbal precision with moral exactness. A working formula for Hill, one that accounts for the moral appeal within the appearance of language, is Kenneth Burke's definition of "workmanship" as "a trait in which the ethical and the esthetic are one." The status of poetry cannot merely be asserted, as Pound could assert that "all values ultimately come from our judicial sentences"; it must be won instance by instance and line by line. The obligation Hill embraces leaves the poet under continual threat, every word a risk, every rhythm a warning: "The status fought for, and accomplished, within the comedy and melodrama of this sequence, is, therefore, that of standing by one's words in a variety of tricky situations." The sequence is *Homage to Sextus Propertius*, but the application is to *The Mystery of the Charity of Charles Péguy:* "Must men stand by what they write . . . ?"

If the status of poetry can be recovered in prose, Hill secures his claim not by his shrewd examples but by his shrewish style. The prose erects the standard it can otherwise only assert, by its strict attention to the possibilities of language within the medium of argument. The position of poetry is an ancient matter, an ancient matter "dark and disputed," and its defense takes place in such charged provisions, "stratagems of the out-manoeuvred man, / the charge and counter-charge." But prose is never wholly sufficient to the necessity of poetry. It is no merciful accident that the only poetry to prove this status is the poetry of atonement, redemption, and bondage Hill has reserved as his domain, the poetry for which Péguy is a sacrificial figure. Martyred for his words, he provides the concluding Passion to the mission of artistic creation begun in "Genesis": "To ravage and redeem the world." The new testament completes the old; the death for words repays the beginning that was the Word.

It is difficult to feel warmth for such difficult splendors or for the moral obligations that prescribe them. The demands made are also denials, the restorations also restrictions. Hill stands by his words by standing apart from everything else, proud of an authority no one wishes to dispute because no one cares to be lord of such limited wasteground. The brilliance of his poetry cannot go unmarked, however limited its effect, however stunted its appeal. It judges the time, and the time stares back blankly. Geoffrey Hill's magnificence is the magnificence of a refusal; and if the poetry, with its tormented recognition of the ethical matter within an aesthetic manner, has been the unacknowledged legislator of the prose, the prose has slowly argued for just such sacrifice and just such fulfillment. To ask otherwise would be absolutely unreasonable.

A Letter
from
Britain

To imagine a language is to imagine a form of life.

WITTGENSTEIN

In 1992 Britain will disappear into the EEC; a state among states, it
will lose its sovereignty, its currency, the control of its borders. The
pound, like the franc and the mark, will eventually be replaced by
the ECU, which young currency dealers in the City, with cunning
intuition of such matters, are already calling the *icky*.* The changes
necessary to social and political life have scarcely been understood,
perhaps scarcely imagined. Britain is living in the ashes of old Europe; and if the founding of a newspaper called the *European* has
been premature, the impulse is the impulse of foresight.

A young British poet faces a more attenuated and more arid condition than a young American. This is not in itself a bad thing,

*Or so matters stood in 1990. The opponents of a united Europe have fought a
long rear-guard action, and the delays are likely to extend into the next century. The
EEC (European Economic Community) became more generally the EC and then
the EU (European Union), and the ECU was renamed the Euro.

though a surprising number of intellectuals in both countries believe starvation is good for poetry. In Britain there are no graduate writing programs in poetry (and only two in fiction, one of which may admit a poet by accident). The American fondness for writing programs is treated with amused condescension if not contempt. Among the sentimentalities still central to British character is the sanctity of the amateur; the world-class cricketer is paid little better than a cab driver. This aversion to poetry workshops derives not just from the fear of what one journalist calls "the American model of high professionalism and low quality," but from prejudice against the formal study of contemporary literature. There are still professors who believe any poet after Tennyson should be read only in private. As for the poets themselves, when Douglas Dunn arrived to teach at the University of Hull, Philip Larkin drew him aside and said, "There's too much poetry on this campus. I'm relying on you to stamp it out."

A poet not discouraged by the attitude may be discouraged by the consequence. Because there are no writing programs, there are no real terms of employment for the poet in the university. The scattered positions of writer-in-residence rarely last longer than a year. British poets are therefore more variously employed, though they concentrate in journalism and publishing. Far too many are virtually unemployed, living piecemeal on the fringes of literary journalism, occasionally invited to a literary festival, an Arvon Foundation course (five-day residential workshops in the country—the only version of the workshop to gain currency), or a poetry reading. The readings are ill paid ($100 is an average fee) and often ill attended. Only a few of the small Arts Council grants are given to poets.

Poetry in the literary magazines is, like British Rail, not dying but endangered. There is no contemporary equivalent of the *Criterion* or *New Verse*, and nothing like the rich variety of American magazines. The most successful literary magazine, *Granta*, doesn't publish poetry. The *New Statesman & Society*, the *Listener,* and the *Literary Review* have given up serious poetry. The *TLS*, the *London Review of Books*, *Encounter,* and the *Spectator* still keep up the tradition, though it is seen as a tradition, and therefore mere obligation or quaint survival. While the significant literary magazines can be counted almost on one hand, their tastes tend to be severe and personal. (Of how many American magazines can that be said?) The list includes, is almost exhausted by, *Agenda, Critical Quarterly, PN Review, Poetry Review*, and *Stand*. The interesting magazines of smaller ambition or scope are *Ambit*, the *Honest Ulsterman, Margin, Quarto, Temenos*, and *Verse*. There are numerous little magazines, few of any quality. By common consent, magazines are a vacant ecological niche in the literary scene. It is hard to know whether the lack of editorial will is responsible for some of the shallows of current poetry, or whether even a great poetry cannot thrive without some constant public outlet. Poets no longer expect—perhaps they never expected—to publish in magazines all the poems they gather into a book. In their acknowledgment pages the same four or five magazines recur, nobly but depressingly.

Trade publishers are only marginally concerned with poetry (they share their distaste with American houses), and most young poets interest a trade publisher only if they win one of the three major poetry competitions. Faber and Faber, Chatto and Windus, and Oxford have large and distinguished lists, and Century-Hutchinson, Secker and Warburg, and Penguin smaller but not inferior ones. Those six houses, however, published fewer than two dozen books by British poets in 1989. The small presses are more lively, and in the same period Bloodaxe, Carcanet, Anvil, Enitharmon, Peterloo, and Seren (*Poetry Wales*) published almost fifty titles.* The small presses provide a necessary alternative to the careful tastes of the large houses and receive the respect and attention reserved for uni-

*A decade later the publishers have thinned. In the fall of 1998, Oxford abandoned its poetry list. There was public uproar; but, by the time Oxford relented and came to a joint agreement with Carcanet, many poets had departed for other publishers. Some years earlier Chatto and Windus let its series decline. Century-Hutchinson and Secker and Warburg are no longer active—the only new publishers among trade houses are Cape and Picador. Smaller houses, especially Bloodaxe and Carcanet, have proved wily and adaptable, though no publisher of poetry goes far into the black and most need subsidies to survive. Among the magazines, there have been further extinctions.

versity presses in America. They are perennially rumored to be in financial straits, though serious poetry sells remarkably well in Britain. In a country with a fifth the population of the United States, almost any old book of poetry can sell a thousand copies. Few American books do as well.

An American view of poetry in Britain is partly an explanation of America. The qualities distinctive to an outsider—even one, like myself, who has often been in residence—may be those that repair the absences of home. They might not seem even worth comment to the British, whose anxieties of tradition are different, though we are haunted by many of the same figures and open to many of the same influences. The aspect of a climate, the accidents of historical accretion, and various estrangements of language have all had effect in the literature; and any view of the estrangements or the accidents must be only a translation, with all the usual error and accommodation. What follows is not a comprehensive survey of British and Irish poetry, but a private and perhaps partial taxonomy.

The Old Guard

Since the death of Philip Larkin in 1985, the appreciations of the British have fallen to Seamus Heaney, Geoffrey Hill, and Ted Hughes. As an Irish poet writing in English, Heaney has been afflicted by the betrayals of language that have left the Irish at war with themselves, and in themselves. For the Irish, language is still a political question, and the tensions in Heaney's work have therefore been more intimate than the affectations of Hill or Hughes. Those tensions have been less a statement than a series of absorptions, and the broader scale of his recent work has disaffected those who prefer the muddy, hoarse, ingrown poems before *Field Work* (1979). Heaney has not written continually to his strengths through the eighties—the middle voice of Lowell has too frequently been echoed in fraternal piety, and his translation *Sweeney Astray* (1984 [UK, 1983]) was half-hearted and clumsy. Nevertheless, his equable tone and linguistic resource, which includes the ability to skate prettily along the surface of language and then plunge deeply into ancient turmoil, conjures up—still too rarely and too fitfully—the mastery of Yeats. Heaney's poetry has suffered the palsy of early canonization, but his criticism was given new spur by his election in 1989 as Professor of Poetry at Oxford. Proudly Romantic, though veined with an austere and old-fashioned responsibility, it has spoken more comprehendingly of the art within the art than any prose since Eliot's.

Geoffrey Hill's austerities have left him an unwelcome presence among British poets. *The Mystery of the Charity of Charles Péguy* (1984) is the most important long English poem since *Four Quartets*; but its cold analysis of religious grace, or disgrace, its self-befouling language games, its marmoreal grandeur, and its difficulty have not permitted it a full appreciation. In a time that has placed its premiums on colloquial insight and easy confession, such a poet's religious qualms are apt to seem queer and forced, as a hothouse plant is forced. Hill was perhaps the only serious poet over forty not mentioned as a candidate for Poet Laureate after the death of John Betjeman; yet no other poet in England has written with his attention to the intensities of the British past and the British landscape, or with his deep sense of the guilt of history and language. The few poems he has published since *Péguy* have reworked the old ground and the old grandeur, and—as so often with Hill—have made self-parody seem a moral provision.

Ted Hughes has written some cheerfully awful and intensely mediocre poems as Poet Laureate. Few things in literature are more depressing than watching a poet mellow into mediocrity, beyond mediocrity, at the price of a butt of sack. Hughes has been a spent force in British poetry for some years, perhaps some decades—there is little in his work after *Wodwo* (1967) except grandiosity, which is very different from grandeur. His most recent book, *Wolfwatching* (1991 [UK, 1989]), has a few moments of the old mystic passion and muscular phrase; but the tone is so frequently embarrassing, so acutely childish, that you wonder if he has lost his hearing:

> *Already dead*
> *The Rhino cried*

From a puddle of blood
Almost dried
In the African dust:
"What can you know
Of wrong or right
Of evil or good?
You are the crime."

Hughes has been generous to fellow poets and to the art, but he long ago contracted the maladies of sentiment that seem to hit muscular poets in middle age and have enervated poets like Galway Kinnell and James Dickey.

The Younger Guard

The categories that follow are a mental inconvenience. Poets rarely choose their alliances or their line of descent, and there are probably subterranean faults and pressures a surface taxonomy cannot reveal—cannot even comprehend. The measure of a poetry is not so much the fittings as the ill-fittings, and there are three poets who deserve consideration beyond the compressions of categories.

James Fenton is the most diversely gifted poet of his generation, with beguiling technical resource and a sweet-tempered, almost dangerously raffish panache. Who after Byron has lived such a life? He has been a foreign correspondent in Germany, a freelance reporter in Vietnam and Cambodia, theater critic for the *Sunday Times*, and most recently foreign correspondent in the Philippines for the *Independent*. His journalism and travel writing, collected in *All the Wrong Places* (1988), display an amateur's knack for being in the wrong place at the right time: he rode a North Vietnamese tank at the fall of Saigon and helped sack the Marcoses' palace, carrying away a towel embroidered with Imelda's initials. He has translated opera libretti and once joined a disastrously funny expedition to Borneo, recounted in Redmond O'Hanlon's *Into the Heart of Borneo*. Some of this restlessness leaks into the poetry, which has varied from desolate war poems to wry and insubstantial surreal vignettes. His most recent work has been a series of light-verse collaborations with John Fuller, *Partingtime Hall* (1987), and the odd self-published *Manila Envelope* (1989), which included (in a "manila" envelope sent from Manila) a book, a manifesto, a poster, and an ad for the printer. The new poems show the usual graceful intelligence and calm inevitability:

> *The sea sounds insincere*
> *Giving and taking with one hand.*
> *It stopped a river here last month*
> *Filling its mouth with sand.*
>
> *They drag the shallows for the milkfish fry—*
> *Two eyes on a glass noodle, nothing more.*
> *Roused by his vigilant young wife*
> *The drowsy stevedore*
>
> *Comes running barefoot past the swamp*
> *To meet a load of wood.*
> *The yellow peaked cap, the patched pink shorts*
> *Seem to be all his worldly goods.*
>
> *The nipa booths along the coast*
> *Protect the milkfish gatherers' rights.*
> *Nothing goes unobserved. My good custodian*
> *Sprawls in the deckchair through the night.*

("Worldly" was misprinted "wordly" in the original.) Fenton has paid a debt here to Elizabeth Bishop, and elsewhere in his life and work larger debts to Auden. For the past half-year he has been conducting a weekly master class in the *Independent on Sunday*, with insights characteristically shrewd and original. Some of his poetry and some of his prose have been slapdash, but there is no other poet of such imaginative demand and reckless range.

Tony Harrison, though a couple of years older than Seamus Heaney, has been too standoffish to gain easy admission to the old guard. His poetry is abrasively polemical, often a little calculatedly so, engaged by the class wars that still rage deeply beneath a heritage of dialect and place. His work is shot with anger and icy irony, and his language takes its tone from the demotic but its words from a rich literary tradition. A poet of such inner torsion cannot help the furies of his work: his long poem *v.* (1985), about the vandalism of his parents' grave in Leeds, caused a tabloid furor in 1987 when it was read on television. Even in Britain, there are words that may be seen but not heard:

> *The language of this graveyard ranges from*
> *a bit of Latin for a former Mayor*
> *or those who laid their lives down at the Somme,*
> *the hymnal fragments and the gilded prayer,*
>
> *how people "fell asleep in the Good Lord,"*
> *brief chisellable bits from the good book*
> *and rhymes whatever length they could afford,*
> *to CUNT, PISS, SHIT and (mostly) FUCK!*

For a poet so sharp-tongued, so wary of conventional grace, he can be unexpectedly tender and even sentimental when writing of family, though he can be unsentimental as well:

> *He keeps back death the way he keeps back phlegm*
> *in company, curled on his tongue. Once left alone*
> *with the last coal fire in the smokeless zone,*
> *he hawks his cold gobful at the brightest flame,*
> *too practised, too contemptuous to miss.*
>
> *Behind the door she hears the hot coals hiss.*

Beyond his stinging rhymes and dramatic angles (Harrison has done significant work in the theater), there is something self-conscious and staged about his emotions and something opportunistic about his subjects: he seems a lace-curtain radical. His poems are better singly than together, but they have—with a want of subtlety—rare vigor and rhetorical flourish.

Michael Hofmann, with his narrow ground and brooding literary air (his poetry is all dark good looks), is the most talented British poet under forty. He has taken much of his manner from Lowell's

Notebook and made Lowell seem younger, more resonant, less brutish. An existential gloom—I don't think it is as serious as angst—
hangs over his work, which finds little honor and less hope in the
collapse of British society. German by birth (his father is a well-
known German novelist) but educated in England, he has spent
most of the past two decades here, reversing the Berlin journeys of
Auden and Isherwood sixty years ago. In the ravaged English landscape and the crumpled cities he has found adequate symbols of
private despair. The clotted turmoil of his first book gave way to the
more personal arguments of *Acrimony* (1986), with its meditations
on the failed provisions of family:

> *Time isn't money, at our age, it's water.*
> *You couldn't say we cupped our hands very tightly . . .*
> *We missed the second-last train, and find ourselves*
> *at the station with half an hour to kill.*

> *The derelicts queue twice round the tearoom.*
> *Outside, the controlled prostitutes move smoothly*
> *through the shoals of men laughing off their fear.*
> *The street-lamps are a dull coral, snakes' heads.*

No British poet has used the flotsam of British culture with such
force. His prose rhythms are a kind of statelessness.

The Irish

Some of the antagonisms and some of the jealousies of poetry in
Britain derive from problems of definition. There is poetry in Britain, but little British poetry. The Irish have perhaps never been British, despite the long, diseased entanglement whose last symptom is
the occupation of Northern Ireland, which continues only by a brilliant mass hypnosis. The IRA bombings and assassinations in England occur in a culture now almost numbed to atrocity. Catholics in
Northern Ireland (and many Protestants as well) are divorced from
any sense of being British—Seamus Heaney has protested his inclu-
sion in an anthology of British poets. The Scots and the Welsh have
more ancient grievances, and despite more complex assimilations

do not consider themselves British except by fiat or default. Even the English, rulers and ruled, find their allegiances are largely to England, its shires and suburbs. The end of the British Empire has in many ways been the end of Britain.

The English are therefore a constituency, but the Irish are still a culture. The language of Irish poetry, despite the diaspora of Irish poets, deepens toward the treasons of religion and politics. That infection of blood, most apparent in the Irish poets born in, raised in, or schooled in Belfast (Heaney, Derek Mahon, Michael Longley, Paul Muldoon, Tom Paulin, Medbh McGuckian), has created a molecular grouping despite transverse differences of class or the more solitary divide of religion.

Derek Mahon and Michael Longley were, with Seamus Heaney, part of a famous gathering of young poets at Queen's University in the early sixties. They have not written as moodily as Heaney—their temperaments are quieter, more classical, less partial. They have at times found in restraint the moral constituent of Irish verse; though they lack Heaney's brilliant appetites, their lower voices have taken possession of the register of moral irony, whether in Longley's victim and nervous assassin:

> *He collapsed beside his carpet-slippers*
> *Without a murmur, shot through the head*
> *By a shivering boy who wandered in*
> *Before they could turn the television down*
> *Or tidy away the supper dishes.*
> *To the children, to a bewildered wife,*
> *I think "Sorry Missus" was what he said.*

or Mahon's self-incriminating inquisition:

> *The ocean glittered quietly in the moonlight*
> *While heavy metal rocked the discotheques;*
> *Space-age Hondas farted half the night,*
> *Fired by the prospect of fortuitous sex.*
> *I sat late at the window, bland with rage,*
> *And listened to the tumult down below,*

Trying to concentrate on the printed page
*As if such obsolete bumf could save us now.**

Their poetry has provided much of the ground that gives Heaney weight and purpose—he has been a brilliant circumstance, like Yeats, but they have been Irish poetry.

Paul Muldoon has proved bad company for many of the young poets who have read him. Like the young Auden, he has a style that seems as easy to imitate as the face in the mirror; but his sidling wit, his punning foolery (sometimes foolishness), and his cunning little rhythms are particulars of character. Young poets think style can be borrowed like a cup of sugar, and there are many young poets carrying around a cup of sugar stenciled MULDOON. Muldoon's poetry is not always easy to admire—he tends to range through the museum of culture like a child with a credit card. Despite his slightness and chilly ingenuity, his awful mugging mannerism, he has a completely original voice and impetuous charm. In a poem about Auden and others, he has Chester Kallman announce,

Among the miscellaneous
Jack Tars
I met last week in a Sands Street bar

I came on one whose uncircumcised dong's
sand-vein was a seam of beryl, abstruse
as this lobster's.

"Please be more serious," the reader might say. And Muldoon might answer, "I *am* serious."

Tom Paulin has gone from early promise to the consolations of seriousness. His poetry has become ever more withdrawn, cantankerous, obscure, and even obtuse, while his criticism has turned embattled and ideological. He reads each poet against a political index, and through his glasses even Larkin's falling leaves become a falling empire, middle age a code for the failure of the Middle Ages.

*In a later book "bland with rage" became "blind with rage" and "bumf" (British colloquialism for "bum-fodder," or toilet paper, hence a contemptuous term for books or documents) was respelled "bumph."

It would be easy to dismiss Paulin's critical motives, if his insights were less provoking. He is perhaps not the only Irish poet to have ruined his poetry for the political rash.

The Scots

Since the battle of Culloden, Scotland has been an identity without a country. The legal system is still arcane and separate (though often fairer and more just than English law); the banks print pound notes rarely seen south of the border, but the border is only a line on a map. Pride is no substitute for sovereignty. A Scottish poet may write in English, Scots, or Scottish Gaelic, but his poetry is riven by subject more than language. A poet like Sorley Maclean, whose poems are printed bilingually in English and Scottish Gaelic, writes as if there had been no poet after Yeats. In English his poems sound harshly aggregate, as if they had borrowed their manner and roughly worn it out. He and George Mackay Brown are the grand old men of Scottish poetry, but they are proudly backward looking.

The younger poets, many of whom write in English, risk sounding like the English (just as the English risk sounding like Americans). Douglas Dunn, whose first books were redolent with place, has lost the precisions of his voice as his work has become unsettled. The restrictions of place perhaps became a limitation he couldn't abide, but limitation is often the resource of character. He now sounds like almost anyone, and he writes as if he lived almost anywhere. Such assimilation undoubtedly has virtues, though it is hard to think of any.

Scots poetry is unassimilable, and therefore almost ignored in England. I've never seen an appreciation of Tom Scott, whose versions of French, Italian, and Old English poetry have a bracing roughness English translations haven't had since the Elizabethans:

Comes the gloamin hour, the cut-throat's freend;
Comes on sleekit fuit wi wowfish mien.
The lift like an auditorium dims doun,
And Man waits till his change til baest comes round.

Lift means sky, but the thorny surface gives back to Baudelaire some of his strangeness.

It may not be perverse to argue that the most important document in recent Scots poetry has been *The New Testament in Scots* (1983), translated by William Laughton Lorimer:

> *Than they crucified him an* haufed *his* claes amang them, castin caivels, *ilkane for his skair. It wis the beginnin o the forenuin whan he wis crucified. A plaicard wis pitten abuin his heid shawin the chairge again him:*
>
> THE KING O JEWS
>
> *An alang wi him they crucified twa reivers, the tane on his richt haund, an the tither on his left.*
>
> *Aa them at gaed by ill-tung'd him,* geckin their heids.

It would have been a nice touch, a mark of the tacit agonies shared between these cultures, had the card over his head been written in English.

Caribbean Poetry

Black poetry exists largely in the underground of letters. Blacks did not come to Britain in any numbers until 1948, when the *Empire Windrush* docked at Tilbury. The black experience in Britain has been one of almost unrelieved hostility and racism—the casual racism is almost as bad as in the America of the early sixties. Racial attacks against blacks and Asians in the tower blocks and on the large housing estates remain one of the shames of modern Britain. The black riots of the early eighties were one reaction against entrenched poverty and unemployment.

These estrangements find further division in the poetry, particularly in the discriminations between literary and oral traditions. The affiliations of black poetry are largely with the Caribbean—though, as David Dabydeen has remarked, after Trinidad and Jamaica Britain is the largest island in the West Indies. Few young black poets have reached a rapprochement with English letters, and many would regard Derek Walcott as a poet of compromise and collaboration. The English language is still a form of empire.

The choice for many black poets is to temper the language with dialect. Dialect has its dangers—on the rare occasions when he has toyed with it, even Walcott has been unconvincing. You could do philosophy in dialect (recall Benjamin Whorf's belief that some problems in modern physics could be conceived better in Hopi), but to such poets it wouldn't *sound* like dialect, because what they are attempting to render is less a language than the experience of the poor. The exception of Scots suggests how varied and rich the possibilities would be, if the politics of writing change.

I can't do justice on the page to the oral tradition, which often sentimentalizes what it would defend. The black poetry most tormented by self-recognition has been written in the difficult transition, and in the difficult tension, between oral and literary culture. David Dabydeen, born in Guyana but educated in Britain, has been drawn to the histories of coolies and slaves:

> *Now that peasantry is in vogue,*
> *Poetry bubbles from peat bogs,*
> *People strain for the old folk's fatal gobs*
> *Coughed up in grates North or North East*
> *'Tween bouts o' living dialect,*
> *It should be time to hymn your own wreck,*
> *Your house the source of ancient song:*
> *Dry coconut shells cackling in the fireside*
> *Smoking up our children's eyes and lungs,*
> *Plantains spitting oil from a clay pot,*
> *Thick sugary black tea gulped down.*

If the peat bogs are Heaney's, the fatal gobs Tony Harrison's, the measure of British and Irish sentiment has been neatly scalpeled for display.

Fred D'Aguiar, born and now living in London but raised in Guyana, has been influenced by Walcott, though he works with more simplicity and wit, and with some reduction in resonance. He has caught the living movement of dialect ("An we all want custom car / fe bun-up a bit a bichemin / com sataday nite"), but his more severe manner is thick with the concerns of exile:

> *You are a traveller to them.*
> A West Indian working in England;
> A Friday, Tonto, or Punkawallah;
> Sponging off the state. *Our languages*
> *Remain pidgin, like our* dark, third,
> Underdeveloped, *world. I mean, their need*
> *To see our children cow-eyed, pot-bellied,*
> *Grouped or alone in photos and naked,*
> *The light darkened between their thighs.*
> *And charity's all they give.*

The voice is that of "Mama Dot," but the displacements are D'Aguiar's. It is one of the ironies of transition that, by the time such poets are listened to, the transition is over.

In America *black* means of African ancestry; in Britain it means of colored ancestry, and may refer to Africans, Indians and Pakistanis, Melanesians, even Asians. Not *European*, in other words. The ancestry of Caribbean peoples is tangled and confused; when any poet may claim forebears from half a dozen cultures, it is perhaps time to dispense with epithets of color or race.

Women

There must be more than one reason, apart from accidents of talent, to explain why women writing poetry in Britain are as daring as library paste. The most striking young poets in America are women, but the conditions of poetry in America have given women closer and more instructive models. The writing workshop, for all its faults, allows a transition to maturity difficult in the closed shop of British education. The position of women here is less indifferent than it was a decade ago; but, when Fleur Adcock writes of the eighties that "it was our decade," the declaration is hollow. The revised edition of

Edward Lucie-Smith's *British Poetry Since 1945*, published in 1985, contained ninety men and six women, one of them Sylvia Plath.

Most British women poets have a subject but no language—they have allowed the vein of experience to substitute for any formal engagement. The few poets of a different order have either accepted the strength of formal poetry or otherwise evaded the logic of prose. Among older poets, Elizabeth Jennings is venerable, perhaps a little too venerable. She is on the syllabus in secondary schools, and she writes good syllabus poems, the sort that begin, "She kept an antique shop—or it kept her." Occasionally, however, she escapes into a dark, frozen eloquence:

> *I have come into the hour of a white healing.*
> *Grief's surgery is over and I wear*
> *The scar of my remorse and of my feeling.*
>
> *I have come into a sudden sunlit hour*
> *When ghosts are scared to corners. I have come*
> *Into the time when grief begins to flower*
>
> *Into a new love. It had filled my room*
> *Long before I recognized it. Now*
> *I speak its name. Grief finds its good way home.*

To such a poet poise is only poison. Her work is most disquieting when most austerely formal, when rhyme seems her only sanity.

Carol Ann Duffy is a slightly awkward poet, and her poems are almost never successful through their whole progress. She stares at the world with suppressed passion, even suppressed panic, but despite her private terrors her poems are marked by their resilience and generosity. It's easy to list her faults, the half notions or partial arguments, the too easy attraction to characters in psychological extremity; but she knows a poem must be constructed, and she has learned much about endings from Larkin:

> *Those streets, the gloomy shortcut by the church,*
> *the triangle from school to home to the high field—*
> *below which all roads sped away and led away—*

and back again. Wherever I went then, I was
still there; fretting for something else, someone else,
somewhere else. Or else, I thought, I shall die.

And so I shall. Decades ahead of this, both of me,
then and now, pass each other like ghosts
in the empty market-place, where I imagine myself

to be older and away, or remember myself
younger, not loving this tuneless, flat bell
marking the time. Or moved to tears by its same sound.

This is almost pure Larkin, though a little shallower and less well deployed. In a time that has given its promise to prose, this pitch and solicitude seem almost aggressive.

Medbh McGuckian is Irish, but unlike the other Belfast poets she prefers a dream logic, and her poems disappear into one another, like ghost into ghost:

The rain has left a scare across the countryside;
The air at the bottom of the sky is swimming closely.
What survives of our garden is held together
By the influence of water, as if we could only live
In the shelter of each other, and just leave the matter
Where we must leave all the doors that matter.

She has borrowed some of her noun stresses from Plath, but a poet with such control of resonance ought to have more control of reason. After three books, McGuckian has been praised too much for what little she does beautifully. Poets of pure language often have this complaint of perspective: they write a poem, then they write another poem.

There are other women of promise, including Eavan Boland and Carol Rumens, but too many women have been fatally attracted to limitations of language and the dead end of mild confession.

Pale Young Men

Every age gets the anthology it deserves, and British poetry for much of the past decade has been measured by *The Penguin Book of Contemporary British Poetry* (1982), edited by Andrew Motion and Blake Morrison. It provoked much anger and argument for its cautious, mild-mannered selections; but caution and mildness have been recent British poetry's mark, if not its virtue. The poets were predominantly male and entirely white; the avant-garde and some of the poets I have called formalists were excluded; and some Irish poets included did not care to be called British. Nevertheless, it missed few poets of value in the generations from which it drew, at the cost of suggesting how narrow a taste had fostered recent British and Irish poetry. The anthologists can't be blamed for the small ambitions of most of their peers, though their claims for some very ordinary poets were needlessly grand. Their advocacy seemed like advertising.

In a small country the literary community is incestuous, and in Britain it is often a boys' club. Many poets have complained that the corridors of power are run by pale young men, among them Motion (formerly poetry editor at Chatto and Windus, now an editor at Faber and Faber) and Morrison (literary editor of the *Observer*). They're both deliberate but not highly distinctive poets (I don't mean they can't be told apart)—even so, Motion's elegy for Philip Larkin and Morrison's "The Yorkshire Ripper" were among the finer poems of the decade. Other pale young men include Alan Jenkins (poetry editor, *TLS*), Mick Imlah (poetry editor, Chatto and Windus), Peter Forbes (editor, *Poetry Review*), and Lachlan Mackinnon (a freelance critic). A long article in the *Guardian* in 1989 traced the daisy chain of interest and influence, how A reviews B who publishes C who gives an award to A. The complaints are more or less valid, but in the next decade some memorable poetry may be written by this group and by other pale young men like Hugo Williams or the American expatriate Michael Donaghy. It would not be the last time literary talent thrived on abuse of power, which may be just use of power.

Formalists

Contemporary British poets who have some interest in formal procedure are often a little lazy about it, as if the tradition were now too agonistic to require any expense of spirit. Geoffrey Hill's *The Mystery of the Charity of Charley Péguy* was written in a stunning rough-footed pentameter, but critics without half his hearing—without any ears at all—took him to task for his flagrancy. Most critics, and many poets who write as if they were critics, prefer the appearance of form without the responsibility.

Jeffrey Wainwright, Hill's nearest protégé (at times it seems his nearest living relative), has written very scantly, as if each word were a worm casting. His formality lies mostly in a diction and an attitude, but when he weakens toward rhyme he has some of Hill's intelligence and cold radiance:

> Un *and* im—*unimaginable, unwageable,*
> *Unprofitable, improbable—will*
> *Keep us calm. Perhaps the dead of those wars*
> *Only pretend: an infantryman clambers*
>
> *From the sticky field, a sapper rises*
> *From a roadside drain, like pearl-divers*
> *Able seamen kick back to the sun*
> *And bob by their children in the warm lagoon.*

Dick Davis, Robert Wells, and Clive Wilmer are, remarkably, middle-aged Wintersians. They have been more stringent than Wainwright in their pursuit of formal graces, and for their stringencies have been ignored. They can be as slight and stilted as Winters, but their work has classical elegance and—when most poets lack an inner ear—classical balance, as in these stanzas by Davis:

> *Unseen, preserved beneath dark velvet, lie*
> *Pale water-colours fugitive to light—*
> *Displayed to none but friendship's gentler eye,*
> *The sanctuaries of her sequestered sight—*

Views of the Rhine and of the Holy Land,
Deep vistas of the spirit's need and rest:
Frail on glass shelves Venetian glasses stand,
The keepsakes of a life secure and blessed.

All the rightness—all the rectitude—of these lines perhaps sets them wrong ("friendship's gentler eye"!), and few readers will bother to breach a distance that marks suppression of desire or oppression of design. Clive Wilmer's recent poems show the reach of personality that all too rarely comes to a poet after the rages of youth. They escape in form from formal rectitude.

Perhaps John Fuller shouldn't be mentioned in this company. Divisively talented, formally ambitious, he has often been suspected of being a dilettante. Most of his poetry, however serious, comes out of Auden's frivolous rib, and he has had difficulty establishing a poetic character. He has sacrificed much for the sake of mere foolery; but his light-verse collaborations with James Fenton, his former student, suggest that in order to make its ascents, form must make its descents as well. Few poets have had such quiet influence—for the past two decades Fuller has almost singlehandedly kept poetry alive at Oxford, fostering two generations of students. Cambridge has had no comparable figure, and Cambridge has been poorer in its poets.

The various allegiances of these poets reveal some of the poor proprieties of formal verse. Younger poets like Craig Raine and James Fenton can be formal when they *wish* to be, but they rarely test their capacities—Raine's delightful songs in his Pasternak adaptation, *The Electrification of the Soviet Union* (1986), were a small revelation, and Fenton has scattered a few simple lyrics among work prosodically less constant if more complicated.

Wits

The tradition of wit in English poetry has been diversely honored, attracting poets as unforgiving and violent as Swift, as crudely ribald as Rochester, as sweet and psychologically peculiar as Carroll.

Americans tend to treat wit dismissively, which explains why Ameri-can poetry is more troubled with sentiment. Craig Raine might be dismissed in America, though he is a deviously ingenuous poet and a terrible model for the young—he and Paul Muldoon are respon-sible for most of the infection of whimsy in contemporary British and Irish poetry. Raine's trademark is the perversely ingenious com-parison, the *discordia concors* of apt unlikeliness: his similes and meta-phors are brilliant and brilliantly irritating. If Aristotle were right about poetry, poetry would be like this: "a glinting beetle on its back / struggled like an orchestra," "Iron filings shine // in her shaven armpits," "Seeing the pagoda / of dirty dinner plates," "Rain is when the earth is television," or

> *the vultures bobbed and trampolined*
>
> *around the bodies, then swirled*
> *a mile above their heads*
>
> *like scalded tea leaves.*

At worst, such cleverness distracts from its object, and the figures become self-amusement if not self-abuse. This combination of vi-sual precision and, for the reader, momentary mental perplexity has given Raine an unusual poetry of unusually small means; he has not found ambitious form for such a gift. He is emperor of a duchy or pocket borough. His poem "A Martian Sends a Postcard Home" gave a name to this alienating style: the Martian School. The name is belittling and reductive, since Raine can be a poet of penetrating affection.

Raine and Fenton have been the most influential young men of letters in British poetry, through their prose as much as their poetry. Raine, whose father was once a boxer, has been a dazzlingly pugna-cious—often needlessly pugnacious—critic, and the recent overlong collection of his prose, *Haydn and the Valve Trumpet* (1990), has re-stored to English criticism a lost manner of attack. As poetry editor of Faber and Faber (in T. S. Eliot's shoes, as he is constantly re-minded), Raine has filled his list with smaller Martians like Christopher Reid and minor wits like Philip Gross. *Poetry Introduction* 7 (1990), the latest in a long series of Faber introductions to young poets, is one stuffed package of the Martian mood. Raine has also taken on Michael Hofmann, Amy Clampitt, and witty and un-Martian poets like Oliver Reynolds and Wendy Cope. Reynolds's work in particular suggests how jazzy and daring a poetry can derive from traditions of wit:

> *A man sits in a blossom-flecked Daimler*
> *and reads the* FT, *stroking his wattles.*
> *All the pinks! It's spring in car-phone country*
> *and every bird's buttonholing the sky*
> *with the latest prices. Worms are up, up!*

Wendy Cope's satires and parodies are a different form of aggression. I should resist quoting her "Waste Land Limericks" entire, but I can't.

> ### I
> *In April one seldom feels cheerful;*
> *Dry stones, sun and dust make me fearful;*
> *Clairvoyantes distress me,*
> *Commuters depress me—*
> *Met Stetson and gave him an earful.*

> ### II
> *She sat on a mighty fine chair,*
> *Sparks flew as she tidied her hair;*
> *She asks many questions,*
> *I make few suggestions—*
> *Bad as Albert and Lil—what a pair!*

> ### III
> *The Thames runs, bones rattle, rats creep;*
> *Tiresias fancies a peep—*
> *A typist is laid,*
> *A record is played—*
> *Wei la la. After this it gets deep.*

IV

A Phoenician called Phlebas forgot
About birds and his business—the lot,
Which is no surprise
Since he'd met his demise
And been left in the ocean to rot.

V

No water. Dry rocks and dry throats,
Then thunder, a shower of quotes
From the Sanskrit and Dante.
Da. Damyata. Shantih.
I hope you'll make sense of the notes.

With cunning insouciance she has exposed the whole banquet of male sensibility. In a civilized time, there would be a Sullivan to her Gilbert.

Eccentrics

Fiona Pitt-Kethley and John Whitworth belong in the lineage of wit, but they have been treated as outsiders. Their wit is perhaps more ill-tempered and antagonistic; but it is their attitude, their not-one-of-you tone, that has proven an effective literary stigma. Pitt-Kethley styles herself a "female Casanova": rude, prejudiced, bawdy, she is disarmingly honest and surprisingly vulnerable. Catullus might have liked her—especially on smoking after sex:

I don't feel easy with a naked flame
too near my vulnerable naked flesh—
you, me, a cigarette, a smoky kiss.
Out of the corner of one eye I see
a toppling inch of ash above a stub,
while lover-boy is fiddling with my tits—
foreplay designed to set the bed on fire.

Her poems have more pathos than her manner, which is increasingly one of complaint. Her most recent book included thirty pages of notes on the adversities of being a poet (you'd think she were suffering like Chatterton), and she has taken out plaintive advertisements in the *London Review of Books* asking for work. I see why people dislike her, but her sexual directness is otherwise absent from British poetry: when you read most British poets you think sex hasn't been invented yet.

John Whitworth has little patience with *poets*. He writes like a recluse or an autodidact—his poems range from technical adroitness to complete flat-footedness, and he favors (when he's not imagining himself Byron or Auden) a sentimental simplicity reminiscent of early Snodgrass, as in this poem of advice to his daughter:

> *Don't pick your friends with too much care,*
> *But such as happen to be there.*
> *Trust—if you must—a pretty face.*
> *There lies disaster, not disgrace.*
> *Love soon, love easily—the fact is,*
> *Like most things love improves with practice.*

Like Pitt-Kethley (*there* would be a marriage), he is a wounded poet, too self-satisfied as the anti-intellectual; they would both go further if they had more technical control, and if they could stop compensating like mad for not being darlings of the literati.

Other eccentrics have occasionally been recommended to me. Frank Kuppner, for example, writes long, crazed, touchingly experimental poems—his *A Bad Day for the Sung Dynasty* (1984), consisting of 511 four-line stanzas, seemed utterly pointless to me, though it was praised by some critics. Lavish attention has been given to Peter Reading, who writes poetry of collage and disjunction, as if he had only old newspapers to work with. His polyphonic voices are meant to draw the mind to Eliot, but when I read his work I thought I was reading Dos Passos on Darvon. Every taste has its limitations, and these are the limits of mine. (I cannot bear the fantastically dull poems of the British avant-garde, who write like a cargo cult with battered copies of Ashbery and Olson to worship.)

Exiles

In the past decade Britain has lost a good proportion of its scientists to America, and it is in danger of losing many of its poets as well. Geoffrey Hill now teaches in the Department of Religion at Boston University. John Ash, Dick Davis, James Lasdun, and, of the Irish, Paul Muldoon now live in the States. Seamus Heaney teaches a semester a year at Harvard and Tony Harrison spends part of each year in New York. A few poets live or have lived in other countries— Robert Wells in France and James Fenton, for three years, in the Philippines—but America, with its university positions, is a constantly dangerous lure.

The effects of exile can be devastating on an imagination tuned to the weights and influences of a certain language. Thom Gunn, long resident in San Francisco, has never regained the tautness and suppressed violence that drove his poetry in the fifties. A poet too long separated from his sources suffers an irreparable deracination. He can turn chameleon, like Auden (or, in prose, Conrad or Nabokov), or become a stately plant, honored for a character he cannot change.

Among the young exiles, James Lasdun is better known as a fiction writer. His poetry has a spritzy, decadent sideshow of a style, sometimes more of a nightclub act than a serious attendance on the art:

> *Here they come, the silver-haired boys,*
> *Minds glandular, tuned to the brine of sex,*
> *Bullion at flinty wrists, carbuncled fingers,*
> *Silk scarves afloat on scalloped necks—*
>
> *You foolish girls, so willingly deceived,*
> *What do you seek, to what ghost of bliss*
> *Glimpsed beyond silver do you cling? Rose flesh*
> *Turning to carrion for the next jackal's kiss.*

It would be a shame to lose such a voice permanently to prose, or to find his poetry consigned to the margins, as Lawrence Durrell's was.

The Ignored

To be ignored is to suffer an internal exile. Poets are ignored for many reasons: their diction falls out of fashion, like an old de la Renta; their concerns never become the rage; they develop too slowly for the critics to notice; their forms offend or afflict. Obscurity can be a compliment when young; when old it is merely another ailment. If the present were just, there would be no employment for future critics, and we would never be able to condescend to the past the way the future will condescend to us.

Thomas Kinsella's recent poetry has gone almost unnoticed in Britain, though he is the most considerable Irish poet after Heaney. *Blood and Family* (1988) is a strangled and disordered work, uncompromising in its claim on traditions of blood, streaked with grave humor, passionate in its reserve. Perhaps, like Geoffrey Hill, he is admired from afar, and because he is Irish the further the better.

Much of Roy Fuller's later poetry has been slight and occasional—it tends to subside into an old buffer's iambic natter. He still commands a wide compass of feeling, sometimes starchy, sometimes as convivial as a lawyer after four double scotches. I prefer his wartime poetry, which has been insufficiently appreciated. He learned from Auden while maintaining a quiet independence from him ("The ridiculous empires break like biscuits. / Ah, life has been abandoned by the boats—/ Only the trodden island and the dead / Remain, and the once inestimable caskets"), and his better work is understated and haunting:

> *Once as we were sitting by*
> *The falling sun, the thickening air,*
> *The chaplain came against the sky*
> *And quietly took a vacant chair.*
>
> *And under the tobacco smoke:*
> *"Freedom," he said, and "Good" and "Duty."*
> *We stared as though a savage spoke.*
> *The scene took on a singular beauty.*

And we made no reply to that
Obscure, remote communication,
But only looked out where the flat
Meadow dissolved in vegetation.

The depth of his work lies in its long devotions and concentrations—it is filled to the limit with a self neither pleading for nor demanding the reader's affection. In the struggle with language he has never succumbed to easy fulfillments.

By choice, John Heath-Stubbs has been a poet of singular interests, almost unaffected by the little whirlpools of fashion. At worst he seems to have dropped in from the nineteenth century, complaining the nineteenth century isn't nearly as fine as the eighteenth century; but he has the ability of Ransom or Hardy to reach, through a superior clumsiness, a rough grace:

Salieri encountered Mozart;
Took him friendly by the arm,
And smiled a thin-lipped ambiguous smile.
This was Italian charm.

Mozart observed the smile of Salieri
But was not enough observant,
(For the Angel of Death had called already
In the guise of an upper servant).

Now past eighty, E. J. Scovell published three books in the forties and fifties and then nothing until *The Space Between* in 1982. Critical memory is short and unforgiving. When most poets temper their talent to a convenient or conversational smoothness—a glazed pastry of a poetry—her work is awkward in the right ways. She is not as peculiar or engaging as Stevie Smith, but even her slightest work has a translucent intensity:

Here is the gate with the young parents waiting there—
Some of them beautiful but not, as once they were,
As flowers are beautiful, no longer in that way.
Their used and hardy beauties are in fruit today.

Life for its reasons has them in its exigent employ—
Talking their in-group talk, watching for girl or boy.
And the children come, flickering like flames over cindery ground.
Each, they reclaim their own. Life has them in its hand.

However ungainly her verse, the calmness of its perceiving intelligence has been lost in recent British and American poetry. American poetry, that melting affection of styles, has little of the aging cantankerousness of these four poets; but British poetry's present defects may be all the plainer when you know its attentions lie elsewhere.

Coda

Both *Poetry Review* and *Agenda* warned the new decade with symposia on the state of poetry in Britain. The poets consulted were unexpectedly dark in their analysis: *marginalized, fairly wretched, undistinguished* were not the most uncomplimentary descriptions. Viewed strictly, British poetry is fiercely competent, with a polyglot variety that obscures its lack of imaginative distinction. The condition is not all that different from the habituations and lack of ambition that afflict American poetry: a gifted mediocrity prevails, and the few poets who transcend the condition work, in the main, in a tradition whose lineaments are fairly certain.

The irrelevance of poetry is often blamed for the irrelevance of poets; but we are not simply in a period of relative dullness compared to the early twenties, the early thirties, or the postwar florescence. Other factors—of education, of culture—have intervened, and it is unlikely that the state of poetry in either country will improve without a viral outbreak of talent. Three or four of the poets I have surveyed have the resources to revive the art; but the British, like us, have often been luckier in their poets than in their poetics.

BOOKS UNDER REVIEW

AUDEN'S DIRTY LAUNDRY

W. H. Auden, *Poems, 1927–1929: A Photographic and Typographic Facsimile.* Ed. Patrick T. Lawlor. The New York Public Library, 1989.
Alan Ansen, *The Table Talk of W. H. Auden.* Ed. Nicholas Jenkins. Sea Cliff Press, 1989.

MODERNISM'S LAST AESTHETE

John Ashbery, *As We Know.* Viking, 1979.

IN AND OUT OF THE AVANT

Allen Ginsberg, *Plutonian Ode: Poems 1977–1980.* City Lights Books, 1982.
Charles Bukowski, *Dangling in the Tournefortia.* Black Sparrow Press, 1981.
Thomas Kinsella, *Blood and Family.* Oxford University Press, 1988.
Michael Palmer, *Sun.* North Point Press, 1988.

MILLIONS OF STRANGE SHADOWS

James Merrill, *From the First Nine: Poems, 1946–1976.* Atheneum, 1982.
———, *The Changing Light at Sandover.* Atheneum, 1982.
———, *Late Settings.* Atheneum, 1985.

BEYOND PSYCHOLOGY

Lorrie Goldensohn, *Elizabeth Bishop: The Biography of a Poetry*. Columbia University Press, 1992.
Bonnie Costello, *Elizabeth Bishop: Questions of Mastery*. Harvard University Press, 1991.

THE HABITS OF THEIR HABITATS

Amy Clampitt, *What the Light Was Like*. Alfred A. Knopf, 1985.
Gjertrud Schnackenberg, *The Lamplit Answer*. Farrar, Straus & Giroux, 1985.

YOUNGER POETS

Tess Gallagher, *Willingly*. Graywolf Press, 1984.
Richard Kenney, *The Evolution of the Flightless Bird*. Yale University Press, 1984.
Melissa Green, *Squanicook Eclogues*. W. W. Norton, 1987.
Timothy Steele, *Sapphics against Anger*. Random House, 1986.

CHRONICLE AT HOME AND ABROAD

James Tate, *Constant Defender*. Ecco Press, 1983.
Alice Fulton, *Dance Script with Electric Ballerina*. University of Pennsylvania Press, 1984.
Albert Goldbarth, *Original Light: New and Selected Poems, 1973–1983*. Ontario Review Press, 1983.
Norman Dubie, *Selected and New Poems*. W. W. Norton, 1983.
Yehuda Amichai, *Great Tranquillity: Questions and Answers*. Tr. Glenda Abramson and Tudor Parfitt. Harper & Row, 1983.
Michael Hofmann, *Nights in the Iron Motel*. Faber & Faber, 1984.
James Fenton, *Children in Exile*. Random House, 1984.

NATURAL SELECTIONS

W. D. Snodgrass, *Selected Poems, 1957–1987*. Soho Press, 1987.

THE MIDDLE GENERATION

Adrienne Rich, *Your Native Land, Your Life*. W. W. Norton, 1986.
Donald Hall, *The Happy Man*. Random House, 1986.
Charles Wright, *Zone Journals*. Farrar, Straus & Giroux, 1988.
C. K. Williams, *Flesh and Blood*. Farrar, Straus & Giroux, 1987.

CHRONICLE OF THE LATE EIGHTIES

Nicholas Christopher, *Desperate Characters*. Viking, 1987.
James Lasdun, *A Jump Start*. W. W. Norton, 1987.
Lucie Brock-Broido, *A Hunger*. Alfred A. Knopf, 1988.
Molly Peacock, *Take Heart*. Random House, 1989.
Edward Hirsch, *The Night Parade*. Alfred A. Knopf, 1989.
Mary Jo Salter, *Unfinished Painting*. Alfred A. Knopf, 1989.
Sandra McPherson, *Streamers*. Ecco Press, 1988.

AT THE HEART OF GRANDEUR

Anthony Hecht, *The Transparent Man*. Alfred A. Knopf, 1990.
———, *Collected Earlier Poems*. Alfred A. Knopf, 1990.

CHRONICLE OF THE EARLY NINETIES

Robert Creeley, *Selected Poems*. University of California Press, 1991.
J. D. McClatchy, *The Rest of the Way*. Alfred A. Knopf, 1990.
Les Murray, *The Rabbiter's Bounty: Collected Poems*. Farrar, Straus & Giroux, 1992.
———, *The Boys Who Stole the Funeral: A Novel Sequence*. Farrar, Straus & Giroux, 1992.
Christopher Logue, *Kings*. Farrar, Straus & Giroux, 1991.
Seamus Heaney, *Seeing Things*. Farrar, Straus & Giroux, 1991.

THE CHARITY OF THE MYSTERY OF GEOFFREY HILL

Geoffrey Hill, *The Mystery of the Charity of Charles Péguy*. Oxford University Press, 1984.

THE ABSOLUTE UNREASONABLENESS OF GEOFFREY HILL

Geoffrey Hill, *The Lords of Limit: Essays on Literature and Ideas*. Oxford University Press, 1984.

CREDITS

Dates in parentheses following chapter titles indicate the year of composition.

"The Condition of the Individual Talent" (1991) originally appeared in *Sewanee Review* 102, no. 1 (winter 1994).

"Auden's Dirty Laundry" (1990) originally appeared in *Parnassus: Poetry in Review* 16, no. 2 (1991).

"Modernism's Last Aesthete" (1979) originally appeared in the *Washington Star*, February 10, 1980.

"In and Out of the Avant" (1982, 1989): Reviews of Allen Ginsberg and Charles Bukowski originally appeared in *TLS*, November 12, 1982. Reviews of Thomas Kinsella and Michael Palmer originally appeared in the *New York Times Book Review*, May 28, 1989. Copyright 1989 by The New York Times Company. Reprinted by permission.

"Millions of Strange Shadows" (1983, 1985): Review of James Merrill's *From the First Nine* and *The Changing Light at Sandover* originally appeared